CRIME AND JUSTICE

CRIME AND JUSTICE

BY

SHELDON GLUECK
Professor of Criminology
Harvard Law School

BOSTON
LITTLE, BROWN, AND COMPANY
1936

Published May, 1936

PRINTED IN THE UNITED STATES OF AMERICA

To the memory of

JAMES ARNOLD LOWELL
(1869–1933)

Upright judge, fearless humanitarian,
valued friend

PREFACE

This book is based on eight lectures delivered to a lay audience at the Lowell Institute, Boston, in the spring of 1935. For those interested professionally in the problems discussed, I have appended detailed notes.

In these pages I have stressed the ills of criminal justice in the belief that by studying the diseased organ we may be able to obtain some light on the destructive forces at work and perhaps some hints as to the therapeutic and prophylactic measures that are indicated. Exactly how extensive this disease process is, it is impossible to say; but, carrying on the analogy, even slight invasions by pathogenic microbes can have serious and pervasive consequences.

Many of the forces involved in the administration of criminal justice and in the careers of offenders are exceedingly complex and subtle, in fact imponderable; a few can to a rough extent be weighed. In an analysis of a social problem involving materials of varying orders of precision, there is always the possibility of differences of opinion, even among those interested professionally, in regard to the conclusions to which the evidence points. This is especially true in the field covered by this book, since very little has thus far been done to develop tests and standards to be applied to the work of police departments, prosecutors' offices, courts, penal and correctional agencies and parole boards.

Whatever their particular approach may be, all serious students of the crime problem must agree (1) that to understand the criminal law and its administration, the culture medium of the time and place cannot be ignored; (2) that corruption and venality should have no place in the administration of justice; and (3) that for the performance of the technical services of the criminal law today a trained personnel is absolutely indispensable. While stressing these last points, I have endeavored to keep in mind others as well.

No one lecturing or writing in the general field covered by these pages can fail to be indebted to the writings of Roscoe Pound and a few other pioneers, as well as to the rapidly growing mass of crime survey reports. I am also grateful to my students, with whom I have discussed many of the problems in the course of a decade of teaching and research.

To Professors Felix Frankfurter, Jerome Hall, Edmund M. Morgan, James J. Robinson, Arthur M. Schlesinger and Edwin H. Sutherland, I am obligated for their careful reading of parts or all of the manuscript and their valuable suggestions. I am also indebted to Messrs. George E. Lodgen and Tuckerman Day, the former for aid in rechecking references and the latter for editorial advice. My wife has given me great encouragement during both the preparation of the lectures and their transformation into a book.

My thanks are also due to the various publishers, F. S. Crofts and Co., Harcourt, Brace and Co., Henry Holt and Co., The Macmillan Co., The University of Chicago Press, and Whittlesey House, McGraw-Hill Book Co., who have so kindly consented to quotations from the works they have brought out.

Cambridge, Massachusetts S. G.
January 5, 1936

CONTENTS

CRIME AND JUSTICE

CHAPTER I

THE CLIMATE OF JUSTICE

1

MANKIND is essentially violent; and every society has had its crime. The content of the term has varied in different civilizations, but the concept itself has existed as long as men have lived together in organized society. From a legal point of view, a crime is any act or failure to act that is prohibited by law and punishable by politically organized society in a formal judicial proceeding initiated in the name of the state. But when we say that the act is prohibited by law, we should bear in mind that this is only the law of a particular time and place. Crime is a relative concept — relative to the society and culture within which the act is prohibited and to the time when it is prohibited. Acts which in some civilized countries are crimes by its laws may not be such in other places; acts which at some periods in any particular country are designated criminal may not be so at other periods. Infanticide and patricide have not been regarded as criminal among some primitive peoples; the prohibition of the manufacture, sale or transportation of liquor rendered certain acts criminal in our own country at one time and not so at another; gold hoarding was lawful but a short time ago; today it is punishable as a crime.

This relativity of crime to place and time makes it difficult to generalize about it. Nevertheless, there are certain acts which have been quite generally condemned and punished in all developed societies. Treason, a very uncommon offense, is one of these; murder, a much more frequent crime, is another. In most civilized communities, also, certain takings of property without the consent of the owner and acts of sexual aggression have long been stigmatized as criminal.

Now while such acts have been punished as crimes in civilized communities of varying degree of development, and by different methods, it is doubtful whether ever before conditions have existed, in the United States particularly, which make it so difficult to cope with them.

In the first place, our ideas of the aims of the state in dealing with criminals are today more complex than they were when the goal was simply to counteract private vengeance and self-help by vindictive punishment in the name of the state; or when punishment was regarded simply as the wages of sin. The introduction of humanitarian ideals of reform, together with the increasing call for the participation of the biologic and social sciences in the administration of justice, and the resultant internal conflict of the criminal law, have rendered its problems much more complex than they were in the past. Men are beginning to wonder whether vengeance, however camouflaged and rationalized in laws and judicial decisions, should have any place in a civilized society well on the way to the second half of the twentieth century. Their misgivings spring partly from increasing evidence of the biologic and social roots of crime, and partly from the accumulating evidence that traditional punitive methods are not bringing the expected results.

In a ruder civilization crime was attributed wholly to a perverse "will", and criminal responsibility was therefore easily determined. The tasks of criminal justice were simple: to fix guilt by some roughly appropriate procedure and to administer a dose of punishment prescribed in advance by parliament or legislature. The punishment was assumed to prevent both the repetition of criminality and its perpetration by others, while at the same time satisfying a natural impulse toward vengeance and restoring the disturbed "jural order." Finding that even reformatories fail in the great majority of cases to reform those entrusted to their care,[1] thoughtful persons are more and more asking whether our methods of coping with offenders do not need to be radically transformed, and whether psychology, psychiatry, sociology and kindred sciences, though far from perfect, should not have a greater place in the administration of justice.

More and more are these inquiring minds recognizing that both humanitarian and scientific considerations should play a prominent role in the coping with acts that involve social derelictions as well as human weaknesses. A social instrument may be nicely scientific, but if it conflicts overmuch with man's hard-won humanitarian impulses, it will sooner or later land in the limbo of unwanted things. Two of the most scientific punitive instruments in existence are the guillotine and the electric chair; but if the next hundred years witness even half the development of humanitarianism that came about in the latter part of the eighteenth and early nineteenth centuries, they will be beaten into more useful medical and social instruments. But unbridled sentimentalism is also bad. Deep though our pity be, we cannot indulge in futile sentimentality while dangerous persons stalk the land. We must discipline our humane impulses with science and good sense. A head without a heart may lead to tyranny; a heart without a head may mean annihilation. These two principles, then, the ethical and the scientific, must both be reckoned with; and their involvement in the current processes of Justice makes her task more difficult than it was in the past.

2

The second reason for the peculiar complexity of the tasks of Justice in the modern scene arises from certain characteristics of our industrialized, dynamic civilization, the changes in human attitudes and mores that it has brought about, and the impairment of traditional sources of authority.[2] These phenomena need to be borne in mind if we would understand the pathology and the problems of American criminal law and procedure. For Justice does not live apart on Olympus, but in the affairs of men. Judges and the judged, guards and prisoners, alike are subject to a pervasive culture which in large measure, though in varying degree, determines their attitudes and behavior. Failure to take into account sufficiently the culture medium of criminals and of those who pursue and punish them may explain to some extent at least the miscarriage of contemporary piecemeal and superficial "reforms."

Analysis of the culture medium of modern crime and justice has extensive ramifications. Some of the roots of the phenomena to be described strike deep into the historic soil; others are more recent; but all appear to have become particularly marked during the past few decades. Mechanization and urbanization, the dramatic history of big business and the excesses of a largely unrestrained private profit motive, changes in psychology and mores, the weakening of home, state, church and other traditional sources of social control accompanied by the overburdening of the law — these and like phenomena are pertinent. A few examples will suffice to illustrate the puzzling complexity of the tasks of Justice in a machine age.

It is well known that the mechanical inventions of the twentieth century have wrought a revolution in American customs and mores no less marked than that induced during the English Industrial Revolution by the steam engine and machines derived from it. The automobile, the radio, the cinema, the long-distance transmission of electric power, and mass production in general have conspired to wrench behavior and attitudes from their accustomed grooves, and with breath-taking speed. In fact a chief characteristic of the industrial revolution is its amazing tempo. Human institutions and human psychology can hardly adapt themselves to such fundamental changes with like speed. Governmental agencies lag limpingly behind. What the potent and restless inventive giant has done to individual habits and attitudes and social customs before man has had time to adjust himself planfully to the new conditions, causes growing concern. As will be seen from many points of view, the dynamic transformations of our epoch have distinct repercussions on crime and its control.

One of the profoundest accompaniments of the modern

industrial revolution has of course been increasing urbanization. In 1900, 40 per cent. of the population lived in cities; in 1930 the proportion had risen to over 56 per cent. The most characteristic patterning has been the clustering of "smaller cities within the orbits of the metropolitan centers", these lesser units having experienced the most rapid growth. Nearly half the population of the United States is located in but ninety-six such regions, whose rates of growth have been much higher than those of other regions.[3] There are pulls toward a new decentralization dictated by economic disillusionments. But it cannot be expected that for a long time to come the stamp of the city matrix on the psychology, customs and mores of the people will be substantially altered.[4] The deeper forces of our dynamic mass-production epoch will continue to do their work for weal or woe. The rapid means of communication which make possible suburban life also facilitate the continued moulding of the people's habits and attitudes by the newspaper, magazine, radio and cinema. Living in suburbs, people are drawn to the city for work and play, read its newspapers, partake of its amusements, and thus remain in spirit denizens of the city. Attitudes toward life, the estimation of values, and habits of conduct are still determined *en masse* by the large centers, and they spread with magical rapidity to suburban satellites and thence into the remotest rural regions. "The concentration of wealth, political influence, cultural advancement, in a population whose young people are as a rule pressing toward the city, combine to make the mores of the city prevail over the more stable mores of the rural dwellers." [5]

The rush to the cities has had profound effects, some of which need but be mentioned to indicate their significance for both crime and the administration of justice. The demands of our industrial civilization have attracted to our cities peoples from various quarters of the earth, presenting wide differences in ethnic, religious, linguistic and cultural backgrounds. Difficulties of adjustment are enhanced by the crowding of these diverse elements into narrow, squalid homes and neighborhoods. Some of the resultant strains are reflected in both delinquency and law enforcement.

As concerns delinquency, modern city life intensifies opportunities for friction and crime. It multiplies the need for regulatory laws and the opportunities for their evasion. Not only do these influences make for increased lawlessness, but the irritation they cause also tends to reduce that "respect for law" which many still attribute to some mysterious ethical organ in the soul of man, but which is in fact the result of complex conditioning factors. City life tends to sharpen and dramatize economic inequalities; side by side with the luxurious displays of shop windows are the miseries of slums; crowded dwellings make wholesome life exceedingly hard to maintain; children seek the streets; recreational outlets tend to be harmful; gang life is stimulated. The rewards of urban criminality are higher than they were in the past. The anonymity of life in the city makes wrongdoing less subject to the criticism and control of neighbors. The surprising mobility of city-dwellers is illustrated by the fact that some two-thirds of the names in the Boston City Directory change addresses every year; [6] this restless movement has a marked effect in preventing the rooting of individuals in definite communities and the building up of a sense of responsibility to one's neighbors.

Law enforcement is also seriously impeded. It is relatively easy to hide away in a large, crowded city, or to escape by automobile. Criminal investigation is much more complicated than in the days when the techniques of crime were simple and when officers, prosecutors and judges knew personally many of those who came into conflict with the law. Policing the city of today is a highly technical task, and the obtaining of well qualified jurors becomes ever more difficult. The tremendous amount of business transacted by urban police officers, prosecutors, judges and correctional administrators makes inefficiency and corruption easier than they were in a closely knit, predominantly rural community where the work of officials was open to direct scrutiny. The diversity in the traditions of the ethnic groups that compose a large part of the population of our cities makes it hard to obtain sufficient agreement on public policies and reform measures.

Whether in city or country, the mechanical inventions and patterns of enterprise of our age have transformed the very nature of crime. The sensational robberies and quick getaways with which we are daily regaled were largely unknown in the horse and buggy era. State lines and the cumbersome, over-technical methods of extradition have been rendered obsolete by the interstate activities of criminals. Such relatively recent correctional devices as probation and parole, of which supervision of offenders outside prisons is the essence, have been greatly weakened by the mobility of those under surveillance. Well organized and widely ramified rackets, employing huge capital, large staffs, branch agencies and standing counsel, are a phenomenon that only the age of "big business" could have given birth to.

Increasing mechanization of industry and the attendant reduction in hours of labor have brought about a marked increase in leisure time, and with this have come wider opportunities not alone for healthful recreational activities but for anti-social conduct as well. "Business, with its advertising and high pressure salesmanship, can exert powerful stimuli on the responding human organism. How can the appeals made by churches, libraries, concerts, museums and adult education for a goodly share in our growing leisure be made to compete effectively with the appeals of commercialized recreation?"[7] This vital question must be answered if growing leisure is to be turned into wholesome channels.

But aside from the influence of increased leisure on delinquency, the exploitation of modern recreational methods complicates the problems of law enforcement. The dramatic devices of the stage and talking picture have been rapidly taken up by the radio, to a point where even courtrooms are invaded and court sessions dramatized. Attorneys in sensational affairs try their cases in the press, the "talkie", over the radio. The sensational sheet pays a high price for the life stories of defendants and jurymen; they and their relatives are painted as colorful figures. Reporters and "ghost writers" churn the most intimate human experiences into the scandal, sex and crime that are fed to a sensation-hungry public.[8] The trials and public hangings of old were known to relatively few persons — those resident in the vicinity; the doings of the underworld and police of today are treated as spicy news, which is disseminated wholesale.

An increasing apprehension of economic insecurity is another significant psychologic phenomenon. The anxiety of the underprivileged has always been extreme; but in more stable times, whether under feudalism, Victorianism or the largely rural economy of our own past, there was a greater sense of security, of "belonging", than in an epoch in which social change is rapid, economic upheavals are vast and mystifying, and unemployment for long periods is the lot of millions. The highly efficient impersonality of the large corporation has doubtless contributed to this feeling. In the past it was much easier for the manufacturer and merchant to be in more or less direct and friendly contact with the problems of their employees as well as those of investors. But corporations have tended to separate ownership from management, to eliminate personal relations and to dehumanize industry. By providing substantial reserves for the protection of ownership while largely overlooking the protection of the workman, they have seriously weakened the security and contentment of the individual.[9] In such a psychologic setting the efforts of even the best intentioned administrators of justice are likely to prove abortive in many instances, if not a sign of hypocrisy in the eyes of offenders.

The effect of the overstimulating machine age on mental health is difficult to gauge. Authoritative sources throw some light on the matter: there are more than 400,000 patients in the mental hospitals of the land, supported at an annual cost of more than $200,000,000, and their population is said to be increasing at the rate of 14,000 a year. About 75,000 cases are newly admitted to mental institutions every year. According to a recent study of mental disease expectancy, "in New York state approximately one person out of every twenty-two of the population becomes a patient in a mental hospital at some time during his lifetime." [10] Whether these figures represent a really substantial growth in mental disorders is uncertain. Improvements in diagnostic technique and commitment laws and enlarged facilities for earlier recognition of mental illness, as well as for hospitalization, complicate the question; perhaps a substantial proportion of the reported increase is due to these factors. It is also authoritatively estimated that "approximately 1,000,000 of the boys and girls now in our public schools will break down mentally at some time in their lives, if the present rate of breakdown continues." [11] The relationship of mental disorder to delinquency and criminality is not yet clearly established; but that it plays a significant role in the etiologic complex has been suggested by several important researches. The wider recognition of this relationship complicates the problems of criminal justice, all the way from arrest and trial to punishment or correction.

3

Another serious phenomenon is the growing disrespect for traditional symbols and agencies of authority, together with failure to substitute others. This is less directly related to the operations of our industrial era and is probably also due to other causes; but it is just as significant and pertinent a sign of the times as those already noted. Family, neighborhood, church, government, law, business — all these erstwhile sources of authority and hence of social control have been gradually loosening their hold on the people.

Consider, for example, family life and parental authority. The progressive disintegration of the family, particularly in urban regions, is evidenced by a number of grave symptoms. In the first place, there has been a persistent increase in divorce. While the trend toward a high rate was already apparent in the 1880's, the increase in more recent years has been such as to cause serious concern. In 1887 the rate of divorce per 1,000 of the total population was .47; in 1916 it had increased to 1.13; [12] by 1929 it had risen to 1.66 per 1,000, although it dropped back in 1931 to 1.48, and in 1932 (the latest year for which published figures are available) to 1.28.[13] Judging by the long-time trend, it is questionable if further declines over a substantial period can be expected.[14] Comparison of the chief countries concerning which information is at hand shows the highest incidence of divorce in the 1920's (though not the highest percentage of increase since 1900) to have been in the United States. Our average rate per 1,000 population in the years 1921–23 was 1.43; not counting Russia, in which the legal bases and customs of divorces are quite atypical, the closest approach to this figure is furnished by Japan, which in 1921–23 had an incidence of .92.[15] From another angle, in 1929 there was in the United States one divorce for every 6.1 marriages contracted; in 1931 one for every 5.8; in 1932 one for every 6.1. The high American rates do not include annulments, of which there were 4,408 in 1929 (one to every 280 marriages), nor desertions (the "poor man's divorce"), which are estimated at 50,000 a year. Moreover, the stability of the family is being destroyed earlier in the marital venture. Recently, the most usual period has been the fourth year; in the span from 1867 to 1886 it was the seventh.[16]

Thus, owing to the heightened speed, intensity and complexity of modern life, as well as to more subtle influences,[17] the marriage tie has been "increasingly regarded as a convenience rather than a sacred obligation." [18] That serious effects on the next generation are to be expected may be inferred from the fact that in 1929, 37.2 per cent of the divorces occurred in families with children.[19]

The instability of the family can also be seen from another angle. Recent researches indicate that pre-marital and extra-marital sex experiences are far more common than many had supposed. This is true not only of delinquent and criminal families and those of low economic status, but also of the so-called normal ones.[20] A mass of books and articles in recent years have been devoted to the effects of the machine age and urban civilization upon the love folkways and mores.[21] A recent penetrating analysis of contemporary morality goes so far as to say that "the emphasis upon sex in fiction, drama, and essay, the radical demands for individual liberty and self-expression in sex relations, both before and after marriage, show a focus of interest comparable to the political focus of the American and French revolutions. . . . The pendulum is swinging from sex repression to sex obsession." [22] At the same time prostitution is on the increase; such is the conclusion of the American Social Hygiene Association, arrived at from a comparison of conditions in 1927–28 with those in 1932–33, after expert observers had collected data in 58 cities in 48 states embracing a population of more than twenty millions.[23]

Not all the causes can be laid at the door of the modern industrial revolution, nor is the conflict between the individual and the group in respect to so fundamental an expression as the sexual impulse something new. Darwinism and the scientific attitude it engendered, the popularization in distorted form of the writings of psychoanalysts, a mounting reaction to the long-enduring religious policy of investing sexual matters with a cloak of uncleanliness, the general greater freedom of the sexes since the World War, are probably all involved.[24] But economic emancipation of youth, the easy anonymity of the individual in the city, the large-scale exploitation of sex-stimulating entertainment and like influences seem to have played conspicuous roles.

In these various ways, by tending to disintegrate the family the forces of industrialism and the other influences noted have contributed to lessen the authority of parents. The old home of rural or small-town America is no more the typical one; no longer is it the center of industry and of social life, no longer the chief school of habit-formation and the inculcation of moral ideals. Its members spend most of their daytime hours outside the home in factory and shop, and many nighttime hours at the movies or in dance-halls and night clubs. With emancipation of youth from family domination have come numerous influences which have subtle but potent relationships to both crime and law enforcement.

Neighborhood authority and control, as we have said, have also been markedly reduced by the growing anonymity of a constantly shifting population. In fact, one of the few places where neighborhood spirit remains in large cities is the slum, which is stable enough to permit the transmission of consistent patterns of culture, many of which are anti-social but satisfying to youth.[25] But in many areas the stabilizing effect of "What will the neighbors think?" is rapidly disappearing.

The church and traditional ethics have also been losing their power to define human values and control conduct. Whether the traditional union of ethics and religion will continue is doubtful.[26] To the extent that the church is able to adapt itself to modern conditions it is apparently holding its own. But there can be little question that the threat of supernatural punishment of sinful acts — so powerful a weapon in the hands of the church in the past — has been decidedly weakened; and with this has come a reduction in the force of religious sanctions as designers of social mores and motivators of law-abiding behavior.[27]

Political prestige, too, has been distinctly weakened. There is a strong tendency to invest long-standing institutions, such as "the State" or "the Law", with mystical significance; but when the sordid realities of practical politics are constantly brought home to the people by press, radio and moving picture, the dogma that "the king [or politician] can do no wrong" is vitiated. No longer is political power widely respected. To have had it survive, undamaged, the frequent dramatic exposures of corruption and incompetence in public office would be too much to expect. Volumes might be written merely recording the outstanding instances of political corruption. We have only to recall that the Tweed Ring of the 1860's controlled practically all branches of municipal and state government, and to realize that the pervasive graft of the New York political fraternity has since been duplicated by similar misappropriation of public funds by politicians in other large cities. The looters and spoilsmen have not been confined to any one party, nor has the source of illicit income been limited to the selling of franchises, granting of contracts or bribing of juries. The systematic alliance of certain municipal political machines with the underworld must also be recalled. At the turn of the century, in New York, Tammany was definitely collaborating with the criminal elements. In Minneapolis, Mayor Albert Alonzo ("Doc") Ames "boldly allied himself with commercialized vice, even allowing his police force to cooperate with thugs in perpetrating robbery upon the citizenry." [28] It took a vigorous crusade to unmask, in all its license, "the shame of the cities." [29]

Nor has graft been confined to municipal government. Particularly in the early years of our century there were wholesale bribings of state legislatures. Says an authoritative historian of the first decade of the present century: "The party machinery was at the beck and call of railroad and corporation interests which understood all too well the means whereby legislators were made their pliant tools. Indeed, bribery was so common in political life that Judge H. S. Priest of Missouri affirmed extenuatingly that it was 'at the most, a conventional crime.' " [30] Not a few corporations pulled the strings that made the state legislative puppets dance. How, in the face of a long story of corruption and waste, could such agencies continue to hold the respect of the people and thereby wield authority?

Respect for the Federal Government has been more slow to fade. Its very size and power, the glorious names with which our national history is studded, have invested it with peculiar sanctity. But the saturnine scandals of the Harding administration gave a telling blow to its prestige and authority. Even in retrospect the record makes one bow one's head in shame. The Attorney General and the "Ohio Gang", the Secretaries of the Interior and Navy and the oil scandals, the head of the Veterans' Bureau and the waste and looting of funds for sick and disabled war veterans, the Alien Property Custodian and the conspiracy to defraud the Government in the sale of assets of foreign corporations — such serious derelictions and betrayals on the part of some of those in high office have besmirched the national Government and lowered its prestige.

That political corruption is not limited to the dimming past is shown by more recent events: the travails of the ill-fated national prohibition experiment added more income to the coffers of organized crime, already well filled by gambling, vice and other illicit businesses. The shocking disclosures of an era during which entire governmental units were in some places in the pay of immune gangsters,[31] the exposures of the Seabury investigation in New York,[32] the later investigations and exposés in many cities and states, some of which are still going on, all indicate that corruption and misfeasance are constantly pressing to invade the body politic. Such pressure has an erosive effect on the authority of government; the memory of the citizens may be short-lived, but (if one may make a new application of a familiar psychoanalytic concept) the emotional effects of continuous shocks of disclosures like these persist in the social "unconscious", breeding cynicism and disrespect.

To be sure, political corruption is probably as old as government itself. But two of its more significant features in the America of the present era — its pervasiveness and its cognizance by millions of people — are essentially recent phenomena. It is not far from the truth to say that political corruption is more and more being accepted as a custom of the times or an unavoidable "price of democracy." An additional result of this attitude is a determination by many to get their own fingers into the political fleshpots. In almost every relation of the citizen to his government, the use of political influence, ranging from friendly contacts with petty officeholders and the asking of insignificant "favors" to attempts at bribery even of those in higher offices, is seemingly common. Is it to be reasonably expected, then, that those we call criminal shall be free from disdain for governmental authority, and should not seize every opportunity to purchase protection and immunity? The cleverer among them, guided by lawyers little concerned with ethical niceties, have made bold to escape the consequences of their crimes by the further offense of unlawful manipulation of the processes of justice. It is sufficient to quote Judge Seabury, writing in 1932: "It is a by-word in the corridors of the Magistrates' Courts of the City of New York that the intervention of a friend in the district political club is much more potent in the disposition of cases than the merits of the cause or the services of the best lawyer and, unfortunately, the truth of the statement alone prevents it from being a slander upon the good name of the City." [33]

In addition to repeated evidence of corruption among public officials, a related potent reason for the growing disrespect for government is its failure in recent years to give adequate protection to legitimate enterprises. It is well known how often gangsters take the law into their own hands to avenge a murder. This is bad; but worse is the fact that businessmen in large cities have preferred the protection of racketeers and gangsters to that of the lawfully constituted agencies. Nothing could be more disgraceful and disheartening than the state of affairs not long ago described by the Attorney General of New York, which typifies conditions that have been developing in other American cities.[34] The metropolitan area of New York in the summer of 1932 contained some seventy-five large plants which cleaned and dyed garments sent them by more than 25,000 small retail tailor shops; about 150,000 persons were involved in this industry. The depression and the advent of chain-store enterprise forced prices down from a rate which rendered a reasonable profit to one which threatened disaster to the industry. The Board of Trade of the Cleaners and Dyers Association at first tried to meet this ruinous competition by legitimate means, bringing in an expert to conduct an advertising campaign which would stress quality rather than cheapness. Let Attorney General Bennett tell the rest of the tale:

Scarcely was his campaign under way when it was abandoned. Events crowded upon the harassed cleaners and dyers. Attempts at conciliation were spurned by the chain stores. Conditions went from bad to worse.

In April of 1932, the industry surrendered to the racketeer. A notorious racketeer with a long criminal record began the work of organizing all phases of the industry. The so-called wholesale cleaners were formed into a metropolitan association. Attempts were then made to organize the 25,000 small shops into various retail associations. . . . The purpose of these associations, as expressly stated in the contracts signed by those who joined, was to stabilize conditions in the industry. A large initiation fee was exacted from the wholesalers who, by their contracts, were also pledged to pay into a common treasury a certain percentage of their weekly gross returns. It was proposed also to charge the retailers an initiation fee and monthly dues. It was estimated at the time, that had the plan been consummated, the take of the racketeer would have approximated $2,000,000 annually.

Coincident with the work of organization, acts of violence were perpetrated. A plant in the County of Queens was bombed. Several defiant retailers were assaulted and reprisals were attempted against the chain stores. In several instances chemicals were hidden under the collars of overcoats which were left at chain stores to be cleaned. When these coats were placed with hundreds of others in the dryers at the plants, the chemicals, because of the high temperature, ignited and destroyed all the garments in the dryers. At the time when these events were transpiring in New York City, similar outrages were being perpetrated in other cities. . . . At most of the meetings called to organize the several groups in the industry, the gangster, whom I have mentioned, was present. At some of them he addressed the gatherings, always carefully stating that the work of organization was being carried out not for his benefit but for the benefit of the industry itself.

When my investigation began, I was at once confronted with the wall of silence which invariably hampers prosecutors when they attempt to get at the racketeer. At the outset, I realized that my investigation under the antiquated Donnelly Act would be futile, because the only remedy therein provided was an injunction to restrain a monopoly. Under that Act, the Attorney General did not have the right to subpoena witnesses. All that we were able to do was to request witnesses to submit to examination. Also a question of law was raised as to whether the Donnelly Act covered the so-called service industries. But despite these difficulties, the facts which I have here recounted were unearthed. Most of the witnesses impressed us as being men solely desirous of saving their businesses which, in several instances, represented the culmination of a lifetime of arduous work. Some of them lied, most of them were reluctant, but quite a few frankly admitted that while they discountenanced violence, they felt that the law afforded them no escape from their difficulties. For that reason they were willing to submit to the coercive threat of the gangster to force competitors to stabilize prices. The racket of course was broken up immediately that the investigation began, but the deeper problem, namely, why was this great industry impelled to resort to racketeering to cure its ills, remained unsolved.[35]

Thus, in the face of the relative impotence of political power and the growing disrespect for it, have governments within government sprung up, captained by modern robber-barons and partially encouraged by citizens who have allied themselves with the agencies of evil — all this in order to control a situation precipitated by modern economic and psychologic trends and the slowness of legitimate government to adapt itself to them.

There are of course earlier causes of the disrespect for and suspicion of governmental authority. Some involve the very nature of our political system and its history, such as strong traditions of individualism (the vestiges of Puritan and pioneer attitudes regarding the rights of the individual against the government), and the division of powers inherent in American political philosophy and governmental structure. In times of great public stress, such as wars and serious economic crises, there is a strengthening of governmental authority both through the tightening of the political system and the centripetal emotional response of the citizenry to a common danger. But in normal periods, and especially in times of reaction to "too much government", such as post-war eras or periods following economic crises, the pulls are in the opposite direction, and are given added momentum by such conditions as have been mentioned.

It is easy to call for a more centralized and stronger government; but the solution of the numerous problems involved in a country in which democracy is, with ample historic justification, regarded as a supreme value is not an easy one. Superficial weighers of relative values of life in a politically organized society are given to stressing the directness, not to say the ruthlessness, with which fascist governments repress crime; they ignore the fact that higher and more pervasive values for which mankind has fought and bled through centuries of oppression are at the same time trampled under foot. How to maintain the true substance of our constitutional bills of rights and yet make law enforcement more effective in an age in which crime has the advantages of efficient organization and the tools of modern inventiveness, is one of the urgent questions to be faced by our generation.

The authority of the courts has also been weakened in our epoch. The soiling of the judicial robe in a number of cities has tended to divest Justice of her traditional sanctity. Publicized exposés of collusion and corruption on the part of law enforcement officers do not make for respect for an institution and its administrators; neither do the widely advertised incidents of "job brokerage in judgeships." [36] So also the tendency of some candidates for judicial office where election is the road to the bench to indulge in ridiculous self-advertisement and similar tactics depresses the judiciary to the lowest level of electioneering instead of investing it with the dignity, prestige and authority it should have. Said the Cleveland Survey, in analyzing the causes for dissatisfaction with the courts: "Most serious is the present cheapening of the judicial office, so that neither the bar, the press, nor the judicial incumbents themselves any longer respect it. Young lawyers who have viewed the bench with reverence formerly, now give voice to their disrespect, and retired and even sitting judges are openly cynical." [37]

The very complexity and technicality of criminal procedure and administration have also aroused antagonism toward an institution that lags lumberingly and stubbornly behind the economic and social changes of a dynamic civilization. And this disrespect is not confined to the underworld; contemptuous of the law and courts, the unscrupulous practitioner and experienced criminal welcome the labyrinthian "system" of criminal procedure which makes evasions of the law a matter of little risk, and criminal procedure itself an elaborate and sometimes farcical game of chance. But unfortunately something like the same attitude too often prevails among those in the higher ranks of the legal profession. Only in very recent years has a substantial body of lawyers shown a real interest in criminal law and procedure, or taken significant steps to bring about its simplification. A few leaders of the bench and bar, some socially minded businessmen and certain experts have long called attention to the more obvious ills of Justice; but until very recently they have been only a small company of voices crying in the wilderness. An authority on government has recently listed among the major phenomena in his field "the massive irresponsiveness of the bar and bench to the challenge of the present system of civil and criminal justice by modern social and economic conditions, and the indifference to the sweeping indictments of the drift by leading jurists."[38] Since legislatures frequently contain lawyers who make their living and reputation through practice in the criminal courts, it is not to be expected that reduction of technicalities and removal of historic encrustations will be very welcome.

Other influences have also been at work. One of these is the widespread evasion of laws not in harmony with the temper of the times, which affects the popular attitude toward laws and courts. The result of the prohibition experiment is by no means the only example. Such a crime as adultery, for instance, is enforced in only a few regions where historic residua and church pressures are still strong; even then, as is well known, many adulterers are never molested. Yet such a law is allowed to remain — a dead vine in the tangle of legislation. But more serious is the mass of unenforceable recent laws. The rapidity of change in the manners, attitudes and habits of America has tended to undermine custom in almost every activity. A frantic attempt to meet the danger is being made through poorly planned and hasty legislation, representing too often not a broad conception of the general welfare but the demands and whims of special groups.[39] To an unprecedented degree our legislative mills are grinding out new laws to regulate an ever more complex social organization.[40] Many of these are passed in complete disregard of the warning forcibly sounded long ago by Bentham, and more recently by Pound, that there are "limits to effective legal action." The law and its techniques cannot take over the full burden heretofore carried by the home, the church, the lodge and other agencies of social control. The load is much too heavy, and legal methods of control are unsuited to many of the problems involved. Bentham's warning of over a century ago is even more pertinent today:

> It is in cases of this kind that legislators have governed too much. Instead of trusting to the prudence of individuals, they have treated them like children or slaves. They have suffered themselves to be carried away by the same passion which has influenced the founders of religious orders, who, to signalize their authority, and through a littleness of spirit, have held their subjects in the most abject dependence, and have traced for them, day by day, and moment by moment, their occupations, their food, their rising up, their lying down, and all the petty details of their life. There are celebrated codes, in which are found a multitude of clogs of this sort; there are useless

> restraints upon marriage; punishments decreed against celibacy; sumptuary laws regulating the fashion of dress, the expense of festivals, the furniture of houses, and the ornaments of women; there are numberless details about aliments permitted or forbidden; about ablutions of such or such a kind; about the purifications which health or cleanliness require; and a thousand similar puerilities, which add, to all the inconvenience of useless restraint, that of besotting the people, by covering these absurdities with a veil of mystery, to disguise their folly.[41]

Unquestionably a serious dilemma is presented by modern social change: the old non-legal agencies of social control are weakening; the new have not yet been sufficiently developed. Control there must be, yet much of the task is burdensome, and unsuited to the law's devices. In the meantime, by its ineffectiveness, the authority of law is itself being seriously impaired.

Finally, it is becoming more and more obvious to the people that "equality before the law" is more figurative than real. As in the purchase of medical service, so in that of legal service it is financial means that determines who is to get the best aid. And this too is eroding the foundations of law and justice.

In all these ways, and for the reasons noted as well as more subtle ones, the authority of law and courts is being reduced. And modern methods of bringing events and personalities to the attention of the man in the street dramatically and speedily have multiplied the effect, engendering cynicism and disrespect.

The authority of business and banking has also weakened materially, particularly in recent years. While the story of business in the United States is one of high adventure, admirable enterprise, inventive genius and shrewd foresight, it is too often also one of unethical and even ruthless practices. The corruption of legislatures, unscrupulous lobbying methods, the exploitation of child and female labor, the freebooter "competitive" tactics of certain businessmen, bankers, insurance companies and other corporations, were exposed during the early years of this century. But the economic depression, the attendant banking and brokerage scandals, the lengths to which certain public utility companies have gone in propagandizing against government regulation or ownership,[42] have besmirched the reputation of business even in a country in which large-scale enterprize and the successful businessman have long been idolized. More than one observer has warned us that in making her fortune America is in danger of losing her soul.[43] The apparent helplessness of private enterprise in the face of the swift-moving events of the depression has given added blows to the prestige of businessmen and bankers. Thus another social institution, "the oldest of the arts and the youngest of the professions", has been losing strength as a means of social control.

In fine, the most cherished social structures of the past are undergoing attack. Their authoritativeness is decreasing; and this despite the fact that the psychologic magnet naturally tends to pull in the opposite direction, since men love to invest familiar institutions with the halo of sanctity and transcendence.[44] As yet there have been but few correctives. The efficiency of city managers; the examples of fearless and high-minded judges, honest and energetic prosecutors; bureaus of "public defenders" for the poor;

the various agencies for dissemination of reliable data regarding the family, sexual hygiene and mental hygiene; progressive schools; wise clergymen; ethical and socially minded businessmen — all these have not yet been able to stem the tide or to provide effective substitutes for our traditional institutions. The perplexing uncertainties and conflicts of morals and mores have a bearing — nobody can say accurately to what extent — on crime and the administration of law. A realistic facing of the problems of justice cannot ignore the crumbling of the familiar monuments of authority and social control and its accompaniments. Not all the influences discussed are necessarily evil; all men would agree, for example, that corruption is undesirable. But would there be equal unanimity about the emancipation of modern youth? The point is not so much whether the influences discussed are making for good or evil in the long run as it is that they complicate the tasks of Justice in the modern scene.

To sum up, two powerful influences have been at work in our age to render the problems of law enforcement much more involved and perplexing. The first is the complication of the aims of Justice through the introduction of humanitarian and scientific considerations. The second is the radical transformation that the culture medium of Justice has undergone. These influences have set the stage for a tragi-comedy in which society is attempting to enforce the laws and to control crime with instruments largely outworn. As if this were not enough, the task of Justice is further complicated by the rapid disintegration of traditional symbols of authority and the attempt to make law do much of the work of social control heretofore performed by the home, the church and other such agencies. Bearing these influences in mind, let us now enter some of the not always sacred temples of Justice.

CHAPTER II

THE HALLS OF JUSTICE

1

Justice performs her functions more in life than in the paragraphs of penal codes. A dignified atmosphere and decent quarters can go a long way toward creating desirable attitudes on the part of her servants, of those who come before her for trial, sentence and correction, and the public. On the other hand, lack of dignity and orderliness, and the housing of Justice in dilapidated and dirty quarters, exert a real if indirect influence not only on the proceedings but on the attitude of all concerned. So also, instruments designed to cope with the intricacies of modern law enforcement make for efficiency and add to the respect in which the agents of Justice are held, while outworn tools have the reverse effects.

If we visit the police headquarters of not a few of the larger American cities, we are as likely as not to find a situation similar to that described in the following sketch of the Chicago police commissioner's office:

> The small anteroom is filling up. Soon there will be nothing but standing room, and very little of that, for those who wish to see the commissioner. Most of them are well known around the City Hall. There are aldermen, ward-heelers, bail-bonds-

> men, police characters, and a few ranking police officers. The latter will have to take their turn. Some of those present have gained admission to the anteroom without passing through the general reception room and stating their business to the commissioner's secretary. They have pass keys which admit them directly from the corridor outside. So they are privileged characters.[1]

In these few words are suggested some of the major evils of the police commissioners' posts: the lack of independence and dignity of the office, the role of special privilege, the overbalancing of professionalism by political influence. Even though the favors actually obtained by the privileged characters who boast of private pass-keys to the commissioner's office may not be great or many, the performance of police work in such an atmosphere is badly handicapped at the outset. Policing a modern city is a highly technical service, to be carried on fairly, fearlessly and efficiently. In the atmosphere described, illegitimate considerations are likely to interfere with professional expertness and just administration.

The station-house is another of the police halls of Justice. Instead of an orderly, quiet, respect-inspiring place, it often presents an appearance like the following, attributed to the desk-room of a typical precinct station in a large Eastern city:

> The desk dominates the whole, and the entire work of the station centers around it. Prisoners stand in front or at one side of it while the facts required in booking an arrest are entered by the desk officer; patrolmen and citizens gather there. . . .
>
> At times great confusion results from such concentration of the station's work. It is not uncommon to find standing side by

> side a person reporting the loss of property, a mother inquiring about her lost child, a policeman waiting for instruction, and one or more prisoners. Citizens upon crossing the threshold are frequently confronted with unpleasant scenes: a violent or abusive woman under arrest for drunkenness, an unspeakably filthy vagabond, or a prisoner struggling to resist search. The atmosphere is often distinctly forbidding to persons whose contact with the police involves no misconduct. In most stations there is no waiting-room except the captain's private office.
>
> Added to the hurly-burly before the desk is the confusion behind it. Officers consulting their record books there must shout orders to the signal man in a room adjoining; typewriters are clicking, telephones ringing, clerks passing to and fro in the cramped space between chairs at the desk and the filing cabinets.[2]

But more important, perhaps, than the atmosphere of police organizations is the fact that they are largely operating with methods long since unadapted to modern crime. In the eighteenth and nineteenth centuries, laws were enforced by officials and agencies taken over originally from England and suited, with little modification, to the American scene. Police organizations in the modern sense were not established in America until the second part of the nineteenth century. Untrained, rough-and-ready constables and sheriffs might have been quite capable of coping with rural or small-town crime and picturesque Western banditry. The police office had little need for more scientific equipment than a club, a gun and a loosely-barred "lockup", for the reason that offenders against the law had at their disposal none of the advantages of modern invention. Moreover, in those times "roving criminals", who give so much concern to the police officials of today, were few. Administration of criminal justice all along the line could therefore quite successfully be local. But in the present American metropolis, all the resources of science and organization that may in any way be helpful in the apprehension of well-armed, resourceful and rapidly moving criminals are indispensable. Yet what is the actual situation?

First, if we examine the tools of not a few municipal police departments, we shall notice that they are not as yet equipped with technical instruments which daily become more essential. Many police departments are without adequate communication systems for keeping in touch with officers on the beats, many have no equipment for photographing criminals, or chemical laboratories and ballistics bureaus; some do not even have sufficient, up-to-date motorized equipment. It is only in recent years, for example, that the Boston police force has been equipped with its own photographic laboratory and radio facilities; and many systems, particularly those in small-city and rural regions, are still without these basic necessities. How useful they are may be inferred from the fact that during 1933, 168,457 broadcasts to Chicago radio cars resulted in 12,688 arrests.[3]

Secondly, in criminal investigation many American police forces still lag behind those of some Continental countries. They are likely to rely more upon chance, or upon the traditional trial-and-error methods of detectives, the use of stool pigeons and the "third degree", than upon that skilful technique of investigation which Continental police administrators have appropriately called *police scientifique*.

Thirdly, in the laying out and patrolling of beats American police organizations have on the whole shown little constructive imagination. Routes designed for residential regions are not altered to meet new conditions arising when industry and commerce invade such localities. Beats do not take into account the economic racial and cultural features of different localities. In Boston, for example, until very recently, no change had "been made in route boundaries for many years; with few exceptions, they . . . remained the same as long as the oldest officers can remember. . . . The city has changed, the character of neighborhoods has undergone modification, habits of the residents of many districts have altered with changes in racial composition — all the factors that influence police work have been subject to considerable change, while patrol methods have remained substantially as they were a quarter of a century ago."[4] A similar state of affairs exists in many other cities, where, although the policing problems differ in volume and kind at various hours of the day and in different localities, little or no accommodation to these facts has been attempted.

A fourth weakness is the inefficiency of internal organization. Responsibility for related activities is likely to be divided among a number of bureaus and officials, with little coordinating mechanism. This results, among other things, in unsystematic planning and in the uneconomical employment of personnel.

Fifthly, instead of a centralized and responsible police authority in each state, there are state, county, city, village and town or township police, as well as police representatives of various federal agencies. "The result," as one informed student of the problem vividly puts it, "is the most complete decentralization of police authority known to the civilized world, accompanied by an extraordinary degree of duplication and conflicting jurisdiction."[5] Even the growth of the state police movement has as yet brought about but little elimination of petty local police offices. The problem is not a simple one; a too efficient, centralized police power might be abused, although the dangers of this in a democracy are far less than they have proved to be in certain European countries.

But the most serious indication that American police systems have, with a few notable exceptions, failed to keep abreast of the needs of the times is the fact that even at this late date they have not established crime prevention bureaus. A city of the rich resources and humanitarian traditions of Boston, for example, has no such unit in its department. The pioneer efforts of Arthur Woods and August Vollmer, who long ago conceived of the police as an agency of crime prevention, have borne little fruit. The typical police office still limits its functions to the traditional activities of patrolling beats and apprehending suspects. To it "crime prevention" has no meaning of protecting wayward children, preventing the origin of criminal careers, extricating children from the pitfalls of modern city life, rooting out the breeding-places of crime. Crime prevention means simply a reliance upon the frightening effect of the presence of the officer on the beat.

Many social workers dealing with delinquents have observed how important to the destiny of the wayward child is the nature of his early contacts with the police; his entire attitude toward law-breaking, and much of his subsequent career, may be affected by it. It is deplorable that in many American cities the first experience of the delinquent child with the police is little different — in points of understanding and insight and of protection against contaminating influences — from the first experience of an adult offender.

One might point to many other faults; but the situation can be summarized by the statement that with notable and very recent exceptions city police departments are little more than physical enlargements of what they were a century ago. Yet recall the transformations that the city has undergone in the past hundred years! Its population has greatly expanded; its racial composition has changed; its business has become technicalized and industrialized; its life has become much more dynamic; opportunities for friction and for violation of laws have multiplied; knowledge of the conditioning factors of delinquency and of methods of social amelioration has increased. While pondering these changes, let us leave the police department and visit the city prosecutor's office.

2

In approaching the portals of this essential agency, we are likely to see groups of police, lawyers and various hangers-on in the corridors, conversing confidentially in an atmosphere of smoke and spittoons. On entering this sanctum of Justice, a similar scene meets the eye. Quarters are crowded, hangers-on are standing about, people are rushing in and out of offices carrying papers, and there is a general impression of confusion, unsystematic conduct of business and, worst of all, lack of dignity. Some of these offices have indeed been referred to as Augean stables requiring the rigorous cleansing of a Hercules. Their equipment and methods are as likely as not to be antiquated and inefficient. The Cleveland Crime Survey vividly portrayed this condition. Describing the office of the municipal prosecutor, the investigators found that there was no office system or organization whatsoever.[6] The report went on to point out that there was "no distribution or specialization of work, whether of preparation or trial, according to classes of cases, importance of cases, or any other basis of classification." Although affidavits setting forth the charges are basic to prosecution, there was dangerous laxity in their care; they were not filed in a central place in charge of a responsible official, but remained with the prosecutor concerned until sent to the clerk for the issuance of warrants; copies were not retained in the latter's files. The office did not even have its own system of records or files, or for that matter a docket of pending or completed cases. Memoranda of the individual prosecutor were kept or disposed of by him at his pleasure, and there was no method within the office itself by which the chief prosecutor could discover the history or status of any case or review the work of an assistant.[7] Thousands of complaints were disposed of without the keeping of records, either as to their merits or their number. There were not even clerical or stenographic aides. The prosecutors were crowded into space inadequate to the efficient and judicious performance of their duties.

The county prosecutor's office in Cleveland, while an improvement over the municipal office in matters of record-keeping, specialization of function, and locale, was also unsuited to the efficient performance of the important functions of the urban district attorney. The county prosecutor, observed the author of the report, "pits his unpreparedness, with such assistance as he may obtain from the police department, against the carefully prepared case of the defendant's attorney. He takes the proof in the way it has been prepared by the police or municipal prosecutor, making the best of what he gets, or, in more serious cases, attempting to remedy the defects or omissions."[8] Given the fact that statutes governing prosecution contain little or no provision for control of the exercise of the prosecutor's discretion,[9] the inefficiency that results, not to speak of possibilities of corruption, may well be imagined. The results of the Cleveland investigation were published in 1922. Improvements have doubtless been made since; but recent reports of the way in which some of the prosecutors' offices perform their functions, and the scanty supervision of the prosecutory arm, suggest that the Cleveland situation of over a decade ago was not then and is not now unique.[10]

Aside from the evidences of an unfavorable atmosphere and inefficient methods in the offices of district attorneys, there is in prosecution, as in police practice, a wasteful and needless decentralization — an independence of each district prosecutor that may have been justified in the past but is intolerable today. The annual meetings of the prosecutors of a state cannot replace a centralized administration of the essential function of bringing suspects to trial. The historic argument of "local rights" has become largely meaningless in this day of rapid communication and liberal opportunities for making public the acts of prosecutors. The notion that a central prosecuting authority of a state will tyrannize over a citizen of one of its counties, or that only local prosecutors can know "local conditions", is in this day far-fetched. If there is any substance to these arguments, the dangers can be counteracted by an appointive system of prosecutors in which local district attorneys will be named from candidates of the regions involved.

3

Continuing our tour of inspection of the halls of Justice, let us next enter the courts. The magistrates', police or district courts, as they are variously denominated — the tribunals of first instance in criminal cases — have the dual function of disposing of the thousands of cases of a minor nature that clog the mills of Justice in our large cities, and of serving as a sifting mechanism for the more serious ones, passing on to the grand jury for indictment and the superior courts for trial those cases in which the magistrate finds probable cause that the accused committed the crime. In most jurisdictions, also, it is these lower courts that are concerned with juvenile cases, no special tribunal for children existing. While the first contact of children with the police is significant, their first treatment at the hands of these courts is perhaps more so. But equally serious is the contact of the vast number of adult offenders with such tribunals, either for preliminary examination or for trial. In these numerous and humble "tribunes of the people",[11] which pass upon offenses ranging from minor automobile infractions or neighborhood quarrels to serious misdemeanors, and sift the felony charges, Justice plays her part for the overwhelming majority of child and adult offenders.

Their task of regulating the relations of people to the legal order in an ever more complex urbanized environment is constantly enlarging with the ceaseless multiplication of criminal statutes. It is from these courts, therefore, that the average citizen gets his impressions of the folkways of Justice. Recognizing their profound meaning in a democracy, orators have eulogized them as "the supreme courts in importance if not in rank", "the most important clearing-houses and sorting stations for keeping the stream of civic life pure", the places where the citizen "might be taught the spirit of our institutions and made to feel that the law was a living force for securing their interests." Being closest to the people, these courts should set an example of dignity, decorum and unimpeachable integrity befitting the holy office of Justice. No one who has visited English courts can fail to be favorably impressed with the part played by orderliness and dignity in impressing upon all concerned that the affairs of Justice should be among the most serious and careful activities of a civilized society. A competent American investigator, who spent five years in the district attorney's office of a large American city before studying the English situation, correctly sums up his observations in the following language:

> The conduct of English trials — both those taking place in courts of summary jurisdiction and before juries — is distinguished by order, dignity, urbanity and dispatch. Professional standards of conduct are on a higher plane than in the United States. There is very little, if any, attempt on the part of either side to get improper testimony before the jury by suggesting it in the form of questions, virtually no attempts to conceal relevant evidence, no dilatory tactics, no bellowing at witnesses,

no derogatory references to the accused, no judicial scolding, very little wrangling among counsel and relatively few objections to testimony.[12]

While in some respects this picture is also descriptive of certain federal and state courts, something different is quite likely to meet the eye as we enter the criminal court of a large American city. Walking through the corridors toward the court room we see the same swarm of officials, police officers, witnesses, bail bondsmen and political hangers-on that we met in approaching the district attorney's office. We enter the court room and are oppressed by its sordidness. As our eyes take in the details, they may see a picture like the following, in which an investigator of court problems describes the municipal court of one of our large midwestern cities:

A room about 40 feet square, walls painted in an ugly yellow, made still more ugly by accumulated soot. . . . Though I sat within 15 feet of the bench and witness-chair and strained my ears, I could seldom catch a word of what was going on. From the beginning to the end the whole proceeding seemed to me one calculated to impress the spectator with at least the suspicion that the main influence at work was not the evidence or judicial procedure as we know it, but either strange influences not audible in the court-room or things that were whispered into the ear of the judge. . . .

The prosecutor had no papers whatever. He lolled against the bench. For each case he was handed a copy of the affidavit and that is all he ever looked at. He took a glance at the paper to ascertain the nature of the case. He then mumbled something to the judge, whereupon the case was often announced as "continued" or "no-papered" or a light fine or sentence given. Other times he called the police officer or other chief prosecuting witness and mumbled some question which started the witness off, and generally that was the full extent of the participation of the prosecutor.

In a few cases the attorney for the defense took part in the interrogation. Generally, however, he seemed to simply wander and stand around, mysteriously going in and out, sometimes approaching the bench, sometimes going to the benches and talking to somebody, and every once in a while somebody would go up and whisper something into the judge's ear. Seldom were all the witnesses sworn in any case actually called to the stand.

While this mumbling and whispering were going on in the immediate vicinity of the bench, the main aisle leading from the door into the court-room and to the bench was the scene of constant goings and comings. It was never quiet a second. Walking around, standing around in groups, moving around hither and thither, went on constantly. Not only was it impossible to hear what was going on in the trial, but it was generally impossible to see what was going on. One or two well tried — that is, by the defense — and well-fought — this is, by the defense — liquor cases were the only exceptions to the above picture.[13]

Other observers, studying this court in action, also stressed the dirty and noisy rooms in which Justice performed her manifold functions, the disorderly flow of visitors, witnesses, court attendants and attorneys, the bantering intimacy of petty politicians and police officers, the crowding of many persons around the witness stand and the judge's desk, the undertone conversations between judge and counsel, involving pleas for continuance, excuses for absence of clients, or appeals for "leniency" — in fine, the lack of dignity and the inefficiency of the entire procedure.[14] In the first chapter we mentioned the mounting disrespect for law and courts. Can the state of affairs here described, which is witnessed daily by thousands of citizens, result otherwise?

Let it not be supposed that such conditions are limited to the lower tribunals of but one city. The revealing Seabury investigation showed, if possible, an even worse picture in some of the magistrates' courts of our largest metropolis, including the sinister fact of corruption of a number of judges themselves.[15] And the Illinois Crime Survey, in summarizing some pertinent findings regarding the Chicago courts, concluded that "the whole proceeding in a preliminary hearing is a *mockery of law administration*. The dockets are badly congested, the physical equipment and atmosphere of the court rooms are usually bad."[16] Describing one of the most important branches of the Chicago Municipal Court, the Survey spoke of the crowding "almost to suffocation", the noise, which at times "rises to almost deafening proportions, due to the shuffling about and the loud shouts of the bailiff and the pounding of the gavel and the remarks of the bystanders and the efforts of the judge to elicit information from reluctant witnesses."[17] As regards the Philadelphia Magistrates' Courts of only a few years ago, a competent observer, under the suggestive heading "Disorder in the Court-Rooms", says, among other things: "Hearings are still conducted . . . in the form of a football conference about the magistrate's desk. Insulting and vulgar remarks, both from the bench and those present, are frequent, and disorder prevails." And discussing how judicial business is conducted, the same investigator gives many illustrations of incompetence and lack of dignity, of which we shall cite but one: "A . . . conductor had a man arrested for obscene conduct in a movie house. The defendant was represented by a lawyer. The magistrate allowed the plaintiff to elaborate his charge in much revolting detail; then discharged the defendant on the lawyer's representation of the defendant's character, though the lawyer said among other things that he had not seen the defendant for two years, and then knew him only slightly."[18]

Similar conditions were found a few years ago in some of the lower courts of Baltimore. In one of these, a small room where the volume of business was greatest, the door had to be closed "to deaden the sound of a piano-player in the police recreation room on the second floor", and "at times the playing of a well known jazz tune would tend to make a farce of certain proceedings which were none too serious at the best."[19] The corridors were crowded with hangers-on. Prosecution in the great majority of cases was by police officers rather than by attorneys, and the magistrate acted "in the double capacity of prosecutor and judge." There were no facilities for ascertaining whether defendants placed on probation carried out the conditions imposed on them by the court. Only in exceptional cases was a record kept of the testimony of witnesses during preliminary hearings, and it was well known that witnesses later changed their testimony before the grand jury and in the higher criminal court — an evil not confined to the place in question. "In a number of cases it was noted that men were tried for drunkenness while so intoxicated as to be unable to understand the proceedings."

Assuredly, the law speaks "too softly to be heard in such

a noise of war." With the conclusions of the Baltimore survey report all thinking citizens must agree:

> Too long have the courts for the trial of minor infractions of the law been undignified, unsystematic, politically-tainted makeshifts. While denying to such courts the right to try major cases, the community intrusts to them the all important power of dismissing the charges in such cases. . . . A system that is perhaps well adapted to rural conditions for which it was conceived is still employed in a great city to meet whose needs and conditions it is totally inadequate. . . . It is an indefensible policy that tolerates the trial of criminal offenses in courts that are for the most part admittedly political and inefficient.[20]

How vital is the role of these courts in conducting preliminary hearings in felony cases, in addition to trying the so-called "minor" ones,[21] is shown by the fact that in recent years these tribunals, operating in six large cities, eliminated as the result of preliminary hearings almost half the serious offenses appearing before them.[22] In determining whether to dismiss a felony charge altogether, or whether the act involved is really a misdemeanor instead of a felony and thereby trying it as such and imposing a sentence, the magistrates' courts exercise an amount of power not justified by the hasty and ill-managed proceedings often found in such tribunals. Here again, then, we see an antiquated and unscientific social institution attempting to solve modern problems with outmoded tools and in an atmosphere that, far from instilling in the citizen a respect for law, is more calculated to disgust him with the agencies of Justice.

The tribunals in which felonies are tried are on the whole a considerable improvement over the lower courts;

but some of these would also benefit from a rise in dignity and efficiency. The same crowd of hangers-on is met with in the corridors, people pass aimlessly in and out, the symbols and essence of dignity are not infrequently lacking. Speaking of the Common Pleas Court in Cleveland, the Survey authorities concluded that while the observation of one judge that "the courts are run like bar-rooms" is an exaggeration, "it is perhaps true that the court-room, in dignity and atmosphere, does not rise above a salesman's display room in a hotel."[23]

Many juvenile courts present a marked improvement in atmosphere and efficiency over tribunals for adults, particularly magistrates' or police courts. The very nature of their problems, their contact with social agencies and their personnel tend to invest them with a cloak that Justice need not usually be ashamed of. But more than one juvenile court bears some of the earmarks of undignified and inefficient procedure, such as the crowding of delinquents, parents and officers around the bench and the presence, in some cases, of politically minded attorneys. When it comes to the instrumentation of juvenile courts and juvenile sessions of adult courts, it must be concluded that many have not reached the reasonable minimum standards set for such tribunals by the Children's Bureau in 1923.[24] The legislation under which they operate still smacks of criminal law rather than equity; their personnel is not adequately trained, and tenure is primarily dependent upon political contacts; their case histories are inadequate; their probation system is behind the times; their case-load per officer is much too heavy; their record system is so poor that valid statistical data are difficult to obtain. Only a few years ago Prentice Murphy, a recognized authority on child welfare problems, pointed out the weaknesses of many juvenile courts in an article bearing the provocative title, "The Juvenile Court at the Bar — A National Challenge", in which he observed that "it is very strange that our various crime commissions have failed to note the close relationship existing between many juvenile courts and the number of juvenile delinquencies in them." [25]

There is, in addition to the evils already noted, an undue decentralization of courts. In many places this tends to duplication and overlapping of jurisdiction and function; prevents a proper superintendence of judicial activity; leaves to each tribunal the appointment of its own politically recommended probation officers and other personnel; and makes it difficult for any judge to have before him the complete criminal record of an offender. While the backwardness of the courts, as of the other agencies discussed, has valid historic reasons, they have been largely outmoded.

But Justice also carries on her labors in other places than police stations, prosecutors' offices and court rooms. Her ministrations are found in industrial schools, jails, prisons and special institutions for certain mental types. What is the condition of these?

4

Consider, first, industrial schools for delinquent children. These institutions have a long history. As far back as 1825 a separate house of refuge was established for juveniles in New York City, and a similar institution was early founded in Boston. These pioneer establishments were admirably described by Beaumont and Tocqueville, who came to America over a hundred years ago to study our penitentiary institutions. Even in those distant days they contained some of the essentials of the subsequently established reformatories for young-adult offenders, including classification of inmates, work at trades, schooling and even systems of partial self-government.[26] They influenced the founding of state institutions for children, such as the one at Westborough, Massachusetts, opened in 1847, which initiated the movement for special correctional-educational establishments for juvenile delinquents throughout the United States.

In practice, these institutions range from a small number of schools in which extraordinary insight into the problems of children is manifest both in program and personnel, to some which can only be called junior prisons. Some still stress repressive and disciplinary features to an extent that in correctional efforts puts them behind the early children's refuges.

Judging from samples of the results of institutional treatment of children, it may be questioned whether the housing of delinquents in public industrial schools does not, on the whole, do as much harm as good. The reasonable Children's Bureau minimal standards that ought to govern such establishments have in a number of respects, notably the quality of the personnel and the intelligent administrative and research use of carefully prepared case histories, not yet been attained in many industrial schools. To be sure, an attempt is made to care for the physical health of the children, but very little is usually done about mental hygiene; part-time psychologists and psychiatrists are not enough in institutions with several hundred children, if more is to be done than to recognize the obviously psychotic.[27] The schooling given in some establishments is of a high order; in others it does not equal the efforts of the better public schools, particularly in the matter of fitting the curriculum to individual needs. In recent years, many schools have experimented with vocational guidance and industrial training; [28] but there is much room for improvement of these aspects of institutional care, particularly in fitting training to modern industrial demands and to the interests and capacities of the individual, and in placing graduates in jobs on the outside. Moreover, the children are often not retained long enough to permit the mastery of trades.

But most damaging is the very fact of institutional routine, which, though less marked in industrial schools than in jails or prisons, is just as likely to result in a mechanization not conducive to healthy self-management on release. While a basic motive for the establishment of industrial schools was to supply as nearly as possible an organization to take the place of family life, the housing of twenty to seventy or more children in one building, even if it is called a "cottage", is not likely to simulate or stimulate wholesome family relations, even assuming the presence of wise and humane house-parents — an assumption not too frequently warranted.

Damaging, also, is the contact of first-offenders with experienced delinquents. The case histories of many criminals indicate that much of their schooling in crime and their attitude of defiance and disrespect for authority is traceable to unfortunate contacts in industrial schools. George W. Kirchwey, formerly warden of Sing Sing Prison, has effectively warned against the damage which improperly staffed and managed industrial schools can do to children. Speaking of the inmates at Sing Sing during his regime, of whom from two-thirds to three-fourths had been in juvenile institutions, he says: "In every case without exception, the individual attributed his criminal career to the experiences of life that he had in that institution . . . and I have seen within these last few years, conditions prevailing which have made me absolutely disillusioned, if not absolutely hopeless, with regard to the possibility of bettering a child through commitment to any institution whatsoever." [29] He illustrates the point with the final letter of "Happy Jack Mulraney", written from the death-house at Sing Sing: "The guard has just touched me on the sleeve; he tells me I have only a minute more. I have not been much use to myself or to anybody else. I do not suppose I would be of any use if I was to live. I would like to have one more year, though, to see what I could do to help you keep the kids out of institutions. No kid ought ever be put in an institution. Yours truly, Happy Jack." [30]

All this is not to say that institutions for juveniles have not on the whole shown considerable improvement during the past decade. The intelligently planned, humanely administered industrial school regimes developed by a few leaders like Calvin Derrick should not be ignored; but by and large the institutions for delinquent children do not seem to have fulfilled their promise.

For these and other reasons thoughtful workers with

juvenile offenders and "problem children" have taken the view expressed in the juvenile court standards of the Children's Bureau that "institutional care should be utilized only when careful study clearly indicates the necessity for it, or when repeated attempts to adjust the child to home life in the community have failed."[31] The retention of delinquents on probation in the community, and their placement in carefully chosen foster-homes, is in a considerable proportion of cases to be preferred. At best, institutions are abnormal environments; at worst they are prison-like establishments. Unfortunately, however, foster-home placement is also inadequately developed in many parts of the country.

What has been said about juvenile institutions applies with slight modification to reformatories for young adults. To judge by an intensive follow-up investigation of the product of one of the oldest and best of these, in which only 22 per cent. of a large number of graduates did not continue in crime during a five-year test period following their release on parole, it is not likely that these institutions are materially reducing recidivism.[32] And many of them, though called reformatories, are little more than traditional prisons in structure, regime and personnel.

5

Justice also does her work in thousands of other institutions: jails, houses of correction, prisons and special establishments for such groups as "defective delinquents." Let us visit some of these.

Throughout the country there are some 2,500 county jails, workhouses, farms and like establishments, and 500 municipal institutions of similar character, maintained for the purpose of punishing misdemeanants and, in most instances, detaining accused persons and witnesses pending trial. They house many thousands, and the turnover of their population is high. Like the lower criminal courts, they are the only official places of punishment with which many citizens have direct experience. Historically, the "gaol" is the oldest punitive establishment in the Anglo-American system, the locale of some of the most comical as well as most poignant scenes in English literature. From the hodgepodge of humanity that it originally housed have been gradually drawn off various special classes of offenders. The process is still going on, and many jails still contain prisoners of both sexes, juveniles and adults, the sick and the healthy, the sane and the mentally ill, including many persons imprisoned and maintained at public expense because they could not afford the payment of a fine.[33]

Upon entering some American jails, aptly called "crucibles of crime",[34] the visitor must be shocked by the picture presented. Sanitary conditions are little short of atrocious, disease is common, food is unwholesome, prisoners are crowded into cells and, worst of all, they rot in idleness and moral contagion. No words of condemnation are strong enough to characterize these venerable institutions of Justice. Implicated in the lowest politics, having no system of industries, possessing no program of education or constructive recreation, trafficking in drugs and immoral practices, staffed by incompetents who are sometimes not distinguishable from the prisoners themselves, many of these institutions are a reeking rebuke to Justice. A heroic effort is being made by the federal

Bureau of Prisons to stimulate local government units to raise the standards of jails. Recently, 2,894 jails throughout the country were rated by federal inspectors under a plan to encourage improvement in jails by paying a graduated scale of compensation for housing federal prisoners, the best jails to receive the highest pay. They were given marks on their condition with regard to such basic matters as administration and discipline, building and equipment, cleanliness and sanitation, employment and industries, hospital facilities, personnel. Only sixteen out of these 2,894 institutions achieved the grade of 80 per cent. or over, while 1,772 (two-thirds of the total) were rated less than 50 per cent. "The Bureau definitely condemned 1,273 and restricted the use of 642 for holdover or emergency cases." The following statement issued by the federal office gives an idea of the major ills of the jail system:

> In about 90% of the jails inspected, no rules concerning the management and discipline had been adopted, or at least, printed or posted for the guidance of the jail officials and inmates. Segregation, except of the sexes, was almost unheard of, and in many instances even this segregation was far from adequate. . . .
>
> It might be generally assumed that local boards of health would be responsible in some degree for checking on the cleanliness and sanitation of jails. The tabulation indicates that 2,204 were never visited or inspected by local boards of health or other sanitary organizations.[35]

Other abuses, such as the notorious "kangaroo courts", in which prisoners tyrannize over their fellows, were also noted.

The recent disclosures of filth, immorality, corruption

and sinister politics in the house of correction on Welfare Island in New York are not the first, nor will they be the last, of their kind. The Cook County Illinois jail survey a few years ago, and other investigations since, have revealed similar conditions. As long as these cesspools remain, Justice will continue to be a sham and a disgrace. For years investigators and reformers have cried death to the county jails of certain states, but those relics of an outworn localism, with its petty grafts and wondrous wastes, are still with us.

It is one of the evidences of the shortsightedness of society that it has stimulated the adoption of child protective laws and juvenile courts, only to compel them in many instances to carry the damage done by previous contacts of delinquents with police stations, lockups and jails. The federal investigation found that, "although the reports show that no juveniles were kept in 1,101 jails the appalling fact is that in 611 jails juveniles were housed with adults. Only 8.5% of the jails where juveniles have been housed have provided separate quarters for them." Another investigation involving 118,772 children detained for hearing or trial in 141 areas throughout the country during the year 1929–30 disclosed that some 14 per cent. had been incarcerated in police stations or jails. In only twenty-two of the areas were no children of juvenile-court age kept in such institutions. Other undesirable parts of police stations — public waiting-rooms, guard- or signal-rooms, unsupervised separate rooms, detective bureaus and the like are also used in a number of communities.[36] In many other places of detention the separation of children from adult offenders is only imaginary, and the cells are unwholesome. Assuredly, the personnel of these establishments is not likely to understand the needs of childhood.[37] The fact must be faced that police lockups and jails too often comprise one of the series of schools of crime that a shortsighted society has set up for its delinquents and first offenders.

Let us next visit the prison, where men serve long terms in "expiation" of serious crimes. Some of the American institutions for felons are a hundred or more years old. Their chief characteristic is their structure of granite and steel, built to endure for all time and to hold fast those deemed to be especially desperate characters. To paraphrase a well-known designation of architecture as "frozen music", the typical penitentiary is frozen penal policy. Because of its fortress-like structure it has rendered almost impossible the introduction of a modernized regime, based on more humane and scientific principles of correctional treatment than it originally embodied. Its cells are narrow, dark, ill-ventilated cubicles, ranged in long rows tier upon tier, the tiers built back to back to form a block separated from the walls of the building by a corridor. Says a reliable authority, in the report of the Wickersham Commission: "There is a very close analogy between the construction of a prison and the construction of the more dangerous parts of a park or circus menagerie; except that it is doubtful if any lion went to sleep in as strongly built a cage as that of a forger or a pick-pocket." [38] Several such buildings, each known as a "wing", comprise the prison, the heart of which is the guard room. In addition to numerous barred and locked doors separating various parts of the prison, the whole is surrounded by a deeply anchored high wall topped by sentry boxes at various points, and in some places electrically charged.

Occasionally prisoners of unusual ingenuity and perseverance escape from even these many-barred fortresses; but a large proportion of felons require no such "maximum security" housing — a fact which it has taken many years to teach to legislators and prison administrators. The penal systems of a few states and the federal Government have in recent years been developing three or four classes of housing, ranging from establishments of highest safety to those in which the inmates can be trusted to live in unbarred dormitories and unwalled colonies. The ever-mounting expense of modern steel and stone structures has thus had the desirable indirect effect of forcing administrators to study their prisoners and classify them in terms of security, which in turn involves considerations not alone of prior criminal behavior but of mentality, trustworthiness, health and other factors. Classification should help to counteract another characteristic of these old "penitentiaries", namely their excessive size; the latter interferes with proper management and, assuredly, with that sympathetic relation between the educative and directive personnel and the inmates which is indispensable if the latter (and to a less extent the former) are to be drawn out of the deadening routine of prison life.

One of the worst features of many prisons is their gross overcrowding. In 1928, for example, federal prisons were compelled to house more than 40 per cent. of their normal capacity, state prisons 11 per cent.[39] In such a situation, two or more prisoners are squeezed into a single cell, the corridors are filled with hastily improvised cots; toilet facilities, already shockingly bad in many prisons, are made worse. Not only does this put a strain on the administrative machinery, but it bedevils any program of industry, training in trades, education and recreation. Most serious, it leads to an even greater moral hazard than is normally to be expected in a prison.

We have said that prison architecture embodies penal policy and in large measure dictates penal practice. This is shown by the life that is led by many thousands of prison inmates. Its chief characteristic is routine; a lockstep mechanization, a mass stamping to and from kitchens and dining-halls, a mass tramping to and from shops, a mass marching into the crowded yard to mill about and snatch some air and conversation — these are the dynamics of prison existence. There are respectable citizens who deplore the alleged luxuries of prison life — the radios in every cell, the baseball games, the moving pictures on Sunday. They have only to spend a brief time in one of the older penitentiaries of the country to be convinced that these reliefs to the tedium of existence do not vitiate whatever deterrent effect there may be in punishment.

While work in prisons is more usual than in jails, the prison labor programs have long been a thorn in the side of penal administrators. Beginning with the abused private contract system and coming down to the "state use" system, they have had to cope with perplexing problems the solution of which involved considerations that did not lie solely in their hands. When prisoners were largely used as the slaves of contractors who purchased their services at a ridiculously low price, there were difficulties of accommodating penal administration to factory administration. When the state began to manufacture articles and sell them on the open market for its own account, there were objections from both manufacturers and organized labor. When the state use system was adopted in a number of places, these obstacles were not wholly overcome; for by selling to the state, prisons and prison laborers were still competing, though indirectly, with private enterprise and free labor. When in 1934 the Hawes-Cooper bill became effective, depriving prison-made goods of their interstate character and thereby empowering a state to ban or control the sale within its borders of articles manufactured in prisons of other states, a deserved blow was struck at the evils of contract labor, which had depended largely on interstate markets. But many states employing the contract labor system did not adapt their labor programs to the new conditions in commerce, and today finds the prison labor situation worse than it has been in the past. Only recently has a competent federal board been set up to attempt to unravel the tangled knot of the prison labor problem on a nation-wide plane.[40] Even at the height of industrial effort, many prisons contained men who, if they could be employed at all, worked only a few hours; later, idleness in prisons increased. Yet experience has shown that unless prisoners are occupied they deteriorate morally and mentally or become difficult to manage because of emotional upsets.

But there is one element of prison life that is even more serious in its consequences than idleness, and that is the crowding together of hundreds of mature men under one roof without contact with those of the opposite sex. This abnormality permeates the whole regime. It is expressed not only in pathologic sex conduct, but, indirectly, in those emotional storms that make discipline so difficult a problem to handle by the familiar punitive methods. Deprived of their womenfolk, of their family life, of the contact with their children except for the eagerly anticipated monthly visiting period of an hour, prisoners are bound to deteriorate. When to this is added the helterskelter association of all sorts and conditions of offenders, the problem becomes greatly complicated.

This treadmill, mechanical, abnormal program, going back largely to monastic-cell punitive and expiative ideas of the eighteenth and nineteenth centuries, is supposed to prevent criminals from repeating their offenses. But the supposition is naive. The high percentage of recidivism — and anyone versed in the facts knows how shockingly high it really is — may in part be attributable to the fiber of criminals, and in part to the inhumanity and stupidity of men in not aiding former prisoners to gain a foothold in some decent occupation. But a large measure of the responsibility must be laid at the door of that hall of Justice that is called a prison.

6

During the past decade, three or four states have in principle recognized the need of a special medical, psychologic and correctional regime for "defective delinquents", that is, offenders whose criminality seems largely associated with limited intelligence and temperamental defects. But though this basis of classification is essentially sound, the institutions intended for defective delinquents receive many other types of prisoners. This is due to the imperfect sentencing practices of the courts, lack of clarity in the concept of defective delinquency itself and the overcrowded condition of other institutions.[41] Moreover, these special establishments must constantly guard against a tendency to become virtual prisons in personnel, housing and regimen. While offering an opportunity for the intensive study of offenders in whose anti-social careers the mental element seems preponderant, they have not as yet sufficiently fulfilled their promise. They might have been staffed with outstanding experts in the study and control of feeblemindedness and other pathologic mental states, but they have not always been so manned.[42] They might have experimented with various special forms of education and trade-training, as do the better schools for the feebleminded; but while some attempts along such lines have recently been made in one or two of these institutions, they have on the whole not yet profited sufficiently from the experience of the more advanced schools for the feebleminded and mental hospitals. Even idleness, and the deterioration that often accompanies it in correctional institutions, have not been eliminated. That such special establishments have a definite place in the correctional program cannot be denied. But they have not yet clearly defined that place for themselves, in accordance with the hopes of their founders and on the basis of adequate legal and sociologic principles of commitment, transfer, housing, mental classification, incorrigibility, anti-social attitude and other pertinent considerations.[43]

These pictures of the temples of Justice are not pleasant to contemplate. But one should not overlook the saving grace that there are some institutions that have adapted their practices to modern needs.[44] There are police organizations, including the federal, which are efficient and orderly. There are prosecutors' offices, particularly in the federal system, in which proceedings are conducted with efficiency and in a businesslike and dignified manner. There are courts in which the decorum of legal practices and the sacredness of the office of Justice are not forgotten. There are correctional establishments, particularly in the federal system and that of Massachusetts, New Jersey and New York, in which some of the most advanced corrective techniques are applied. Owing largely to exceptional leadership, they have somehow managed to cling to a reasonably decent standard of administrative efficiency and honesty. This should lead us to hope that despite the numerous unfavorable influences at work, progress is feasible.

CHAPTER III

THE LAMENESS OF JUSTICE

1

NUMEROUS and Gordian are the knots that bind Justice and render her progress clumsy, difficult and uninspired. Some are tied by certain protections of the liberties of the people — in large part as valuable and necessary today as they were when jealously embodied in constitutional bills of rights or enunciated in historic judicial pronouncements as priceless bulwarks against oppression. Others are the result of the complicated and awkward procedure that Justice has by law and custom adopted. Still others are due to an antiquated criminal law, not clear in its aims, overly technical in some of its definitions and distinctions, not always realistic in its application to modern crime. Some of the evidences of these three chief sources of the lameness of Justice merit examination.

The layman is inclined to attribute poor law enforcement almost exclusively to insufficient intelligence and to corruption on the part of certain police officers and prosecuting attorneys. He overlooks the fact that in addition to efficiency and honesty, *legality* is called for. It has taken men centuries of courageous action to establish a regime of legality in the enforcement of justice. The elements of civilized proceedings in the arrest, trial and punishment of offenders are too precious to sacrifice upon the altar of ruthless repression of crime at all costs. Many of the practices of police and prosecutor involve the fundamental difficulty of accommodating the need for protecting society against criminal aggressions to the equal or greater need of protecting it against lawless law enforcement.[1] How difficult it is to adhere to a regime of strict legality, particularly in dealing with modern crime, is shown by the problem of "unreasonable searches and seizures",[2] which may be taken as a good illustration of the first source of the lameness of Justice.

The Fourth Amendment to the federal Constitution guarantees the common law "right of the people to be secure in their persons, houses, papers and effects, against unreasonable searches and seizures." It provides also that warrants shall issue only upon "probable cause, supported by oath or affirmation, and particularly describing the place to be searched, and the persons or things to be seized." These provisions, together with the related clause of the Fifth Amendment which provides that no person "shall be compelled in any criminal case to be a witness against himself", [3] apply to prosecutions in federal courts only, being protections against the possibly tyranny of the central government. There are, however, similar provisions in state constitutions or laws.[4] These protections are the crystallizations of a long and colorful history of the struggle of the individual against unfair tactics in the prosecution of crime by governmental officers. One of its American chapters was the opposition of the Colonists to the oppressive, irresponsible searchings and seizures under the infamous "Writs of Assistance." [5]

In attempting to pour a content into the constitutional phrase "unreasonable searches and seizures", courts have wrestled with two main questions: what is an "unreasonable" search and seizure, and what shall be the consequence in practice of the obtaining of evidence through such methods? This is not the place to explore minutely the web of legal interpretation which the courts have woven into the law on this subject. Suffice it to say that in the light of the types of crime involved and the techniques of modern criminals, some of the leading decisions are considered by persons versed in the practical difficulties of police administration in the modern scene to be unrealistic and needlessly detrimental to its work. Many decisions recognize the right of the police to search the person of a suspect as well as the room he occupies, when making a lawful arrest even without a search warrant, and to seize both instruments and evidence of crime thus obtained.[6] But when it is not an incident of arrest, on the authority of the Supreme Court of the United States it is "unreasonable" for government officials to make a search, with or without a warrant, the exclusive aim of which is to obtain evidence of the suspect's guilt.[7] This was the opinion in an important case in which the pertinent facts were as follows:

The accused was suspected of conspiring with an army officer to defraud the Government in connection with contracts for supplies. Upon direction of his superior officers in the Intelligence Department of the Army, a soldier acquainted with the suspect gained admission to his office in his absence under pretense of a friendly call, and without a warrant carried off several documents, one of which, "of evidential value only", was turned over to the prosecutor. Later, an agent of the Department of Justice swore out search warrants under which other papers were taken from the accused's office, among them being contracts between him and other persons. These papers were apparently alleged in the affidavits for the warrants to have been used as instruments in the commission of the felonies of bribery of an officer of the United States and conspiracy to defraud the Government, but in fact were only useful to the prosecution as *evidence* against the defendant. Before and during the trial the defendant moved to have this property restored to him, but the motions were denied,[8] and the documents were admitted in evidence over his objection that his constitutional rights had been violated.

The lower court certified a number of questions to the Supreme Court, among which was the query, concerning the material seized without a warrant, whether the secret abstraction, without force, by a representative of the Government, "of a paper writing of evidential value only belonging to one suspected of crime and from the house or office of such person", constituted a violation of the Fourth Amendment. The question was answered in the affirmative. The court reasoned that the invasion of the security and privacy of the home or office exists whether done through stealth or by force. And since "the result is the same to one accused of crime, whether he be obliged to supply evidence against himself or whether such evidence be obtained by an illegal search of his premises and seizure of his private papers", he being "in either case . . . the unwilling source of the evidence", the privilege against self-incrimination (Fifth Amendment) was also violated.

As to the materials seized under the warrants, the question was whether taking papers "of no pecuniary value but possessing evidential value against persons presently suspected and subsequently indicted" was a violation of constitutional protections. This too was answered in the affirmative, the court holding that a search warrant

> may not be used as a means of gaining access to a man's house or office and papers solely for the purpose of making search to secure evidence to be used against him in a criminal or penal proceeding, but . . . may be resorted to only when a primary right to such search and seizure may be found in the interest which the public or the complainant may have in the property to be seized, or in the right to the possession of it, or when a valid exercise of the police power renders possession of the property by the accused unlawful and provides that it may be taken.[9]

Since the documents seized under the warrants were of such nature that the Government could desire their possession only to use as evidence against the accused, to search for them was violative of the constitutional prohibition of unreasonable search and seizure, and to use them would be "to compel the defendant to become a witness against himself."

Especially in crimes in which the point of departure and chief basis of detection and proof are likely to be the seizure of articles, their barring from evidence may seriously hamper the administration of justice. As Chafee points out,

> a criminal, who is clever enough to gather into his possession all the damaging documents which are not actually instruments

of crime, will always be able to defy the Government to make the slightest use of such papers against him. What are the police to do, even though they know exactly where the evidence is? They cannot obtain a subpoena *duces tecum* ordering him to bring the papers into court himself, for that would violate his privilege against self-incrimination. They cannot break into his house with a search warrant and take the papers from him by force, because the warrant would be invalid and the evidence wholly inadmissible, at least if the accused made a seasonable demand for its return. This "astonishing situation" stirs the *Yale Law Journal* to apply Wigmore's phrase, "justice tampered with mercy." [10]

The courts are, however, divided on the question of permitting the use at the trial of illegally obtained materials in order to bring about the conviction of the person whose constitutional privileges have been violated. The Supreme Court, as we have seen, and a minority of the state tribunals bar such evidence; a majority of the courts admit it.

One has only to consider some of the reasoning of the two sets of courts to see that the questions of policy involved do not admit of any easy solution. They therefore interfere with the smooth progress of justice. The position of the first group might be summarized as follows:

If evidence unlawfully seized were allowed to be used, the constitutional protection against unreasonable searches and seizures would have little or no value.[11] Balancing the social interest in maintaining the force of constitutional protections against that of convicting offenders, it is better that a guilty person should escape punishment than that a court should ignore a fundamental constitutional principle in order to convict him.[12] Courts ought not, by permitting the use of evidence unlawfully seized, to encourage public officers to violate the law, thereby putting themselves in the position of apparently winking at illegality of one sort while punishing illegality of another. A legally sanctioned license (or even the appearance of one) to go on a fishing expedition to find evidence of the alleged guilt of a suspect who may or may not be guilty might well develop into a modern form of that tyrannical invasion of security and privacy (with its reflex of hatred of law-enforcing officers on the part of decent citizens) of which there is ample evidence in Anglo-American history [13] (and, one may add, sufficient example in the contemporary doings of certain foreign countries).

> If officers of the law were given unlimited license to search persons, homes, offices, automobiles, and effects whenever they desire, the nation would be saddled with a nuisance of the first magnitude which, in itself, would tend to bring all laws into disrepute. If, for example (as has frequently been the case), an over-zealous officer might station himself on one of our trunk highways, over which thousands of automobiles travel every day, stop every car and search the occupants, greatly to the annoyance and humiliation of the many innocent people, would not such a practice tend to bring unnecessary prejudice and odium upon the law itself? [14]

Far from indirectly condoning or seeming to condone illegality, it is the duty of the organs of justice to insist at all times upon just methods throughout the criminal proceedings, thereby helping to encourage a fairer and more scientific technique on the part of law enforcers. Constitutional provisions are meant to protect not merely the law-abiding but also those charged with crime. It is the duty of courts to insist upon fair play even toward one strongly suspected of crime, in order to retain and increase the general respect for and confidence in the fairness of the law. In the eloquent language of Mr. Justice Brandeis, dissenting from a decision in a case in which admission of evidence obtained through tapping of telephone wires outside the premises of the accused was held by the majority of the court not to infringe upon the defendant's constitutional rights:

> Our government is the potent, the omnipresent teacher. For good or for ill, it teaches the whole people by example. Crime is contagious. If the government becomes a lawbreaker, it breeds contempt for the law; it invites every man to become a law unto himself; it invites anarchy. To declare that in the administration of the criminal law the end justifies the means — to declare that the government may commit crimes in order to secure the conviction of a private criminal — would bring terrible retribution.[15]

The evil results might not be immediately discernible, but in the long run they would taint the moral atmosphere in which Justice is required to live.

In weighing this last argument, it is of course difficult to obtain conclusive proof that there is more lawless enforcement of criminal justice by police, as well as greater disrespect for the law and courts on the part of the general public, in jurisdictions which admit in evidence material illegally obtained than in the others. The variables are too numerous to permit of assigning a true weight to the single factor under examination. But it seems reasonable to assume that by insisting where possible upon lawful methods courts can reduce the number of unlawful ones, and that by publicly demanding fair play even for probable criminals they can aid in increasing respect for the fairness of law and thereby help to bolster up its waning authority.

The courts which do permit the use of unlawfully obtained evidence argue that the real right of the defendant is not to have the incriminating articles excluded, but to recover possession of them because they were wrongfully taken from him, this right existing independently of any use to be made of them by the state in prosecuting him for a crime.[16] The officer who acts without a warrant (or on a void warrant) is acting without state authority and thereby ceases to be an agent of the state — a fact which makes him alone responsible for his illegal act and has nothing to do with the later use of the materials he seized as evidence.[17] Why, then, should the state be handicapped in its law enforcement by barring such materials? Judge Cardozo points out that thereby, "the pettiest peace officer would have it in his power through overzeal or indiscretion to confer immunity upon an offender"; and one decision calls the exclusionary rule a "bomb proof dugout" for the enemies of the state.[18]

To the position taken by Mr. Justice Holmes that "we have to choose, and for my part I think it a less evil that some criminals should escape than that the Government should play an ignoble part",[19] comes the reply by an experienced investigator of the practical aspects of the problem, that "It is not a matter merely of 'some' criminals escaping justice. . . . Hundreds have been freed every year. In Detroit during a year when 1347 armed robberies occurred, one out of every four guilty gun-carriers arrested by the police was again turned loose upon the public because of this rule."[20] Nevertheless, one might legitimately inquire, how much of their discharge was owing to the operation of this rule and how much to insufficient skill on the part of the police and prosecutors in obtaining and organizing the proof of guilt acceptably, despite the rule? It would be interesting to obtain figures on the same point from other jurisdictions in which the exclusionary rule is followed.[21]

In courts which adhere to the common law practice of admitting evidence illegally obtained, it is also argued that there are more direct and pertinent ways of disciplining the overzealous police officer who resorts to unreasonable searches and seizures than by throwing out the evidence he obtains.[22] It is pointed out, for example, that a civil suit for damages is open to the person whose premises and privacy have been unlawfully invaded. But such recourse is not likely to be translated into a collectable judgment, since the plaintiff in such a suit is typically a humble person without funds to employ competent counsel, while the police officer enjoys the aid of the city's legal staff; besides, officers as a rule have little property on which to levy a judgment, even where the plaintiff is successful. Moreover, not all jurisdictions allow a suit for the invasion of privacy, which is the real injury in many cases. Remedies against the governmental units involved in unlawful searches and seizures either do not exist or are inadequate. Prosecutions for criminal trespass, or under special statutes which provide specifically for fines and jail sentences as punishments of unlawful searches and seizures, may theoretically discourage "dirty business" on the part of the police. But prosecutors rarely take action against the police, who are, after all, fellow-officers; and even where they do, such prosecutions are but little satisfaction to the victim. These personal remedies, finally, leave almost untouched the larger issue, namely, that the general public has an interest in seeing that law enforcement is proper and lawful. Such an interest is not secured by giving the injured person a remedy; it must be vindicated on behalf of Justice itself.

Those who would admit illegally obtained evidence also argue that the refinements and exceptions to the exclusionary rule which courts have developed, in themselves demonstrate the unwiseness of the rule. One of these is, for example, that "a warrantless search-and-seizure by some *third person* not acting in collusion with the Federal officer, is not within the exclusionary rule." [23] It can also be urged that courts which adhere to the exclusionary rule are inconsistent in barring evidence unlawfully obtained yet allowing the conviction of a defendant who has been kidnaped elsewhere and forcibly brought into their jurisdiction for trial.[24] But such an argument amounts to saying that if courts cannot for some reason demand legality in all proceedings they should not demand it in any. When it concerns the implementing of constitutional safeguards, it may well be that half a loaf is better than none.

We have not exhausted the arguments for and against the exclusion of evidence illegally obtained; but the points given are enough to illustrate some of the practical difficulties of a legal nature met with by the police and prosecutor in the administration of justice, particularly under modern social conditions. It is unnecessary to take a definite position on the basic issue involved in this particular example, in order to recognize that constitutional safeguards make it very difficult in certain types of cases for the police to remove some offenders from harm-dealing circulation. When it is considered that there are seven or eight constitutional protections involved in criminal trials,[25] part of the clumsiness of Justice is readily accounted for. If the police and prosecutor were given a free hand, many more criminals would be behind bars than at present; yet in a civilized community, unfair and lawless law enforcement should be kept at an irreducible minimum. The escape of a proportion of criminals is the price society must pay for its constitutional protections. While certain procedural improvements would be helpful in enlarging the legitimate activities of police and prosecutor, it is doubtful whether they are more valuable than the staffing of police and prosecutory agencies with high-minded, ingenious and technically trained personnel who will devise means of fighting crime efficiently yet fairly.

Other shackles of Justice in investigating and detecting crime are the technical legal rules respecting interstate rendition (extradition) and "close pursuit" of offenders across state lines[26] — which present problems of increasing importance with the growing mobility of modern criminals; arrest, with or without a warrant;[27] and "entrapment", or incitation of the prospective offender by an officer to commit a crime.[28] We cannot go into these and related matters in detail, but it ought to be pointed out that before the arrested person is taken into court on the preliminary hearing as to the existence of "probable cause" for holding him for prosecution, overly zealous police officers have ample opportunity to resort to all sorts of illegal and unfair practices. The reality of the dangers to constitutional rights and fundamental traditions of personal liberty has been forcibly brought home by the report on "Lawlessness in Law Enforcement" of the National Commission on Law Observance and Enforcement. Not only has the privilege against self-incrimination been violated in numerous instances, but also "such fundamental rights as those of (1) personal liberty; (2) bail; (3) protection from personal assault and battery; (4) the presumption of innocence until conviction of guilt by due process of law; and (5) the right to employ counsel, "who shall have access" to the accused "at reasonable hours." [29] These all indicate overzealousness on the part of the police in attempting to make the machinery of justice function more directly and expeditiously.

In justifying the "third degree", as in arguing for the admission of evidence unlawfully obtained, it is frequently urged by police officials that without such methods the obtaining of the proof would in many cases be impossible. But there is evidence that such methods, aside from their brutality, tend in the long run to defeat their own purpose; they encourage inefficiency on the part of the police. The use of the third degree, for example, "tends to make police and prosecutors less zealous in the search for objective evidence . . . 'It is a short cut and makes the police lazy and unenterprising.' " [30] Unfair methods also tend to turn loose as many criminals as they bring into custody:

> The statement of a Chicago lawyer . . . is enlightening. He says:

"I have tried 130 murder cases and I have won 126 of them. Many of these cases were based as far as the prosecution was concerned, on confessions extorted from the defendant by the 'third degree.' I have won almost all of the cases in which such confessions were obtained. If it had not been for the dishonest methods used by the police towards these defendants, I could not have won 10 of the 130 cases. In almost all the cases the police used illegal methods with the prisoners, deceiving, cajoling or bullying them. The jury saw that their methods had been unfair and acquitted defendants who might have been convicted except for the police." [31]

Finally, such unfair methods further contribute to the already too unwholesome moral climate of Justice, by lowering the esteem in which her administrators are held by the public. Here again, more high-minded and intelligent officials would find ways of loosening the shackles of Justice lawfully yet efficiently.

2

Consider, next, some of the procedural obstacles thrown in the path of Justice. Assuming that the state effects a lawful arrest of a person accused of crime and obtains evidence legitimately, it still may, in order to prove him guilty, have to tread a tortuous path through the magistrate's court, the grand jury and the petty or trial jury, not to speak of appellate tribunals. As has been indicated, in a felony case the accused is usually given a preliminary hearing on a complaint filed in a magistrate's court. If the magistrate finds probable cause that the accused committed the offense, the latter is "bound over" to await the action of the grand jury. Sometimes cases are brought directly to the grand jury. If a majority of that body think there is probable cause of his guilt, an indictment ("true bill") is returned. The indictment, among other features, names the defendant, states the acts constituting the criminal charge against him and indicates the time and place of their alleged commission. Though a simplified indictment form has in recent years been provided in some states, some jurisdictions still employ a highly technical instrument, full of saws and catches, reflecting in part the judicial psychology of the days when the possible consequence of conviction of any one of a long list of crimes was the punishment of death. These technicalities may make the indictment vulnerable to attack before or after trial and conviction. After indictment the accused is arraigned in open court, the charge is read to him and he is asked how he wishes to plead. If he pleads guilty, he is usually sentenced without further proceedings unless, in serious cases, a special hearing in mitigation of punishment is provided. If he pleads not guilty, a trial before the petty jury follows.

At the outset of the trial the defendant may attack the indictment because of defects in the composition of the grand jury, or its departure from statutory requisites. He may challenge the entire petty jury panel for similar reasons. If these attacks are repulsed, the selection of the jurors for the trial proceeds. Both the state and the defendant may eliminate by challenge for adequate cause any jurors not meeting statutory qualifications; they may also turn away a specified number for no assigned reason. After the twelve jurors have been selected, the state through its prosecutor first sketches for the jury what it proposes to prove. This is followed by the introduction of its witnesses. Being subject to strict rules of evidence, their testimony is given not in unhampered narrative form but by question and answer. Their veracity and reliability are tested by the device of cross-examination. Counsel for the defense then go through a like procedure of addressing the jury [32] and introducing and questioning witnesses, who are also open to cross-examination. Finally come the summings up by the defense and prosecution, the judge's charge to the jury on the law applicable to the case and the jury's deliberations. Throughout these proceedings there are numerous opportunities for motions, all of which must be passed upon by the judge, each adding to the delay, technicality and possible ultimate futility of the process. During the trial, counsel note numerous exceptions to rulings by the court on objections to evidence or to the judge's charge to the jury. These form the basis for review of the conviction by higher courts, on appeal by the defendant.

In most states, if the jury is not unanimous a mistrial results. If it returns a verdict of guilty the judge imposes sentence; it is the common practice to dispose of this important duty quite summarily and perfunctorily. In deploring the "law's delays", Hamlet could not have had the sentencing procedure in mind. Days, weeks and sometimes months are devoted to the trial; minutes are usually given over to the solution of the difficult problem — and the most serious one from both a social and an individual standpoint — of what to do with the defendant after he has been found guilty.

For the sake of clarity we have greatly simplified the

highly technical and shrewd game that is the criminal trial. The proceedings do not run off as smoothly as may have been suggested. There are opportunities for delay at every turn: continuances for absence of witnesses or for other engagements of counsel, attacks on the jurisdiction of the court by motion or by *habeas corpus*, and the like. In fact it is not uncommon to find a dozen or more steps in the proceedings, each of which gives some chance for delay and tactical manipulation of the "system" at its vulnerable points. The clever criminal lawyer is quick to shift his attack to the Achilles' heel. If magistrates become more strict in their preliminary examinations, he directs his attention to the district attorney's office. If the prosecutor is criticized in the press for his apparent leniency and thereafter for a time bears down hard on defendants, counsel's attack may stress loopholes in the indictment, or may shift to getting numerous technical errors into the record to serve as grounds for appeal and possible reversal of the conviction with the result of a retrial or sometimes of a dismissal of the charge. If appellate tribunals begin to look with disfavor upon errors that have not substantially affected the rights of the accused, the lawyer seeks leniency from the trial court in the form of suspended sentences or probation or a short term of imprisonment, whether or not the social good will be served thereby. And so with the various other parts of the process.

Indeed the chief qualification of the successful criminal lawyer is an ability to keep constantly alert to discover open or rusty joints in the armor of Justice. Aside from the fact that the prosecution usually has no appeal from a verdict of acquittal however much it appears to be a miscarriage of justice,[33] the Wickersham Commission listed no fewer than ten "mitigating devices" that must be reckoned with before a defendant can be convicted and stay convicted; [34] these are in addition to the constitutional guaranties. The history of criminal procedure shows that originally most of its technicalities were defense mechanisms against the unrestrained arbitrariness and tyranny of royal officials. Despite changed conditions, these have persisted in twentieth century American criminal procedure. The American Law Institute in 1930, after five years of work by authorities, completed a Code of Criminal Procedure in which some of the complicated steps of Justice are simplified, a few eliminated. But its provisions have as yet been adopted only partially, and then in but a few states.[35]

Perhaps under modern conditions the loosening of some of these shackles will benefit Justice without depriving accused persons of any essential safeguards against oppression. For example, cannot the four-fold sifting of many cases — by the police, magistrate, prosecutor and grand jury — be reduced? Is the preliminary hearing necessary, and if so does it not require revision? Is the grand jury still needed, and if so cannot its functions be limited to a few situations in which it still serves a useful purpose? These questions may be profitably pondered.

Recent investigations indicate that substantial proportions — in some cities as many as half or more — of the serious charges are dropped as the result of preliminary hearings. In such inquiries magistrates have the serious task of sifting felony charges, thereby preventing unjust prosecutions and reducing the burden of the district attorney and the grand jury. These preliminary proceedings in the lower courts are as a rule not carefully recorded, so that it is difficult to check up on the efficiency of the magistrates who wield so great a power at the early stage of criminal proceedings.[36] Yet the quality of the work done at the preliminary examination may be sufficiently determined. In many jurisdictions the prosecutor is not represented; where he is, his work seems to be largely a waste of time and money. Speaking of the preliminary hearing in the criminal branches of the Chicago Municipal Court, the Illinois Crime Survey concluded: "The cases are not well prepared, witnesses are almost never interviewed before their appearance, the assistant state's attorneys who are present appear to the have the attitude represented by . . . the opinion it doesn't matter much — 'It's only a preliminary hearing.' "[37] The seriousness of such a situation may be inferred from the fact that in one recent year, in Chicago alone, of 10,829 felony cases entering the preliminary hearing, no fewer than 6,124, or almost 60 per cent., were disposed of as the result of this sifting process; in New York State, in 1930, 51 per cent. were thus eliminated. A similar picture of the preliminary hearing and of its importance in terms of the proportion of cases handled has in recent years been sketched by investigators in Cleveland and Philadelphia, and would probably also be found in many other cities.[38]

Not all the fault for questionable dismissals lies with the magistrate and the preliminary hearing; the numerous arrests, many of which are evidently unnecessary, and the poor preparation of the evidence are also to blame. Without the magistrate's elimination of many charges, the mills of Justice would be unable to grind out the heavy stream of cases fed into them. But the evidence so far available shows that rural magistrates are far less willing to drop cases at the preliminary investigation. Thus, compared to the 57 per cent. of the eliminations in Chicago only 11 per cent. were dropped in rural Illinois counties; the respective percentages in Missouri cities and rural districts were 42 and 11; in the three largest cities of New York compared to places with a population of less than 50,000, the proportions of major offenses disposed of (acquitted or dismissed without going to the grand jury) in the lower courts in 1933 were 38.2 per cent. and 17.4 per cent. These differences, plus the fact that in Milwaukee, a city favorably known for its low crime rate, only 17 per cent. of the felonies are eliminated at the preliminary hearing, suggest that in the nature of the problem there is no inherent necessity for the high percentage of dismissals by magistrates.[39] In considering this matter it should be borne in mind that while the accused is permitted to be represented by counsel at the preliminary investigation, only the state is represented in the grand jury room; however, at the preliminary hearing the state is often represented only by the arresting officer or complaining witness and is therefore at a disadvantage because the defendant has an attorney. These considerations imply that while the proceedings in the magistrates' courts might well be retained, they need to be raised in efficiency. In addition to various necessary improvements in preparation and presentation of cases at the preliminary hearing, the question should be raised whether the grand jury sifting is still called for in most cases.

Constitutions customarily provide that no person is to be convicted of a serious offense (usually a felony) except upon indictment by a grand jury. In the proportion of cases disposed of, however, the grand jury plays a much smaller part today than do the magistrates at the preliminary hearing. Thus, in Illinois it was found that only 12 per cent. of the charges were eliminated at the grand jury stage, compared to 44 per cent. at the preliminary hearing; in New York State (1933) 12 per cent., compared to 55 per cent. In Missouri and certain other jurisdictions the grand jury has an even smaller part in disposing of cases.[40] In practice, in many jurisdictions the grand jury is inclined to be the creature of the prosecutor, customarily following his recommendations as to whether or not an indictment should be brought in. In England for many years the grand jury did little more than ratify the findings of the examining magistrates. "Here and there a bill was thrown out, but on no discoverable principle. It is a fact that the court usher, the only official allowed to be with the grand jury, frequently guided their deliberations."[41]

Both because of the proportionately small number of cases handled by it and for reasons discussed in the note,[42] the grand jury, except for purposes later mentioned, appears to be a superfluous luxury in the administration of justice. It adds to delay, it inconveniences witnesses and those who serve on it, it multiplies opportunities for escape of the guilty through technicalities; finally, in this day it rarely gives the accused any greater protection than do proceedings initiated by the prosecutor's statement of the offense, known as the "information." For these and other reasons the grand jury has been virtually eliminated in about half the states, which provide that indictable offenses may also be prosecuted by information. Studies of the procedure in those states indicate that prosecution by information is more efficient and less expensive than prosecution by indictment.[43] During the next few years we may expect the function of the grand jury in most states to be reduced to a task that still remains legitimate — the making of special investigations of a broad nature, such as inquiries into the conduct of public officials or institutions, or into widespread corruption.[44]

The trial jury has also been subjected to attack. Judged by the percentage of cases that today go to trial, however, the petty jury has shrunk to relatively little importance in the procedural scheme.[45] The unrestrained waxing of the prosecutor's role in American polity has been compensated by a corresponding waning of the jury's. Thus in recent years in New York City but 4.7 per cent. of the cases ever reached trial; in Chicago, only 3.8 per cent; in Cleveland, 13.6 per cent; in Cincinnati, 11.8 per cent; in Franklin County, Ohio, 10 per cent; in St. Louis, 13 per cent; and in New Jersey (1934), but 7.8 per cent.[46] If the jury is still a desirable institution, it ought to be strengthened as regards the machinery for selecting jurors and for determining their qualifications. The immediate issue, however, is whether the objectives of the trial are more likely to be achieved expeditiously and fairly by a judge or by a jury. In discussing this problem we are concerned essentially with serious criminal charges which involve oversight of the trial proceedings by judges who as a rule are of greater competence than the magistrates in the lower courts.

What are the defects with which modern trial by jury stands charged? It has been attacked on the ground of technicalities involved in the selection of jurors, which tend to fill the jury-box with incompetent, overly emotional or prejudiced assayers of facts, and to slow up proceedings. It has been charged with needless waste. It has been chided for acquitting too many guilty defendants. It has been accused of being just one more institution in the complicated system that is susceptible of corrupt influence to the detriment of Justice. These alleged stigmata of the jury system deserve some consideration.

Compulsory resort to jury trial in felony cases has a much greater retarding effect than might be inferred from the relatively low percentage of cases that reach the trial stage. Jury trials absorb a disproportionately high proportion of the time and effort of court and prosecutor. Sometimes hundreds of men are drawn and qualify for jury service, report for duty over a period ranging from days to weeks or more, and although paid, do not serve. In dramatic cases, or those involving wealthy defendants, the public is regaled with the spectacle of hundreds of prospective jurors being examined before the magic twelve are finally chosen. In one Chicago case, 1,350 jurymen were summoned and 646 examined before twelve were selected.[47] In a San Francisco case a few years ago it took ninety days to choose the jury.[48] These are, to be sure, atypical instances. Such scandals need not necessarily attend trial by jury; they are largely due to weak judges and to their lack of authority themselves to examine and qualify jurors.[49] They are foreign to proceedings in federal courts and those in England and Canada. But a realistic account of modern jury trials cannot ignore their existence, both because they illustrate the depths to which trial by jury is capable of sinking, and because of their effect on the public's conception of criminal justice. To all the delay involved in drawing the panel and selecting jurors for the trial is added the slowing up of proceedings by the numerous contests over the admissibility of much of the evidence, a condition that is not nearly so marked where the judge tries the case himself.

The equipment of jurors for their tasks is gone into in detail in a later chapter. Here it need only be mentioned that by the method of their selection, their occupational background and their lack of training for the weighing of evidence and discounting the effect of emotional appeals by counsel, typical jurors are not the best triers of facts. Of course, juries in criminal cases are expected to temper justice with mercy, to represent, as it were, a sample of the sentiments of the community. In some states they are even judges of the law as well as the facts, and in some they are permitted considerable latitude in determining the punishment. But if emotional considerations are to be permitted, it must be remembered that a jury not only can be humane but can be swayed equally in the opposite direction when an innocent defendant happens to be unpopular. The contents and titles of recent books, such as "Convicting the Innocent" and "Trial by Prejudice",[50] are eloquent of this truth. It is moreover questionable whether sentimental considerations are appropriate in ascertaining the basic fact of whether the accused did or did not commit the offense charged.[51] They belong more properly, if anywhere, at the sentencing stage, when it is to be determined what form of correctional treatment is best suited to the offender.[52]

Do juries acquit an unduly high proportion of those tried? The answer cannot of course be definite, for the reason that a careful analysis of each case is needed in order to determine whether the evidence justified an acquittal, and even then there may be legitimate differences of opinion. A finding of "probable cause" in the preliminary examination, or indictment by the grand jury, does not necessarily mean that the defendant is really guilty. The case is not fully tried at either of these early stages, and the requirement at the trial that guilt be established beyond a reasonable doubt is a higher standard than those that govern in holding the defendant for the action of the grand jury or in finding an indictment. It is therefore hard to fix upon a reasonable rate of acquittals to be expected of jury trials. However, available statistics disclose such considerable proportions of acquittals as to demonstrate that there is something wrong with jury trials in many places. To mention a few of the figures, in recent years the proportion of acquittals in jury-tried cases in New York City was 56 per cent., in Chicago 57, in Cincinnati 23, in Cleveland 38, in St. Louis 43, in New Jersey (1934) 47.[53] Since the final results of the activities of Justice are attributable to an interplay of many influences, not all of the responsibility for what appears to be an unduly high acquittal rate can be laid at the door of the jury. Some of it doubtless belongs in the police department and prosecutor's office, since a fair proportion of the cases are not properly prepared or presented for trial.

No statistical data are available regarding the corruption of juries; however, not a few cities have in recent years been aware that the practice exists. It is frequently argued that one reason why the jury can be "reached" is the requirement of a unanimous verdict: the venality of one juror is enough to "hang" a jury or force a compromise verdict. On this assumption it has been suggested that a three-fourths or five-sixths verdict replace the unanimous one. In support of this it is pointed out that unanimity is not required in any other branch of our polity, including decisions by the Supreme Court of the United States. It has also been suggested that a thirteenth juror be impanneled to prevent mistrials due to illness or death of a regular juror.

These and similar details of administration are important, but they are subsidiary to the larger question whether jury trials should be retained. Complete abolition would require constitutional amendments, and would meet with considerable hostility. At the present stage professional opinion seems to be in favor of retaining the jury, but providing for and encouraging waiver of jury trial at the option of the defendant. Such a provision, for all except capital cases, is embodied in the American Law Institute's Code of Criminal Procedure (section 266), and has been recommended in most recent investigations.[54] Not only does this give the innocent defendant a chance to present his case to a better trier of the facts, but it partly shields him against newspaper publicity. On the part of the state, in turn, time and money are saved, the proportion of nolles is likely to be reduced, and the chances of reversal are lessened. For over a hundred years Maryland has permitted defendants to elect whether they will be tried by judge or jury. The constitutions of six states have long provided for waiver without regard to class of case, and a few other states have enacted legislation permitting waiver in all cases. Many states have abolished jury trial in petty offenses.[55] Over nine-tenths of the tried felony cases in Maryland are disposed of by a judge without a jury. The proportions in other jurisdictions, while not as high, may be expected to increase with the passage of time and the establishment of a tradition in favor of trial before judges.

Another factor that is both symptom and cause of the clumsiness of Justice is the hesitancy of courts, until very recently and then only with great reservation, to make use of the possible contributions of extra-legal sciences in the trial of cases. When the issue of guilt or innocence is tried, the admission of proof is governed by highly technical rules of evidence designed to keep out irrelevant matters. While the basic principles of the law of evidence reflect shrewd judicial experience and knowledge of human nature as crystallized in countless litigations, others might be improved by the freer admission into the trial forum of some of the attitudes and techniques of investigation used in psychology and other disciplines. These would aid in getting at the truth of facts of a litigated issue.[56] Leading students of the law of evidence are on the whole not unsympathetic to the introduction of points of view and data from the experimental sciences, provided these have received general acceptance among authorities in the pertinent fields; but courts and legislatures are inclined to be excessively conservative in this respect. "The road to judicial recognition of scientific evidence," says a recent explorer of this subject, "is not always an easy one, as indicated by the historical development of firearms identification testimony in the state of Illinois. In examples like this the layman finds some support for his criticism of the courts concerning such matters."[57] Fortunately, there is a growing even if cautious tendency of the courts in recent years to call to the aid of the traditional techniques of the legal forum the findings of the scientific laboratory. Fingerprint similarities, photomicrographs revealing the crystalline structure of metal in weapons, findings of likenesses in bullets as revealed by the comparison microscope, results of chemical tests and spectographic analyses, as well as other data of this type, are increasingly being admitted into evidence.

The conservatism of the courts is illustrated, however, by the fact that it was not until 1911, years after expert experience proved the reliability of fingerprint evidence, that an American appellate tribunal "took judicial notice of the fact that fingerprints of any individual are so distinctive as to permit their use for the purpose of identification, and admitted expert testimony as to the similarity between the evidence print and that of the defendant."[58] So also, courts have long hesitated to admit blood tests in evidence to disprove paternity, although these have won favor on the Continent. Only recently (1935) has the enactment of a statute in New York providing for the use of blood tests in criminal cases been hailed as "another forward step in medico-legal jurisprudence." [59] But the few instances in which the question has been considered by appellate tribunals are not very encouraging as regards the judicial attitude.[60] Again, although scientifically valid proof exists of the reasonable, though not perfect, reliability of the polygraph deception test ("lie-detector"), courts still refuse to admit evidence based on its use.[61] In a recent case counsel offered to prove by means of the polygraph the truth of the defendant's alibi. The trial court barred such evidence, and on appeal the Supreme Court of Wisconsin was of opinion that while this instrument "may have some utility at present, and may ultimately be of great value in the administration of justice," its acceptance "during this stage of its development may bring complications and abuses which will overbalance whatever utility it may be assumed to have." [62]

More fundamental difficulties, however, are contributed by the very essence of the proceedings in American courts. The trial is a contentious performance in which the give and take of opposing counsel, under highly technical rules, is assuredly not the most scientific or just way of getting at the facts. The modern criminal trial may be described as a polite version of at least one of its oldest progenitors — trial by combat. The mental climate of the forum, and its historic traditions, are such as to give too much weight to the rules and their clever manipulation, and too little to the ascertainment of the truth. Under this "sporting theory of justice", and with weak judges exercising an authority that is sometimes insufficient even for strong ones, the search for the facts is very likely to degenerate into a vigorous forensic battle marked by trickiness and surprise. Neither side is as a rule willing to disclose its full case to the other before trial. Alibis and pleas of insanity may be concocted at the last moment.[63] In sensational cases, though the fiction is encouraged that the trial is carried on in the supposedly sober and dignified atmosphere of the courtroom, the press and other outside influences exert their pressures.

It is in such an atmosphere and under such a system that unrealistic rules of evidence are very likely to defeat the ends of Justice. Wigmore, the chief authority on the law of evidence, has aptly summarized the faults and needs of the system. He calls, first, for a greater flexibility in the rules themselves, pointing out that the technical rigidity of the mechanism of proof is "due to the exaltation of the rule into an end in itself, instead of a means to an end, viz. a correct verdict." In his opinion, "the law of Evidence needs a good deal of loosening." Secondly, he suggests the need of a counteractive to the tendency, in applying the rules at the trial, to magnify petty technical details. Thirdly, he demands that appellate tribunals cease overemphasizing the significance of technical errors committed at the trial. "The nauseous and intellectually disgraceful doctrine of 'reversible error' has too long stained the pages of our appellate opinions." [64] Other authorities have likewise criticized certain of the rules of evidence as not realistic enough or overly technical.[65] Indeed a judge of unusual wisdom deemed it necessary to remind the legal profession that the doctrines of evidence may blind them to the fact that the rules were after all never intended to supplant sound reasoning:

> The custom [says Learned Hand] of attributing to the rules of evidence the relevancy or irrelevancy of the proof is certainly an inversion. An issue is a proposition of fact, asserted by one side and denied by the other. The canon for its proof is not prima facie anyway, legal at all, but rational, and in a court room men's minds should operate no differently from outside. That evidence is relevant which human beings would think to prove the issue, if they had never heard of a court, and the test of its relevancy depends altogether upon what the proposition truly is. Now of course a judge may misunderstand what the issue is, and the poor wretch is lucky if he can find it at all amid the usual pleadings as they are drawn, but if he has found it, his ruling is right or wrong, not as he is a learned lawyer, but a sensible man.[66]

It has been proposed by various reformers that trial rules be modified. The defendant should be required to give the prosecutor advance notice of the nature of his defense, so as to reduce the elements of surprise, perjury and manufactured alibis. The number of motions should be cut, and notice should be given before they are made. The historic privilege against compelling the accused to testify should be abolished; and the prosecutor should be permitted to comment to the jury on the defendant's failure to take the stand in his own defense. The presumption of innocence to which the defendant is entitled should be done away with, and the state should not have to prove its case "beyond a reasonable doubt" but only by a preponderance of the evidence, even if thereafter a reasonable doubt of guilt still remains in the mind of the jury. The hypothetical question and partisan expert testimony, particularly in insanity trials, should be eliminated.

Some of these proposals are valuable and timely; others, such as the abolition of the privilege against compulsory testimony, the presumption of innocence and the requirement of proof of guilt beyond a reasonable doubt, seem to be abandonments of protections too vital to destroy unless more efficient safeguards are substituted. Present events in parts of Europe should convince the most ardent reformers that the evil practices which gave birth to these protections may once again prevail. That even a cabinet officer sees fit to shield himself with the constitutional privilege against self-incrimination when charged with an offense, is a disgraceful spectacle. But it is doubtful whether more would not be lost than gained if these historic privileges, grounded in a tyrannical past capable of rebirth, were lightly abandoned for the sake of convicting more offenders.

But all the proposals mentioned seem to avoid the basic problem of securing more adequate servants of Justice. True, elaborate rules exist primarily because the Anglo-American trial, unlike the continental one, is an adversary or contentious, rather than an inquisitorial, proceeding. But even with this characteristic it might be greatly improved with more skilful and high-minded personnel. The decorum of the English criminal court, its adroit guidance of the trial by the judge, its elimination of haggling over extremely technical rules of evidence and requested instructions to the jury, the smoothness and expeditiousness of its trial procedure, indicate that the chief weaknesses of the adversary system of criminal procedure may be markedly reduced by raising the standards of the bench and bar and then giving trial judges more power to guide the proceedings than they now have in most courts. As Wigmore aptly puts it,

> Judges must become stronger and better equipped at the trial bench, and more liberal and more justice-seeking on the appellate bench. The rules must be treated only as means to an end; and this cannot be until the men on the bench see them in that light and make it a prime aim to treat them so. The rule is the complement of the man. The weaker the man, as a dispenser of justice, the more the rule is exalted and the stiffer its bonds become. Improvement of the rules will need more sympathy and intelligence to handle them effectively.
>
> All the rules in the world will not get us substantial justice if the judges and the counsel have not the correct living moral attitude towards substantial justice.[67]

3

Aside from personnel, the difficulties of Justice are not exclusively attributable to constitutional or procedural complications and methods of proving guilt or innocence, even if we stress these aspects of an organic whole. Among the most serious causes for the lameness and awkwardness of Justice are those that spring from the substantive criminal law itself. Basically it is still grounded on naive conceptions of human mind and behavior and their relation to "responsibility." Volumes could be written on the recondite technicalities of its various branches, but a few references must suffice.

Consider, first, the very foundation of criminal liability. The traditional basis, both in the definition of crimes and the provision of punishments, is "intent", founded on a naive conception of freedom of will from which "responsibility" is assumed to flow. "Historically," as Pound puts it, "our substantive criminal law is based upon a theory of punishing the vicious will. It postulates a free agent confronted with a choice between doing right and doing wrong and choosing freely to do wrong. It assumes that the social interest in the general security and the social interest in the general morals are to be maintained by imposing upon him a penalty corresponding exactly to the gravity of his offense." [68] Yet study of the motivating factors of criminality shows how little, in most instances, there is of "free will" in so simple a sense.

This is not to say that the recognition of biologic and social causality in human behavior excludes altogether a realistic concept of the capacity for choice which different persons possess in varying degree. From the presence of mechanism in one aspect of personality and conduct it does not necessarily follow that human beings have not some spark of capacity for consciously and purposefully guiding their behavior to conform to legal sanctions.[69] In recent years even physical science has rejected a rigid determinism for a theory of "indeterminacy" or "probability." In the view of Eddington, while "the admission of indeterminism in the physical universe does not immediately clear up all the difficulties — not even all the physical difficulties — connected with Free Will . . . it so far modifies the problem that the door is not barred and bolted for a solution less repugnant to our deepest intuitions than that which has hitherto seemed to be forced upon us." [70] But if the criminal law and its punitive provisions are to continue to be founded on an unsophisticated theory of freedom of will, then both in logic and in fairness responsibility and punishment ought to be accommodated to the precise degree of free will and blameworthiness existing in the particular defendant, or, at any rate, in the fictional "reasonable man" of the law.[71] Human ingenuity has, however, not yet invented a machine for measuring this. The most that can be said about the defendant at the bar is that he did or did not do the prohibited act. Even the question of whether he did it intentionally or not is sometimes very difficult to answer; in practice it is often merely inferred from the fact that he did it. What role unconscious motivation may have played in formulating or biasing the "criminal intent" is not inquired into.

But aside from more subtle motivating forces, the criminal law is unrealistic in not taking into account sufficiently the fact that many criminals suffer from defective intelligence, mental disease,[72] abnormal emotional makeup, overly strong instinctual drives, and like handicaps.[73] Finally, the fact needs to be faced in any just philosophy of responsibility that many criminals are more or less victims of the poverty and other unwholesome social influences over which they have little control.

To be sure, some of these factors are provided for in the rules respecting the irresponsibility of the insane. Yet, on examination, the law on this subject only discloses its fundamental inadequacies. Unworkable "tests" of ancient vintage are given to juries to apply to the hopelessly confused conflicting testimony of partisan medical experts. This subject has been explored in detail elsewhere;[74] here we can only indicate a few of the basic imperfections of this branch of the criminal law, due to its origin in days before there were sciences of biology, psychology and psychiatry.

The modern English law, though reaching back to distant times, rests essentially upon the famous M'Naghten Case, decided in 1843.[75] In that historic opinion the rules of responsibility were crystallized in the well known answers of the judges of England to certain questions propounded by the House of Lords as the result of an unpopular acquittal of M'Naghten, a paranoiac who killed Sir Robert Peel's secretary, mistaking him for the statesman. The judges replied that "to establish a defence on the ground of insanity, it must be clearly proved that, at the time of committing the act, the party accused was labouring under such a defect of reason, from disease of the mind, as not to know the nature and quality of the act he was doing, or, if he did know it, that he did not know he was doing what was wrong." This simple-sounding "test" of the irresponsibility of the mentally ill has in practice led to great confusion and difficulty of application. Almost every phrase in the classic judicial utterance is open to criticism from both a legal and a psychiatric point of view. The same is true of the further opinion of the judges in this case that a person who suffered from delusion might be liable to punishment if he knew that he was acting contrary to law.

Most courts still refuse to consider any criterion of the irresponsibility of the insane other than some local variation in phraseology of the "nature-and-quality" or "right-and-wrong" test. In a number of jurisdictions, however, under the influence of both legal theory and attacks by psychiatrists, it has been held that irresponsibility may under certain conditions result from the presence of an "insane, irresistible impulse" even though knowledge of the nature and quality and wrongfulness of an act exists. The New Hampshire law expresses the doctrine that the question of irresponsibility by reason of insanity is altogether one of fact for the jury, since there is in truth no particular legal test which they must (or in fact always do) observe. Reviewing all the "symptoms, phases, or manifestations, of mental disease as legal tests of capacity to entertain a criminal intent," Judge Ladd, in a classic decision in 1871, concluded that "they are all clearly matters of evidence, to be weighed by the jury." [76] But other courts have shrunk from this cutting of the intricate Gordian knot of responsibility, both on authoritarian grounds and for the reason that juries might easily acquit many offenders who are not clearly insane if the entire question were left to them without any binding rules in the form of "tests."

While it is true that the law has never held that the mere existence of mental disease or defect in itself constitutes an exemption from criminal liability,[77] the fact remains that the attempted drawing of the line in insanity cases has resulted in confusion worse confounded. Moreover, the standard tests today proceed more or less upon the following assumptions, which from the viewpoints of psychiatry and psychology are open to question: that lack of knowledge of the nature or quality of an act or incapacity to know right from wrong (assuming the meaning of such terms to be clearly defined in the minds of juries and in judicial decisions, which they too often are not) is the sole or even the most significant symptom of mental disorder of all types; that such knowledge is the exclusive instigator and guide of conduct or at least the most vital element therein, and consequently should be the only criterion of responsibility when mental disorder is involved; and that the capacity of knowing right from wrong may be completely intact and may function normally even though a defendant be otherwise of disordered mind.

The irresistible impulse test supplies in a measure the deficiencies of the knowledge tests; for it takes into account disturbances in the volitional-inhibitory mode of mental life. It recognizes that although the disorder in the cognitive sphere may not be such as to prevent a defendant from having had some conception of the nature of his act and its wrongfulness when he committed the offense, he may none the less have been suffering from a deep-seated mental disturbance which markedly affected his capacity for self-management. Emphasis of delusion as a test may be criticized in that it represents a singling out of one symptom from a general disease syndrome in the delusional mental disorders, a symptom which is not necessarily more significant than others and which is not always present in all mental disturbances. There are some decisions, going back also to the M'Naghten Case, to the effect that a delusion will exempt from responsibility only in case the facts of the delusional belief, if they had actually been true, would have justified or excused the act. This is founded on the naive assumption that the reasoning of a mentally ill person with respect to "mistake of fact" is the same as that of a mentally sound one.

All three of these chief concepts — knowledge, irresistible impulse and delusion — are open to criticism as tests of irresponsibility, because their employment neglects the fundamental fact of the interrelationship and interdependence of mental processes. A serious disturbance in the cognitive or volitional or emotional sphere can hardly occur without its affecting the personality as a whole and the conduct that flows from it. One could readily show that these outworn preconceptions of the law may work injustice to offenders suffering from various forms of mental illness, particularly those with pronounced psychoneuroses, in whom unconscious motivation of conduct is more and more conceded to play a major role.

To be sure, the number of cases in which the defense of insanity is resorted to is small compared to the total of prosecutions; but the doctrines of the criminal law are most clearly shown to be inadequate when the crucial question of responsibility is subjected to analysis through the approach of the liability of mentally ill offenders.

There is questionable psychology, also, at the basis of the fine-spun distinctions between various degrees of crime. To cite one example, Mr. Justice Cardozo has called attention to the unsatisfactory nature of the distinction in the New York penal law between murder in the first and murder in the second degree, which turns on whether "premeditation" was present or absent. How the case is decided means the difference between life imprisonment (which often results in incarceration for a period less than life) and the death penalty. Yet there is great confusion in the judicial interpretation of the distinction. "The presence of a sudden impulse [Judge Cardozo points out] is said to mark the dividing line, but how can an impulse be anything but sudden when the time for its formation is measured by the lapse of seconds? Yet the decisions are to the effect that seconds may be enough." [78]

One final illustration of the inadequacies of the criminal law is furnished by the law of larceny, which involves a very considerable proportion of crimes. A careful investigator of this field has recently concluded "that the rules defining the subject-matter of larceny have become so highly involved, numerous and technical that they are extremely difficult to apply competently," and that results are therefore reached "which are irrational and unjust," because many persons who are as guilty as those punished escape through accumulated technical loopholes.[79] This has a harmful effect upon the community's sense of justice. This writer gives very convincing evidence in support of his conclusions.

But the clumsiness of Justice attributable to weaknesses in the criminal law springs from deeper cleavages. These reflect the law's fundamental inconsistency: it is a house divided. Basically, the cloven hoof of the ancestral vengefulness of our criminal law still marks and mars it after centuries of piecemeal reform, despite its camouflage of questionable psychologic and ethical notions. On top of this, with the passage of time, various contradictory theories have dictated the addition to the historic mass of common law, of statutes whose inconsistency with the whole has rarely been noted by enthusiastic reformers. Contrivance upon contrivance has been attached to the common law core with no attempt at a basic redesign of the structure.

One of the most obvious inconsistencies arises from the

punishments provided. In the same jurisdiction various offenses are punished on two contradictory theories: for one group fixed sentences are provided, for another indeterminate ones.[80] The penocorrectional philosophies behind the two are different. The one is a survival of the naive belief that the appropriate dose of punishment can be determined in advance and measured out legislatively on the basis of the relative heinousness or danger to social security of the crime in question. The other reflects the opinion that the length of punishment cannot be stated in advance, but must be modified by a parole board on the basis of each prisoner's dangerousness as determined by his reaction to imprisonment and by his characteristics and socio-economic background; the offender, rather than the offense, is the point of orientation.

Such contradictions permeate the system, varying in different states only in degree. On turning the pages of a modern statute book on criminal law, procedure and administration one becomes convinced of the prime need of introducing order and a clearer definition of aims. Ideas of crime causation and responsibility going back to medieval or early modern times jostle the most up-to-date statutes pertaining to the psychiatric examination of prisoners. Like the temple of some insane architect who, with little rhyme and less reason, has embodied his delusional dreams in a conglomerate of Egyptian and Assyrian, Greek and Roman, Gothic and Renaissance elements, the criminal law and its associated statutes form a bizarre edifice. In the center squats the pyramid of vindictiveness, its peak of deterrence rising above the rest of the structure; its chief function seems to be much the same as that of its Egyptian prototype, — entombment. Attached to one side is the Assyrian wingéd bull of "reformation", reflected in those reformatories which too often are in fact junior prisons. Another side is Doric, its strong, simple columns embodying the Classical, "even-handed justice" theories of Beccaria, — equal punishment of all offenders who commit outwardly similar crimes. But even here, the purity of the structure is adulterated by the over-ornate Corinthian columns, which reflect the ridiculous refinements that many judges go to in the exercise of discretion within the bounds of the indeterminate sentence. On another side of the pyramidal core abuts a court of Roman arches, representing the stiffening of the indeterminate sentence by the rules governing parole. The fourth wing is a melange of Gothic pointed arches, embodying the aspirations of the juvenile court and supported by the flying buttresses of the psychiatric clinic and social case work. Perched precariously on the peak of the pyramid rises the dome of the probation system, representing, like those of the massive churches and palaces of the Renaissance, a rebirth of old ideas garnished with new. Is it any wonder that such a disharmonious edifice is unesthetic, illogical and ineffective? [81]

These contradictions of what should be a system of justice, but is in fact most unsystematic, are reflected in the attitudes of those who administer the law. Each is typically inclined to regard his particular job as an end in itself, unrelated to the tasks of those who come before or after. The institutional administrator is concerned with seeing that inmates who adhere to the rules of the prison shall be rewarded by early release on parole; his job is to have harmony in the institution. The parole board is concerned with seeing that dangerous offenders are not released on parole until absolutely necessary; it sees its task from the point of view of protecting society. We may marvel that the product of Justice is as good as it is, being conceived in a welter of contradiction and tended by nurses with inconsistent notions of what is best for the patient.

Of course it is possible that the fundamental attitudes toward crime are basically irreconcilable.[82] Or it may be that one approach is suited to one type of offense or offender, the other to a second. At all events, the time is ripe for a radical reëxamination and overhauling of the complicated and ill-arranged structure of criminal justice. For it is clear that many of the definitions of the criminal law, and the procedural and evidential devices that accompany it, originated in simpler times and places. Some of the technicalities hark back to the days when a petty offense was punishable by death, and when as a result technical loopholes were invented as escapes from the rigors of the law and the tyrannies of royal judges. Others were designed for a much simpler economy and a freer play of individualism. The provisions have on the whole not kept abreast of the rapid and radical transformations of the American scene: the industrialization and urbanization discussed in the opening chapter and their attendant changes in the habits and customs of the people; the modification of attitudes toward crime and punishment; the rise of the disciplines of sociology, statistics, psychiatry, psychology. The more technical the provisions have become, the more difficult has it been to convict the guilty and the more specious has become the claim that the rich and the poor

— those who can afford expensive counsel and those who cannot — are really equal before the law.

Basic to the necessary redesign of the criminal law and its associated apparatus is a realistic, unbiased examination into its fundamentals; into the practical work of the agents of Justice; into the results of their efforts in terms of reducing crime, rehabilitating offenders and deterring prospective wrongdoers; and into the relationship of the criminal law and its agencies to other social institutions and other sources of authority and control. It is gratifying to report that, under the auspices of the American Law Institute, a responsible movement is under way for such fundamental explorations.[83] We may hope that completion of the work will result in a more efficient as well as a more ethical Justice; a goddess freed of at least some of the historic shackles that today impede her progress. For Webster was not indulging in mere oratorical hyperbole when, in his oft-quoted but still vital encomium on Judge Story, he exclaimed: "Justice, sir, is the great interest of man on earth."

CHAPTER IV

THE BLINDNESS OF JUSTICE

1

"WHAT have we better than a blind guess to show that the criminal law in its present form does more good than harm? I do not stop to refer to the effect which it has had in degrading prisoners and in plunging them further into crime, or to the question whether fine and imprisonment do not fall more heavily on a criminal's wife and children than on himself. I have in mind more far-reaching questions. Does punishment deter? Do we deal with criminals on proper principles?" [1] These are the words of Mr. Justice Holmes, spoken four decades ago. Since then we have made a little progress. The "born criminal" theory of Lombroso has come and gone, though it is perhaps in some of its aspects about to receive a new lease on life.[2] The development of statistical technique has enabled investigators to draw some rough generalizations about the characteristics of criminals and the results of peno-correctional treatment. The case-history method has suggested a fruitful hypothesis or two regarding the interplay of individual and cultural factors in the etiology of crime. The recent investigations of police and prosecutors' offices, courts and prisons, have given some insight into the anatomy and pathology of these bodies, less into their physiology. A few studies have thrown some light on the results of different types of correctional treatment. But there is still a vast amount to be learned about the influences operative in crime and punishment, the processes of reformation, the questions put by Holmes, indeed the day to day tasks that Justice is called upon to perform.

Traditionally the goddess is represented as blindfolded. This pretty custom is supposed to suggest her impartiality, but ironically enough it may come to be a symbol of her actual blindness. It may also be deemed a symbol of society engaged in a tragi-comic game of blindman's buff. Some of the evidences of this situation deserve consideration.

2

If a criminologist were asked to give more than a very rough estimate of the amount of crime existing in any community, or to calculate whether crime has increased or decreased in proportion to the population, or whether one type of punishment or correction is more effective than another; if he were required to answer with precision many other questions the answering of which is essential to the improvement of social policy, he would be put in a difficult position. Some of the reasons for this are inherent in the problem itself; only the needless blindness of society and of Justice is responsible for others. An inherent barrier to light is the fact that varying proportions of crimes of different sorts are never reported to the police, and that even among those reported it is difficult to determine the true percentage who are guilty. Criminal statistics, however carefully gathered, are only samples, and not always reliable ones, of the actual crimes. It is fundamentally impossible to determine the exact ratio that any such statistical index — be it of crimes known to the police, or arrests, or prosecutions, or convictions, or imprisonments — bears to the total of crimes committed. And the ratios vary with the seriousness or other quality of the crimes and the regions in which the statistics are compiled. Only recently, after years of study and experience, an authority on criminal statistics was frank to admit that he could not tell how much crime there was in Boston, and this though the collections of crime statistics in Massachusetts have long been among the best in the country.[3]

But what about the reasonably possible? What is the status of crime statistics reported to the police, or those in which arrests have been made, or in which there were prosecutions, or convictions, or those in which peno-correctional instruments have been applied? Aside from the inherent difficulty noted, in many regions no count is kept of crimes reported to the police, and in not a few even the tally that is made is for various reasons unreliable. Not so long ago a recognized expert admitted that not more than "a very conservative guess" could be made of the amount of crime in the nation.[4] But even his rough estimate, admirable for its careful analysis, would but a few years ago have had to be based only on "pure speculation." It was not until 1930 that a central clearing-house, the United States Department of Justice, began to gather and interpret statistics of a sample of police department records in the United States sufficiently large to promise reasonable reliability. A like situation exists with regard to judicial statistics. As recently as 1930 it was reported enthusiastically by one active in the movement that after years of preoccupation with the problem of basic criminal statistics in the United States, the Federal Census "is definitely going through with the task of gathering statistics from the courts of general criminal jurisdiction (probably not from the minor courts this year). Some eight jurisdictions seem quite certain to contribute data this first year, and I am inclined to think the number will rise above twelve." [5] In fact it was not until late in 1932 that the Bureau of Investigation of the federal Department of Justice adopted a standard classification for police, penal and judicial statistics. In contrast to this state of affairs, English criminal statistics have been compiled satisfactorily for many years.

Accurate bookkeeping in private business is as old as arithmetic. Reliable accounting in the important branch of public business concerned with crime is, in most jurisdictions, as young as a new-born babe. In some states it has not yet been born, even if conceived. In not a few cities crimes known to the police are not even recorded; in others they are recorded unreliably. In some states figures of arrests are not accurately compiled. Many have fair and some have excellent judicial statistics, but some of these have unreliable prison statistics. A major weakness of available data springs from the varying reliability of the different fact-gathering agencies in any one state and in the several states. This makes comparisons almost impossible.

Moreover, nobody can say with assurance how trustworthy is the raw material that daily enters into the police, prosecutory, judicial and other records, to be later compiled into annual statistics. Research experience has proved that much of the data recorded in courts, prisons and parole boards is inaccurate and unreliable, because it is not contemporaneously and expertly verified.[6] Furthermore, in many jurisdictions much of the material necessary for the compilation of useful statistics does not even exist. Experts attempting to compile their own figures from existing raw materials are met with this insuperable obstacle. Speaking of the attempt to work out the average time intervals between the various steps in criminal procedure in Illinois, the investigators complained that outside of Cook County, including Chicago, it was usually impossible to find recorded the date of arraignment — surely a basic item to be entered routinely in any adequate record system. And the Missouri Crime Survey report points out that one handicap under which a major part of the investigation labored was that it was not always feasible to determine the dates defining the four chief stages in the criminal proceedings.

Even where fairly reliable, the figures are not so compiled and analyzed as to lend themselves readily to administrative and legislative uses. The crime surveys have had to make independent analyses of the number of cases entering and leaving the various halls of Justice. These functional statistics, or "mortality tables", first systematically compiled in the Cleveland Crime Survey in 1922, are invaluable guides to the analysis of procedural and administrative steps and thence to the location of responsibility for weaknesses in the system of justice as a whole.[7] Yet such tables are kept in only a few places, though years have passed since the first surveys demonstrated their value.

Thus it is that after centuries of activity Justice is blind to the very fundamentals of her work. In many places she does not know how many crimes are reported to the police, she does not know how efficient her various knights are in terms of the numbers and proportions of cases they dispose of and the manner of disposition. Except in one or two states she does not know the results of her efforts to punish and correct offenders. She merely assumes that her police and prosecutors are efficient; that industrial schools and reformatories must "reform" those sent to them, because they are intended to reform; that indeterminate sentence legislation is generally applied with an exercise of wise discretion, because such was the aim of the framers of the laws; that fines for various types of offenses are effective in preventing those fined from repetition of their acts, because it seems logical that they should be so.

The gathering of statistics of the administration of Justice *as a unified process* depends upon the existence of a central, responsible statistical bureau. In most of the states of the Union, however, there are no central clearing-houses of criminal statistics; [8] and it is doubtful if there are more than two or three states which, having set up standards for the gathering and compilation of statistics, maintain a service for teaching the numerous police and court officials how to compile them.[9] Even where such records are kept under compulsory legislation, there is hardly ever any inspection of the actual work. Here, as in practically every branch of administration in connection with crime, there exists an exaggerated historical localism, an assumed right to be independent of a standard-setting central authority. "The present lack of unification is reflected in the methods now used to record the activities of the county officials. Each maintains his own records, quite often inadequately, frequently negligently kept, and usually with no regard to interrelated records of other officials. The consequent inability to fix responsibility for failure is a distinct and serious deterrent to effective law enforcement."[10] So spoke the Missouri Crime Survey report. But the situation it described is by no means confined to Missouri counties. Nor does the failure to keep interrelated records apply only to county authorities: it pervades the entire unsystematic "system." Anyone with experience in gathering even a meager outline of the facts in the career of an offender knows that many offices must be consulted in order to piece together a record that ought to be available at some central bureau.

Society enacts all sorts of criminal laws, such as legislation providing life imprisonment for a fourth offense, without knowing how they are enforced; without even furnishing her judges accurate prior criminal records of offenders, upon which the very essence of such laws depends. Court A does not always know that an offender has previously appeared in Court B, which may be not only in the same jurisdiction but sometimes even in the same building. Probationers may be under supervision of two or more courts at the same time, without each knowing of the others' interest in the case. A defendant who has jumped bail in one court may be haled before a neighboring tribunal for another offense, without that court's knowing of the former one's claim. The following extract from the

Missouri Crime Survey illustrates another weakness of Justice chargeable to failure to centralize records:

> Under the present practice, it has frequently happened that defendants who have been convicted, but released on bail pending appeal, have failed to prosecute their appeal and the appellate courts therefore have been unaware that any appeal has been taken. The local officers, meanwhile, thinking the case transferred to the appellate court have given it no further attention. This defect in the procedure has been termed "the double shuffle" and makes it possible for a convicted man to remain unpunished indefinitely unless the facts are discovered. When the writer was Attorney-General of Missouri, he instituted an investigation and found that the appeals of several hundred convicted men had thus been lost sight of.[11]

So it transpires that both in the mass and in her dealings with individual offenders, Justice gropes blindly, an easy prey to her betrayers, to uninformed and equally blind reformers, to her own mistakes. Without adequate records, her efforts to improve are futile, and those of her servants who are inclined to betray their trust know how difficult it will be to pursue and punish them.

3

But Justice is blind in other vital respects as well, and particularly in the balancing of her scales. There has been considerable talk in recent years about the "individualization of punishment" and the classification of prisoners. In both these processes the sentencing function of the courts is of high significance. Courts are engaged in a primary classification of those convicted; that is, in choosing, from among several alternative prescriptions, that specific correctional remedy which is supposedly most suited to the particular offender and at the same time most protective of society through the exercise of deterrence. Now in sentencing offenders, two extremes are possible: either courts will sentence uniformly all offenders who have committed outwardly similar crimes — the method of Beccaria's Classical School of penology — or they will focus attention on the offender, with the result that sentences for similar offenses will not be the same. In America today courts have in most states been given considerable discretion in imposing sentences. That they should have such discretion cannot be doubted in sound theory, in which it is deemed more important to fit the correctional plan to the needs of the individual offender than the punishment to the abstract crime. But when analysis of sentences imposed for similar offenses discloses a wide variation among judges and among courts of like jurisdiction, there is evidently no guaranty that the result is due largely to the exercise of wise discretion instead of to questionable motives and inefficiency.

In his reminiscences regarding sentencing practices of judges in England some years ago, Sir Henry Hawkins, an experienced magistrate, summarized his observations in this wise:

> The want of even an approach to uniformity in criminal sentences is no doubt a very serious matter, and is due, not to any defect in the criminal law (much as I think that might be improved in many respects), but . . . to the great diversity of opinion, and therefore of action, which not unnaturally exists among criminal judges. . . .
>
> The result of this state of things is extremely unsatisfactory,

and the most glaring irregularities, diversity and variety of sentences, are daily brought to our notice, the same offence committed under similar circumstances being visited by one Judge with a long term of penal servitude, by another with simple imprisonment, with nothing appreciable to account for the difference.

In one or the other of these sentences discretion must have been erroneously exercised. . . . Experience, however, has told us that the profoundest lawyers are not always the best administrators of the criminal law.[12]

This quotation suggests several elements of the problem we are discussing: the fact that similar types of offenses are variously punished by judges; the question whether the wide variations in sentence are really due to the judge's individualization on the basis of the needs of different prisoners rather than on the nature of offenses; the fact that judicial discretion is, if not entirely unrestricted, at least so unchecked as to permit of unfairness and inefficiency; the question whether some principles of individualization, based on a more scientific approach to the entire problem, cannot be evolved for the use of judges, and what methods shall be employed in the application of such principles; and the fact that the sentencing function requires special qualifications not guaranteed by the mere possession of a legal education.

To determine some of the results of the blindness of Justice, let us first see whether the evidence does disclose a wide variation of sentencing practices. Some twenty years ago, the annual report of the New York magistrates' courts called special attention to the wide range of variance in the sentences imposed for like offenses by different judges. Here are a few illustrations dealing with drunkenness cases: Judge A in one year suspended sentence in 56 per cent., imposed fines in 25. Judge B's percentages were 35 and 20, Judge C's 61 and 28, D's 65 and 18, E's 74 and 5, F's 28 and 25 (he sent 44 per cent. to the workhouse, compared to 21 per cent. by Judge E.). Judge G suspended sentence in 72 per cent. of his drunkenness cases, imposed fines in 23 per cent. and committed but 4 per cent. to the workhouse. The percentages of suspensions and fines, respectively, on the part of other magistrates who disposed of the correct number of cases to make their work statistically comparable, were as follows: Judge H, 23 and 67; Judge I, practically the reverse, that is, 67 and 20; J, 2 and 68; K, 59 and 35. Judge L, with a total of 205 convictions, sent 19 per cent. of the defendants to reformatories; Judge M, with 213, sent only half of one per cent. to reformatories.[13]

Other offenses disposed of in the New York magistrates' courts showed similar variations. In the 1914 report, the chief justice of those tribunals seems to have condoned this practice. "I have never attempted," he said, "although the power of assignment of magistrates to this court is vested in me, to lay down any iron-clad rules as to punishments, because individual cases exceptional in nature so often arise." [14] This is theoretically a sound reason for such a policy; but the fact remains that the lower courts are extremely hurried, and the information on which they must base sentences is far from adequate to permit taking much account of exceptional circumstances.

Similar findings have been made regarding courts in other jurisdictions and at other times. Thus, in 1912, under the leadership of Chief Justice Bolster, a Commission on the Inferior Courts of the County of Suffolk, Massachusetts, prepared a report showing wide differences in dispositions by total offenses in the various courts involved. The investigation concluded that "these courts . . . exercise within their several districts the same criminal jurisdiction, . . . and although the social and economic conditions of their various districts do not differ essentially, there exists a radical and multiform variation and antagonism of practice in matters essential to the enforcement of law." [15] Analysis of the business of these courts in more recent years compels one to concur in this conclusion. It demonstrates that the disposition of criminal cases in the courts of Greater Boston having jurisdiction over like offenses varies markedly and on no observable principle. Of all cases disposed of in the Boston Municipal Court in a single recent year, imprisonment was ordered in 8 per cent., fines were imposed in 50, and probation was granted in 19. In District Court A, with similar cases, the respective percentages were found to be 3, 27 and 32; in Court B, 5, 32 and 39; in C, 1, 10, 64; in D, 2, 34, 31; in E, 3, 32, 40; in F, 10, 12, 38; in G, 4, 14, 43.[16] Analysis of the disposition of separate offenses shows similar variations.

Thus far we have spoken only of minor offenses. Like discrepancies have been shown in respect to serious crimes. A recent analysis of over 7,000 sentences imposed by six judges over a period of nine years in a New Jersey county shows considerable variation in sentences for similar offenses. Taking the total of such serious crimes as larceny, robbery, burglary, embezzlement, assault and battery, rape and the like, it was found that while Judge A imposed sentences of imprisonment in 36 per cent. of his cases and Judge B in 34 of his, Judges C, D, E and F imposed such sentences in 53, 58, 45 and 50 per cent., respectively, of their cases. Judges A, B and C sat at the same time throughout several years. Thus a prisoner found guilty of a serious crime had about three chances out of ten of going to jail or penitentiary under Judges A and B, five out of ten if sentenced by Judge C, "for the same crime and under the same circumstances." [17] Placing the defendant on probation instead of sending him to prison ranged among the various judges from a proportion of 20 to 32 per cent.; suspension of sentence from 16 to 34 per cent.

Bearing in mind the reflex effect of any process of justice on every other, it must be concluded that not all the responsibility of the sentencing situation is the judges'; district attorneys must take their share, for their recommendations as to sentence are frequently involved. But primarily judges are the officials entrusted with the determination of sentence. Commenting on the New Jersey study, the investigators fixed the judges' responsibility in the following reasonable manner:

> Since the rule is that there is no selection of the cases which the judge is to sentence but that the sentencing of a particular prisoner by a particular judge is a matter of chance (the judges rotate), it is obvious that, by chance, each judge should get an equal number of cases whose sentences would normally be long or short. . . . Given a sufficient number of cases, one could expect that two judges would give sentences whose average severity would be about equal (providing that the judges were influenced only by the circumstances of the crime and those

of the prisoner). Conversely, given a sufficiently large number of cases, if one finds that the average severity of the sentences of two judges is appreciably different, one is justified in saying that the factors which determine this difference in the sentencing tendencies are to be found outside the circumstances of the crime and those of the prisoner and hence probably in the judge since he is the other factor which is always present.[18]

The blindness of Justice operating through judges is further illustrated by the manner in which indeterminate sentences are applied. Frequently these sentences, designed to balance legislative, judicial and administrative discretion, provide for a definite minimum and maximum. For example, for assault with a dangerous weapon with intent to rob or murder the legislative prescription may be a sentence of two-and-a-half to not more than twenty years; for assault with intent to rob or steal without use of a dangerous weapon, it may be a span of two-and-a-half to ten years. The variations in the outer limits express the legislative opinion of the difference in gravity of the two crimes; but within two-and-a-half years and the upper bounds, the *judge* is supposed to individualize the penalty. For the first-named offense, for example, he may sentence X for two-and-a-half to three years, Y for two-and-a-half to twenty. In the case of X he will thereby cut the zone of discretion of the parole authorities to a very thin slice; in the case of Y he will allow them considerable leeway, so that if they choose they may, subject of course to regulations, release Y after he has served, say, only three years of his possible twenty-year term.

A recent unpublished analysis of sentences of judges in Massachusetts over a period of years shows a refinement in the exercise of judicial discretion in imposing sentences that would be difficult to justify even if it represented the work of Solomon. In 194 successive admissions to prison in one year no fewer than fifty-three separate types of indeterminate sentences were imposed. The sentences varied to such an extent that there was great difficulty in reducing them to a few categories. Not counting life sentences, they ranged from between two-and-a-half years and three years at one extreme to between forty-two-and-a-half and forty-five at the other. Even if the best available information as to the characteristics and background of the offender were laid before judges as a basis for the exercise of their discretion — which is not often the case — they could not reasonably tell in advance that it would take X from two-and-a-half to three years to reform, Y from two-and-a-half to three-and-a-half; A from forty to forty-five, B from forty-two to forty-five; or, if deterrence be stressed, that X's punishment should be half a year shorter or longer than Y's because they require these different sentences to prevent them from repeating their crimes, or because the public requires this fine distinction to deter it from violating the respective laws. Such ultra-precision is on its face irrational. It satisfies neither the prisoner's nor the public's conception of justice; nor does it meet the demands of a realistic individualization of punishment.

Consider still another illustration of the blindness of Justice in the matter of sentencing. The first section of the Massachusetts law governing defective delinquents states, among other provisions, that "at any time prior to the final disposition of a case in which the court might commit an offender to the state prison, the reformatory for women, any jail or house of correction, the Massachusetts reformatory, the state farm", and certain other corrective institutions, "for any offense not punishable by death or imprisonment for life", any proper official, including the district attorney, may file an application for the accused's commitment to a special institution for defective delinquents. It then provides that "if, on a hearing on an application for commitment as a defective delinquent, the court finds the defendant to be mentally defective and, after examination into his record, character and personality, that he has shown himself to be an habitual delinquent" and that other necessary conditions exist, "the court shall make and record a finding to the effect that the defendant is a defective delinquent and may commit him" to an appropriate institution for defective delinquents.[19] This is not the place for a discussion of the concept of defective delinquency or the treatment of those committed under the law. Attention is called merely to the basic requirement that the person must be found to be mentally defective. Yet persons have been committed, theoretically for a wholly indeterminate sentence (meaning, if need be, life imprisonment), whose intelligence quotients were found later to be over 105. To be sure, "the vast majority of those with high I.Q.'s have [later] either been paroled or discharged as responsible offenders" because of these "erroneous commitments as mental defectives";[20] but such commitments further emphasize the limited vision of Justice in performing the sentencing function.

So much for the evidence of variations in sentences. Are the wide differences largely due to scientific individualization? That this is doubtful has already been suggested.

But a conclusive answer depends on considering, first, the nature of the materials customarily consulted by judges in imposing sentences, and secondly, the education, experience and outlook of the judges themselves. The amount and nature of data supplied to courts to guide them in imposing sentence vary considerably, but in not a few regions even the basic materials of the prior criminal record are, as we have seen, unavailable. A Wisconsin judge, after a quarter of a century of dealing with criminals, recently complained that during all that time he had been working in the dark, as evidenced by the fact that he was without even an accurate record of defendants' prior criminal activity. Having on one occasion obtained a convincing story from a defendant convicted of burglary, the judge believed his statement that the offense was the first he had committed. Here is the rest of his experience with this offender: "I sent him to the Green Bay Reformatory for the shortest term I could impose. Later I saw the superintendent, who took from his pocket a packet of cards, each of which contained the record of the confinement of this man in some prison or reformatory. This illustrates the helplessness of the trial judge."[21] The illustration could be multiplied many times.

But even in some of the jurisdictions which do supply fairly complete data regarding the offender's prior criminal record, there is little in the way of a case history going into the industrial career, family situation, and other relevant matters respecting the prisoner about to be sentenced. In most places, moreover, an insufficient number of probation officers, lack of training of such investigators, procedural complications, the fact that judges do not devote enough time to the study of case histories before imposing sentence, or their lack of training in the interpretation of materials involving medical, psychiatric, psychologic and sociologic data, renders it questionable whether the wide differences in sentence described reflect a high form of individualization.

Indeed, the blindness of Justice in the sentencing of offenders is most convincingly demonstrated by disposition of cases in the light of the actual characteristics of offenders of different types. A recent intensive research into the sentencing practices employed with female offenders shows that the courts sentenced to a reformatory substantial numbers of patently irreformable prostitutes and feeble-minded or psychopathic women, including many who had previously suffered deterioration in jails and houses of correction; that they committed many promising women (those shown by sociologic and psychiatric factors to be essentially nondelinquent) to an institution when they might better have been treated in the community under probationary supervision, with less expense to the state and less opportunity for moral contagion; that they frequently gave sentences far too brief for achieving the goals of the reformatory in the training of the offenders; and that they often imposed fines which did very little good in preventing offenders from repeating their crimes.[22] Of course the fault is not all with the judges. It must be remembered that society has thus far supplied them with but a few bottles of peno-correctional medicine. Insufficient experimentation with new methods of treating offenders is a characteristic of even twentieth century penology; but inadequate employment of the existing remedies is also a feature.

More basic, however, is the fact that after all Justice must depend on human beings to carry out her sacred mandates. The study of New Jersey sentencing practices disclosed that "the sentencing tendency of the judge seems to be fairly well determined before he sits on the bench. In other words what determines whether a judge will be severe or lenient is to be found in the environment to which the judge has been subjected previous to his becoming an administrator of sentences."[23] It is only reasonable to expect that as long as virtually uncontrolled discretion is lodged with judges, sentences are likely to be dictated, to a greater degree than is desirable or necessary, by their cultural backgrounds and the prejudiced attitudes they bring to their tasks. A century and a quarter ago, Sir Samuel Romilly, the great reformer of the criminal law of England, made some shrewd observations in this connection:

> It has often happened, it necessarily must have happened, that the very same circumstance which is considered by one judge as matter of extenuation, is deemed by another a high aggravation of the crime. The former good character of the delinquent, his having come into a country in which he was a stranger to commit the offence, the frequency or the novelty of the crime, are all circumstances which have been upon some occasions considered by different judges in those opposite lights; and it is not merely the particular circumstances attending the crime, it is the crime itself, which different judges sometimes consider in quite different points of view.[24]

To believe that by donning the judicial robe a person doffs his prejudices is to be superlatively naive. Discussing judicial "freedom of decision" on the Continent, Ehrlich regards the personality of the judge as the very crux of the problem. The administration of justice, he says,

> has always contained a personal element. In all ages, social, political and cultural movements have necessarily exerted an influence upon it; but whether any individual jurist yields more or less to such influences . . . depends of course less on any theory of legal method than on his own personal temperament. The point is that this fact should not be tolerated as something unavoidable, but should be gladly welcomed. For the one important desideratum is that his personality must be great enough to be properly entrusted with such functions. The principle of free decision is really not concerned with the substance of the law, but with the proper selection of judges; in other words, it is the problem of how to organize the judiciary so as to give plenty of scope to strong personalities. Everything depends upon that.[25]

So also, Mr. Justice Cordozo has somewhere emphasized that "there is no guarantee of Justice except the personality of the Judge." How these "strong personalities" are to be brought into the service, and how their scope is to be enlarged without jeopardizing individual rights, are basic problems. Discretion there should be; but the difficulty is to develop a formula and a technique whereby discretion shall be allowed ample scope and yet be subjected to proper discipline.

That judicial discretion is to-day so uncontrolled as to permit of inefficiency and unfairness and occasionally venality, is a conclusion supported by several considerations. First is the fact that sentences are not as a rule reviewed by a controlling tribunal. Since 1907 England has found it necessary to have a special Court of Criminal Appeal.[26] In American polity there is usually no appeal from the sentence, the only review being on questions of law. In some jurisdictions an appeal is obtained indirectly by a provision permitting a retrial in a superior criminal court of a case in which the defendant has already been convicted and sentenced in the lower court. Where this practice of double trials prevails, the procedure tends to become a sort of amiable competition. The lower courts, anticipating that the upper ones will usually revise sentences downward, fix higher penalties than they otherwise would have imposed; the upper courts, anticipating that the lower ones will probably make their sentences excessive, are inclined to reduce them. Says a competent observer of the system in Massachusetts: "A lower court judge may well feel that his careful work on a case is no more than a sigh in a gale." [27]

Secondly, a number of investigations have shown that clever attorneys and their habitually criminal clients have been quick to seize upon the blindness of Justice and the eccentricities of her ministers. A significant section of the Cleveland Crime Survey is entitled "How the System is 'Worked' for Weak Spots"; it shows clearly the manipulation of cases by political lawyers as compared to others. Before Judge A, who suspended sentences in 31 per cent. of his cases, 80 per cent. of the defendants pleaded guilty; before Judge I, who suspended sentences in only 6 per cent. of his cases, only 30 per cent. pleaded guilty.[28] In many places lawyers manage to bring their cases before judges who have a reputation for being "easy", utilizing postponements, transfers and other technical manoeuvers as the means.

Thirdly, it must be remembered that even in very

serious cases judges do not customarily write opinions explaining and justifying the sentences they impose.[29] This not only prevents a check upon their exercise of discretion, but makes it impossible to develop inductively a body of experience from which scientific sentencing principles might be developed. It is no exaggeration to say that in all the years that judges have been imposing sentences they have made little contribution to a possible science of penology. They have been going through the motions of "individualizing punishment." Some have gone to great pains to understand the motivation of the misconduct they are being asked to deal with; others have disgraced their office by imposing some drastic or dramatic sentence to "fit the crime" by way of misplaced poetic justice. But as a class they have failed to develop a method of comparing the individual case with similar ones to evolve a useful typology of both offenders and sentences.

Yet a chief prerequisite of a realistic administration of criminal justice is a scientific means of distinguishing between various classes of offenders and predicting their subsequent careers when subjected to one form of peno-correctional treatment as opposed to another. Without some such technique, even the best intentioned judge can do as much harm as good; for the right medicine applied to the wrong disease rarely effects a cure and may kill the patient. This is particularly true of probation, a most promising and inexpensive correctional instrument. It is wasteful and socially dangerous to apply this method of treatment on any shortsighted, mechanically administered basis.

4

So much for evidences of blindness in gathering fundamental records and exercising discretion in imposing sentence. Let us now consider a number of the signs of the blindness of organized society on behalf of Justice.

Take social planning in the penologic field. Time and again a law is passed or an institution established for dealing with crime, without previous account having been taken of the techniques to be employed or the equipment to be possessed by the personnel. Again and again a court clinic, an institution for defective delinquents, a special prison for the insane, or a reformatory has been provided by legislation, with few if any informed persons concerned about these basic considerations. So, too, judges have been given wide discretion in many places before instruments for its intelligent exercise were supplied. The result of such planless "reforms" has been that agencies and institutions theoretically sound were sooner or later discredited; they had not been given a chance to show their true value, because that could only have been brought out by the proper personnel and equipment. The statutes creating such reforms have a noble ring: they speak of a house of "correction", of a "reformatory", of an institution for the professional care of offenders with mental problems, of a probation bureau. But the reality is often likely to be a far different affair. This is an old story. In 1822 Josiah Quincy, then "Judge of the Municipal Court for the Town of Boston", was addressing the grand jury of the county of Suffolk on "some of the provisions of the laws of Massachusetts affecting poverty, vice, and crime", and he said some plain, blunt things on this point:

> There is, in the general features of this act, much that is admirable. Considered as the commencement of a system, it is worthy of all praise. The great means of reformation, solitary imprisonment, and hard labor, are ordered. The great evil of county gaols, want of air, exercise and employment, are obviated. Means are provided for its execution. Penalties are inflicted upon counties in case they fail of erecting the prescribed accommodation. All this is wise, practical, efficient, honorable. But, alas! with what regret and disgust must it be added, all this is false, hollow and deceptive! This act stands little more than a dead letter upon the statute book; absolutely so, except as to some of its minor and less important provisions.[30]

Another evidence of blindness in social planning on behalf of Justice is the way in which society deploys its funds in the fight on crime. It typically devotes far less to preventive agencies dealing with pre-delinquent and delinquent children than to prisons for habituated offenders difficult to reform by any known method. A state will pour hundreds of thousands of dollars into a modernized institution for adult offenders while its establishments for juvenile delinquents are outdated. It will set up expensive psychiatric clinics to deal with confirmed chronic alcoholics and vagrants, but stint on clinics for children, or on expansion of extra-curricular school activities. It will provide much more elaborate case-records at the hopeless end of a criminal career than at its hopeful beginning. It will pay much higher salaries to probation officers in adult criminal courts than to those in juvenile courts.

5

In conclusion we may stress the most serious aspect of the blindness of Justice, namely, the relative unacquaintance on the part of those who carry on her affairs with the disciplines basic to both an efficient and a fair administration. Not only judges but all the other enforcers of the criminal law need to have training in the interpretation of adequate case-histories and the understanding of treatment methods. They should know enough of psychology, sociology and other disciplines to employ intelligently the data indispensable to an effective yet just treatment of offenders. With outstanding exceptions here and there, police investigator, criminal court judge, probation officer, penal institution administrator, parole board member and parole agent have not enjoyed such training. As has already been suggested, unconscious or conscious prejudices against type of offense or race or class of offender, or a technically narrow legalistic attitude, rather than a broad training in pertinent disciplines, is still too often the basis of a sentence. Ignorance of even rudimentary psychologic considerations still marks the work of many a probation officer, prison attendant and parole agent.

To be sure, the blindness of Justice and her ministers is partially dependent upon the imperfection of the very sciences which ought to be drawn upon in the sentencing and corrective procedures. The objection has been made against the more widespread use of psychiatry, psychology and social case work in the administration of criminal justice, that these disciplines are still in a highly experimental and formative state, and that experts representing such bodies of knowledge frequently disagree. The criticism has gone so far that certain recent writers have naively recommended the application of the technique of the test-tube and the microscope to the complex problems of human behavior, motivation and values, as well as the shifting sands of social transformation. They have spoken of the ideal as if it were possible to achieve it the day after tomorrow. They have not seemed to realize that where human beings and human values are concerned, it is still largely figurative to speak of "the experimental method." However desirable it may be to experiment with human beings, unfortunately there exist vast realms of human conduct in which people will not yield themselves or their cherished religious, family or other institutions as willingly to experiment as do the relatively docile white mice, guinea-pigs, dogs and monkeys of the laboratory. No doubt had Pasteur directed his genius to the study of human psychology and social problems, he would have made some brilliant contributions. But even he would have been faced with the basic difficulty of inability to control a good many of the variables that enter into human and social situations. There is, besides, the question of the appropriateness of the tool to the task in hand. One does not hunt elephants with bean-blowers or attack microbes with sledgehammers. Without reduction of the activities of human nature to their ultimate elements — whatever these may turn out to be — psychology and psychiatry have been able to assemble and organize a good deal of information about mind and behavior, some of which can be of immediate practical value. All this is not to say that the methodology of "pure science", so far as it is applicable, should not be introduced into the social sciences including the law; [31] it is merely to take account of the practical difficulties in the way of such application.

But though it may be conceded that psychology, psychiatry, sociology and like disciplines are still not fully developed sciences, and that a wise legal system should proceed cautiously in absorbing methods or attitudes from outside the law, there is enough available in extra-legal disciplines even today to render Justice less blind. The disagreement between psychiatric experts where they are not employed by different sides but asked to give unbiased professional opinions is not as great as is generally assumed.[32] On the significant symptoms of the various mental and behavior disorders well-trained psychiatrists are likely to agree. True, there are some serious differences of opinion on questions of theory, on attempts to account for the phenomena observed; there are also differences of view respecting the merits of various therapeutic methods. But these are healthy signs of a growing discipline. Difference of opinion among experts is not absent in the law itself, as much litigation, not to dwell upon the divided opinions of appellate tribunals, would indicate. Again, in the realm of psychology, standardized intelligence tests of various kinds are admittedly far from perfect and are undergoing continuous revision on the basis of experience; yet their use is becoming more and more widespread and at the same time more discriminating. And there are other possible uses of psychology in the administration of justice.[33] Further, a complete, perfectly logical set of principles of social case-work to be used in the institutional treatment of offenders and in probation and parole work has not yet been developed; but a body of wisdom, based on experience, is gradually crystallizing, and scientific attitude and method are little by little being infused.

At all events it must be conceded that a mature approach to a social problem like crime should take advantage of the best of available techniques; it should place itself in a position to profit by their future improvement. Such an attitude is superior to a blindfolded, routine approach or to one based on rationalization of fear-responses or anger-responses to behavior that is annoying or dangerous to social security.

CHAPTER V

THE KNIGHTS OF JUSTICE

1

Few assemblies of men in government are entrusted with more power than the knights who do battle on behalf of Justice. These officials — the police, district attorneys, defense counsel, judges, juries, penal and correctional administrators — deal with the very lives and liberties of the people; upon them rests the chief burden of maintaining the general security. We need to know something of their essential functions, their qualifications for the performance of these tasks, their compensation and their integrity. Consider first the police.

What are the functions of police officers? The layman is likely to describe them as controlling traffic, patrolling beats and making arrests. We have already alluded to the important but as yet poorly performed function of preventing the origin of delinquent careers and eliminating the breeding-places of crime. But even with respect to their traditional duties, police officers wield a tremendous power requiring high intelligence, sound judgment and incorruptibility. The officer on the beat is in some respects a judge; indeed, he must carry out his duties more quickly and with more direct accountability than the ordinary judge. In arresting without a warrant, he must rapidly decide whether an offense is a misdemeanor or felony, and if the latter, whether the suspect committed it; he must be discreet as to the amount of force to be used in making an arrest. He is, as has been pointed out, required to keep within highly technical provisions of the law in respect to the search of persons and premises and the seizure of evidence. For illegal arrest, imprisonment or lawlessness in obtaining evidence he is liable to civil suits and sometimes to criminal prosecution. But apart from the work of identifying and apprehending the person accused of crime, the police officer has a host of functions to perform which call for rare talents. In petty offenses or neighborhood squabbles he must use tact, sound discretion and a knowledge of human nature in determining whether more harm than good will not result from making a formal arrest instead of merely giving a friendly warning.

Besides all this, he is supposed to carry around in his head an ever-multiplying mass of statutes pertaining to myriads of minor offenses, such as regulations in respect to building and sanitation, stolen goods, pawnshops, and the like; to be able to give intelligent testimony in the courts; to be on the alert for any significant changes in the police problems of his neighborhood; and to perform many other widely varied functions. It has been said with little exaggeration that "there are few vocations which, if adequately performed, require so much of a man — physical courage, tact, disciplined temper, good judgment, alertness of observation, and specialized knowledge of law and procedure." [1]

What kind of qualifications do the police bring to these essential and difficult services? The methods of selecting recruits are in many regions not calculated to enlist men of adequate physical, mental and moral caliber. In the first place, there are few branches of public service in which politics, and low politics, plays so prominent a part. As a rule the chief of police is appointed by the mayor and council, and the post is a recognized political plum. What this may mean in practice may be inferred from the fact that while the late police commissioner of Vienna was a man of sufficient caliber to be called to the post of Vice Chancellor of Austria, the mayor of Indianapolis a few years ago introduced his appointee with the remark, "I know that my man is going to be a good chief because he has been my tailor for twenty years. He knows how to make good clothes; he ought to be a good chief." [2]

It is notorious that in many cities chiefs of police are changed with each administration and that appointments to such posts carry with them generally conceded obligations to betray Justice when the political whip is cracked. In thirty years Chicago has had fourteen chiefs of police. It may not be wholly a coincidence that the nearby city of Milwaukee, which has had but two new chiefs in forty-six years, is also one of the least crime-infested cities in the country.

But even the rank and file are in many regions still appointed through political connection, this having more to do with selection than does the meeting of mental and physical qualifications. Not only has this system resulted in the appointment of some police officers who themselves have criminal records, but in various cities from coast to coast it has made it easier for the police to have too intimate and illegitimate a relation with vice-rings, racketeers and gamblers. Equally serious, political intervention has resulted in so high a turnover in police personnel as to render impossible continuity of policy by the chief, the learning of duties by the men, and the establishment of a fine professional tradition. A recent investigation disclosed that in Kansas City over half the police had less than three years' service, and wholesale dismissals — in 1921, 350 of them — followed upon changes in administration. In another city 214 men left the service in a single year.[3]

Civil service reform has doubtless improved conditions in some places, but it is naive to assume that civil service commissions are always free of political influence;[4] and even where appointments are not frankly controlled by local politicians, the methods of selection — whether largely through the civil service or through direct appointment by police authorities — are, with certain exceptions, ill adapted to the needs.[5] Recent investigations of the matter make one wonder whether a substantial proportion of police officers are at all fitted to cope with the complex problems of the large American city; and whether, despite the growing recognition of the difficulty of police work, and the large volume of writing on training methods recently produced,[6] we are not still really governed by the notion that brute strength, "a police manual, a uniform, a club, a revolver", form the sole necessary equipment of the guardians of peace. In Boston, for example, as late as 1929, the physical examination was given the same weight as the educational test in grading the papers of candidates.[7]

The prior experience necessary for successful police work has not yet been carefully analyzed, although notable beginnings have recently been made.[8] Candidates usually come from the unskilled and semi-skilled sections of the population. Study of a sample of police officers appointed in Boston in 1928 disclosed that a fifth had previously been chauffeurs or taxicab or truck drivers; a substantial proportion had been either laborers or other workers requiring little skill or education.[9] Similar findings were made in Chicago and Cleveland.[10] Even under civil service, the basis of grading prior experience is extremely vague, and in Chicago "the heavy weighting accorded to 'experience'" was said to assume "a peculiar, if not sinister, appearance."[11]

The mental examinations given police candidates often do not test either innate or permanently acquired intelligence. The answers required by the civil service examination are likely to be "crammed" by rote from pamphlets or digests of statutes supplied to applicants. A few of the more forward-looking police experts have long recognized the value of both psychologic and psychiatric tests, and the recent development of rating scales for determining to what extent police departments meet definite standards may stimulate the adoption of more intelligent ways of selection.[12] But thus far methods of appointment and promotion are on the whole inadequate.

Delinquents and criminals are as a rule markedly deficient in educational equipment. What about those who arrest them? In Boston, in the four-year span 1924–27, out of 656 appointees to the force, 231 (35.1 per cent.) had gone to high-school for various periods. This leaves two-thirds of the police force with only elementary school equipment, many not having even completed the grammar-school grades. In fact it was only in 1926 that the Massachusetts Civil Service Commission raised the minimum educational requirement to graduation from a grammar-school, and even this was later abandoned.[13] The situation seems to be as bad, if not worse, in a number of other cities. Thus in Los Angeles in 1924 over 60 per cent. of the police personnel had never entered high-school. In Detroit in 1925, of a sample of 143 patrolmen, over 70 per cent. had gone no farther than grammar-school [14] — this in the face of the intricate problems the modern police officer must cope with!

Delinquent and criminal groups tend to contain an appreciable incidence of mental defectives. What about the police? Under the Army Alpha examination, 979 officers and patrolmen of the Cleveland police force were tested a few years ago. Some 40 per cent. of the officers were found to be of superior intelligence, 32 per cent. of high average, 20 per cent. of average, 6 per cent. of low average. Twelve per cent. of the patrolmen were of superior intelligence, 29 of high average, 34 of average, and 20 of low average or inferior intelligence. This relatively favorable picture is marred by the somewhat amusing finding that of all classes of officers and men tested the detectives rated the lowest, having only 5 per cent. in the superior category compared to 12 per cent. for the patrolmen.[15] Other police forces disclose lower ranges of intelligence. An experienced civil service examiner has concluded that "unless a candidate can make a score of 120 [out of a possible 212 points] in any one of the Alpha tests it is useless to appoint him as a patrolman." [16] This means that even some of those in the B grade, which ranges from 105 to 134 points, ought to be disqualified. The D category usually typifies persons of such inferior intelligence that they cannot go beyond third or fourth grade, some of them even being of the moron class of feebleminded. A test of the freshmen at the University of California disclosed that 60 per cent. of the students were in the A class, 31 in the B, and none in the C–, D or D– grades. Compared to these figures, the Los Angeles police force had only 9 per cent. in the A category, 18 in the B, and 16 in the C–, D or D–. The Minneapolis police had but 7 and 19 per cent. in the two highest grades, 18 in the three lowest; the Kansas City, 5 and 13 in the highest, 25 in the lowest; the Cleveland, 4 and 13 in the highest, 22 in the lowest.[17] Placing such findings beside those concerning the intelligence of delinquents and criminals, we may well ask whether we are not too often setting a dullard to catch a dullard.

Nor are such meager educational achievements and intellectual gifts materially remedied by systems of training after appointment. The experts consulted by the Wickersham Commission sampled training facilities throughout the country and concluded that in towns of less than 10,000 population "there is absolutely nothing done which by any stretch of the imagination could be considered as police training"; 185 of 225 towns investigated reporting that a new officer is sent out on duty with neither instructions nor the assistance of an experienced officer.[18] Speaking of the preparation he gives a new recruit, the police head of one of the smaller cities of New York graphically described his simple method:

I say to him that now he is a policeman, and I hope that he will be a credit to the force. I tell him that he doesn't need anybody to tell him now to enforce the law; that all he needs to do is to go out on the street and keep his eyes open. I say: "You know the Ten Commandments, don't you? Well, if you know the Ten Commandments and you go out on your beat and you see somebody violating one of those Commandments, you can be sure that he is also violating some law." [19]

If legislators were only less inventive of all sorts of diabolical crimes not catalogued in the Lexicon of Mt. Sinai, this simple theologic approach to the police problem might be sufficient.

Even in larger cities training is in many regions woefully inadequate, although the list of educational facilities for police is now rapidly expanding.[20] Only 78 (20 per cent.) of 383 larger cities which responded to questionnaires sent out by the Wickersham Commission reported some method of training recruits, and only 29 of the 78 provided schooling for at least a two-month period.[21] The Boston training period has been raised to two months only recently. While a few cities, notably New York and Berkeley, California, have comprehensive training provisions, only fifteen of those who reported could be said to have properly qualifying courses. Compared to those of certain European cities, American training methods are, with a few notable exceptions, but poorly adapted to the intricate functions of modern police duty.

By and large, compensation for police service is too low to attract persons of the proper caliber. The maximum salaries for patrolmen in a good many large-sized cities do not run much beyond $1,000 or $2,000; in many they are much lower, while relatively few cities extend the annual income to $3,000. The maxima for sergeants are not much higher, and even the salaries of superior officers are as a rule not attractive to men with capacity for leadership and executive ability.[22] While the compensation of superintendents is more reasonable, vacancies in this post are relatively few and the tenure is most insecure. Many cities provide some form of pension. But the low wages of the rank and file, in addition to the political nature of many appointments, the type of men recruited and the great temptations to which they are subjected, are bound to make for some corruption. If one turns to the index to Bryce's widely read *American Commonwealth* for the topic "Police Administration in New York", he finds the pointed cross-reference, "See Tammany Ring." It has become popular to say that Bryce was guilty of an exaggeration founded upon a sense of British superiority. But if this distinguished political Bosworth were recording his observations in more recent times, he might honestly make similar cryptic references to many other political rings that have more than a nodding acquaintance with the police departments of our large cities. New York and Chicago, the two large cities that have received the most unfavorable publicity over the sinister partnership of politicians and police, are not the only ones in which police graft betrays the high calling of Justice.[23]

But what of the second order of knights of Justice, the prosecuting attorneys? It is little exaggeration to say that the prosecutor has more power with less accountability than any other officer. In some jurisdictions he controls the issuance of warrants of arrest. He dominates grand jury proceedings (at which defendants are not represented) and can therefore influence in one direction or another the bringing in of indictments. He has a vast and almost unchecked authority to dismiss even the most serious of cases through the little-controlled device of *nolle prosequi*, by which he declares his intention not to prosecute further, without necessarily having to give his reasons. He has virtually unlimited power to bargain with defense counsel regarding the charge to which the accused will plead guilty — a power that can easily be exercised corruptly. His ways of influencing the sentencing procedure of the courts range from a legitimate presentation of mitigating and aggravating circumstances to the exertion of subterranean pressure.

The statistics reflecting the untrammeled exercise of these powers by prosecutors in large American cities demonstrate how relatively small is the amount of criminal business that is left to juries after the district attorney has acted.[24] Consider the nol-prossing of cases. In 1925, in Cleveland, 11 per cent. of indictable cases were nol-prossed; in 1930, in Franklin County, Ohio, 14 per cent; in 1923, in the county containing Minneapolis, 29 per cent; in 1923–24 in St. Louis, 10 per cent; in the county containing Atlanta, Georgia, 13 per cent; in Cook County, Illinois, in a recent year, more than 25 per cent. In Detroit, in the statistical years 1927–28 almost a third of the felony complaints were either nol-prossed or otherwise "dismissed" by the prosecutor; and in New Jersey, as recently as 1934, 15.6 per cent. of offenders charged with serious crimes had their cases disposed of by the prosecutors' exercise of discretion, the proportions in the various counties ranging from 3.2 per cent. to 38.4 per cent.[25] Such wide variations in the rates of dismissals of cases by district attorneys make it probable that even where consent of the court must first be obtained for the entry of a *nolle prosequi*, there is something fundamentally wrong in the exercise of discretion by prosecutors. It should be recalled, in this connection, that as a rule the cases so disposed of by district attorneys have undergone at least one, sometimes two, prior siftings — at the preliminary hearing and in the grand jury room — before the defendant is held for trial.

Equally indicative of the prosecutor's great power are the figures as to the acceptance of a plea of "guilty", which not infrequently means that an arrangement has been made between the district attorney and defense counsel involving either a reduction in the grade of the offense originally charged or a promise of recommendation for leniency in sentence. In New York State the plea of "guilty of another offense", which customarily means guilty of a lesser offense than that originally charged, is the most common one, involving in 1925 no less than 36 per cent. of pleas to 25,000 felony cases initiated in the courts throughout the state, and almost 50 per cent. in those of New York City. In New Jersey in 1934 there was a plea of guilty in 81.6 per cent. of those found guilty of the offense-charged and in 75 per cent. of those convicted of some lesser offense.[26]

But it is in instituting proceedings in the first place that the prosecutor has perhaps the most influence. A recent sketch of this field, in which statistical recording is difficult, rightly points out that what goes on "behind the closed doors in the prosecutor's office" when he is deciding whether or not to prosecute may be of even more importance than those other acts of his that are at least susceptible of record and are done more or less in the open. "Nowhere is it more apparent that our government is a government of men, not of laws. Nowhere do the very human elements of dishonesty, ambition, greed, lust for power, laziness, or bigotry have more room for development. Also, there is no office where an able and honest public servant can be more effective." [27]

There are of course perfectly legitimate reasons for nol-prossing cases, and there are occasions when for reasons of economy or difficulty of proof, or the very size of the case-load the prosecutor is expected to handle, he is forced not to initiate proceedings, or when it is wise social policy for him to accept a plea of guilt to a lower offense than that actually committed or originally charged. But this very fact indicates how the system puts into the hands of those prosecutors who have but a warped conception of social responsibility an armory of powerful weapons with which to defeat the legitimate ends of Justice without leaving behind embarrassing footprints in the sands of time. Various devices — the abolition of the *nolle prosequi*, the requirement that the prosecutor record his reasons for its exercise, the written consent of the judge — have been resorted to as safeguards against the arbitrary and corrupt exercise of the powers of the district attorney. But each has its Achilles' heel so long as the mental and moral standards of many public prosecutors are not raised.

Who, then, are these men who exercise such vast powers with such slight oversight? Our prosecutors, particularly assistant district attorneys, are in many places relatively young men. The median age of prosecutors in Missouri, as determined a few years ago, was between twenty-five and twenty-nine; and although in some places it is higher, the age of assistants is customarily low.[28] In education and experience assistant district attorneys, who carry the burden of prosecution, are not infrequently maladapted to the exercise of their princely functions. Many of them are graduates of inferior law schools. Most of them have practiced but a very short time before becoming assistant prosecutors. With each election there is a turnover in the office, faithful political workers being given preference in appointment. The salaries of assistant prosecutors are low considering the importance of their functions and the qualifications required; but in many instances they are higher than the young "counsel for the people" could earn in the practice of law.

But the typical feature of the office of prosecutor is that it is staffed with perhaps the most politically minded of our officials. In most jurisdictions prosecutors take office by election, and the multiplicity of valuable favors they can grant to political ward-heelers makes them peculiarly vulnerable to sinister influence. Moreover, there is no public office that more generally is regarded as, and in fact is, a stepping-stone to higher political preferment, than that of the prosecutor. Moley studied the careers of 767 lawyers who in our generation have held high political office, "including all lawyer members of Congress in 1914, 1920 and 1926, and governors of states in 1920 and in

1924", and found that 319 (42 per cent.) had been prosecuting attorneys.[29]

The political background of the vast majority of prosecutors, and the obligations they assume in coming into office, have led to disclosures of atrocious conditions. Chicago, New York, Boston are only some of the leading cities of the nation that have in recent years been regaled with appalling spectacles of the iniquitous alliance of prosecutors with leaders of criminal gangs, vice-ring operators, blackmailers, or dishonest lawyers. Racketeers and gangsters have won long-standing immunity; innocent women have been "framed" as prostitutes and "shaken down" of all their possessions; innocent men have been blackmailed. It has taken ingenious and daring investigations to bring some of the official malefactors to account through prosecution and disbarment, after years of immunity. But the resultant reforms have too often been short-lived, and a familiar sequel has been the return of the guilty to public office through "vindication" reelections.

Despite the fact that in most prosecutors' offices there will be found a few public-spirited men who place devotion to duty above neglect and corruption, the picture sketched by the recent surveys is one to make Justice hide her head in shame.

What now of those who make a business of defending criminals in our courts? Among the servitors of Justice has penetrated a corrupt crew who feed upon her bounty and repay her with betrayal. Less elegantly they are known as "shysters." Their "runners" are versed in the arts of getting business through splitting fees with police and court attendants. Often wearing the mask of Robin Goodfellow, these unclean spirits make and take every opportunity to bring Justice into disrepute, while putting money in their purses. They are likely to have minor political connections or friendships with someone in the district attorney's office, which they manipulate to their own gain. To them the Canons of Legal Ethics, which emphasize the lawyer's obligation to maintain the dignity and honor of the profession and to improve the administration of justice, are merely ornamental, if indeed they have even read them. Professional criminal lawyers have commodities to sell which the legitimate practitioner shrinks from handling, so that they are in great demand by the criminal classes; and such is their power and knowledge of "the ropes" that even some innocent first offenders, fearing a miscarriage of justice, are inclined to seek them out in preference to more respectable lawyers, loftily unfamiliar with the traps and mazes of criminal procedure. Most lawyers shrink from criminal practice because they regard it as a shabby business and feel it to be detrimental to civil practice. In a recent discussion with some of the best students at the Harvard Law School it was discovered that not one of them was even interested in criminal practice, a point of view generally shared by students in the better law schools. This leaves the field largely to professional criminal lawyers, shysters and novices.[80] With the evolution of organized crime, criminal lawyers who do not have such scruples are even retained on a yearly fee basis; and in some cities defendants brought in by police raids from different regions are mysteriously represented by identical lawyers. Even a recent notorious kidnaping and jail delivery involved a member of the bar in a very questionable way. The methods of professional criminal lawyers range all the way from the use of every ingenious procedural technicality to gain an acquittal, to the exercise of downright political influence in the district attorney's office, the obtaining of perjured testimony and jury-fixing.

These abuses have ordinarily been dealt with by sporadic and long-delayed disciplinary action on the part of local bar associations. While in some states, during the years 1929–34, there have been as many as ten to twelve disbarments per 1,000 of the lawyer population, and many reprimands and suspensions,[31] the problem of the unethical practitioner is still an acute one. This is indicated by the frank challenge of the Attorney General of the United States only a short time ago:

> The American Bar is confronted with a vital problem growing out of the improper activities of certain of its members in their contacts with the criminal classes. There have been repeated instances of a studied abuse of the privileges of the profession. A startlingly large number of lawyers have not only misconceived their duties as advocates but have, in effect, actually participated in criminal activities. . . . It is no exaggeration to say that the Bar of this country is on trial before the public.[32]

Not until recently has the American Bar Association entered energetically upon a study of the extent of the evil and methods for its elimination. More rigorous selection of candidates for the bar, more intensive control of their activities and greater leadership on the part of the judiciary will doubtless help, at least to the extent that the moral climate of the times permits.

A considerable proportion of persons accused of crime have no professional defense at all — it is a luxury they can ill afford. In cases where the charge is a serious one, statutes in most states provide for appointment of assigned counsel by the court. Since, for the less serious offenses, either no fee at all or only a small one is provided, counsel assigned in such cases are either fledglings at the bar or older lawyers of limited capacity. It is felt by many authorities that while relatively capable lawyers are assigned to the poor in capital cases, the assignment system in the general run of cases fails to give the offender that degree of protection implied by the maxim of "equality before the law", by the presumption of innocence and by the constitutional guaranties that the accused shall be represented by counsel. The public defender system, first established in Los Angeles in 1913 and now provided for in some of the larger cities, has on the whole been more protective of the rights of accused, more efficient in reducing delays and eliminating corruption, more economical, than the assigned counsel practice.[33] But in many places the problem of the corrupt or incompetent lawyer in the criminal courts remains unsolved.

2

Consider, next, some of those who carry out the mandates of Justice on the bench.

Judges in criminal sessions have the dual function of conducting the trial according to the procedural and evidentiary rules, and of imposing sentence. It will be recalled that those in courts of first instance have tremendous power as examining magistrates, in which capacity they decide whether to dismiss the accused or "bind him over" for the action of the grand jury. The high percentages of charges dismissed by these magistrates have already been stressed.[34] These justices also act as trial judges, disposing, without a jury, of the vast proportion of lesser criminal charges that go to trial. In addition, judges of criminal courts have wide discretion in granting or withholding bail and in fixing its amount.

It is indeed true that "an inch of judge is worth more than a yard of justice." But that even the judicial robe has been soiled by certain unworthy place-holders on the bench was disclosed with dramatic force by the Seabury investigations of the manner of appointment and the doings of certain magistrates in New York City.[35] The picture should be kept before the public as a constant reminder. Asked on the stand to state how they obtained their appointments, many judges pointed to their political connections, the work they had done for the party in the various districts, the recognition that was due them as a matter of course or for favors done to politicians, their long membership in Tammany Hall, their becoming known as the political leader's "right bower", and the time and money they had spent on behalf of the party.[36] Hardly one alluded to more appropriate qualifications for the office. Here are two illustrations of how judicial place may be obtained in some of the American cities of our age.

Magistrate A, whose practice was dwindling, went to his district political leader, who later became a judge of the superior criminal court, and insisted that he was "entitled to get a judgeship" for the eighteen years he had worked in the organization, without even getting so much as a receivership or a guardianship or even a "5-cent piece." The leader replied, "I will be honest with you, you are entitled to some recognition. You never annoyed me or bothered me, other lawyers were after me to see what I could get for them." [37] When the next vacancy went to another, Magistrate A was "blue", but his leader cheered him up and told him not to "give up hopes." Finally this aspirant to judicial honors went to the mayor, and pleaded: "I am a Democrat, and here you have been a classmate of mine, and when the time came you asked me to do a favor and I did it for you. Many an afternoon I stayed in and told you just what happened. Now, there is an opportunity for you to help me." But for some time Magistrate A received no help; so one day he went to the "organization" to "have it over with" and find out if his name was being sent in or whether he "was being fooled around with." Subsequently the Mayor appointed him.

Magistrate B threatened to desert the party unless he got recognition. When his leader failed to present his name to Tammany Hall, he "had it out" with him in the street one day, and told him he felt his "political career was at an end", that he was "growing old in service", and that if he were "not to receive any further recognition" he would like to know it so that he could devote his time much more profitably to his profession. He was told to be patient, and when the next judicial vacancy in the district occurred he got it as the "logical candidate." Asked why he thought himself the logical candidate, he replied:

> For twenty odd years I was a public speaker enunciating the principles of my organization in the streets, using my voice during campaigns, spending my evenings at the clubhouse trying to help those in the district after I became an attorney by being a free eleemosynary institution around there for years and rendering much more service than I felt I should have rendered for the organization. I will say this now, I have always felt and I frequently complained that I have not adequately been rewarded for my work for the organization. I feel that I should have been elevated to a much higher bench many years ago. I complained about that.[38]

And so with other magistrates. The same refrain — activity on behalf of the party in power and endorsement by the district political leader — is repeated with wearisome iteration throughout the testimony.[39] Judge Seabury bluntly and justifiably concluded his penetrating exposé with a diagnosis that is not limited alone to New York City:

> The demoralization of the Magistrates' Courts resulting from the political considerations governing the appointment of Magistrates finds expression not only in the subserviency of the Magistrates to the dictation of politicians in the disposition of court business, but also in the very type and quality of the men appointed. Ability and fitness for the office, where they exist, are, as a rule, purely accidental. The selection is made primarily to strengthen the power of the party. This explains the principle by which appointments are parcelled out to meet the alleged claims of particular political districts; it also explains the even more vicious principle by which race, nationality and creed often dictate the selection of Magistrates.[40]

Contrast this picture with the specifications laid down long ago by Livingston:

> If an ordinary court of justice be properly called the temple of that high attribute of the deity, we may, without too far extending the metaphor, term the tribunal of criminal jurisdiction, a shrine in that temple; the holy of holies, into which impure or unworthy passion should find no admittance, and where no one ought to officiate until he has put off the habits of ordinary life, and assumed, with the holy robes of his function, that purity of intention, that ardent worship of truth, so inconsistent with the low pursuits of interest, the views of ambition or the vanity of false talent. Party spirit unfortunately will, in some degree, influence every other department; from the nature of our government it must exist, but it will do no material injury, while it is felt in the legislative, or even in the executive branches; but if it once find admittance to the sanctuary of justice, we may be assured that the vitals of our political constitution are affected.[41]

The removal of a number of the New York magistrates because they were influenced in large measure by politicians and were therefore "unfair and unjudicial", or because they altered official records to the prejudice of defendants in order to cover up unjudicial remarks and rulings at the trial, or because of their connection with bonding companies upon whose business transactions they passed in their judicial capacity, or because they accepted loans from notorious racketeers and gamblers, or because they sponsored the sale of stock in questionable enterprises or had interests in gambling establishments;[42] and the resignation of others under fire, disclosed only the cruder aspects of judicial unfitness. Politically appointed justices, as well as those elected largely because of long-standing political connections (it apparently makes little difference), are in a position to grant, and are customarily expected to grant, many less flagrant favors to the "boss", that peculiarly American Warwick who is the real king-maker that plays so powerful a role in not a few large cities.

For the forces tending to select incompetent judicial agents of Justice are not confined to any one place. Much is revealed in the admission of outstanding legal scholars that one of the chief reasons why many lawyers object to permitting the judge to guide juries by commenting on the weight and credibility of the evidence is their conviction that "trial judges of today are so unlearned and inexperienced and of such poor ability and character as to be incapable of performing this function impartially and efficiently."[43] The Illinois Crime Survey, discovering an increase since 1917 in the election or appointment of young men to judicial posts, pointed out as one of the most significant reasons "the fact that there is greater tendency for judges to ascend to the bench in these days as the result of holding some minor political position rather than through long service as practicing attorneys." Comparing the caliber of judges who mounted the bench before 1917 with that of later ones, the report concluded that "we are getting poorer judges from the standpoint of ability, courage and independence, we are getting more political judges and younger judges. We are getting judges whose experience at the bar has covered fewer years."[44]

The political connection and incompetence of many justices of the lower courts — those judges who, because of their frequent contacts with the people, ought above all to set a high example — cannot be said to be mainly due to their low compensation. In fact, in many cities judges are quite adequately paid, and in some their incomes are envied by practicing lawyers. It might even be said as to a few places that the salaries are so high compared to the incomes to be earned in practice that the political organization expects and receives handsome contributions from the wearers of the judicial silk. However, in some cities the low salary of judges possibly has the same influence in making them open to manipulation as it does in the case of police officers. In some states, such as Pennsylvania and Virginia, the vicious fee system of compensating the minor judiciary is still in effect. In others, the hardly less desirable system of part-time special justices presents a number of unhealthy aspects, among which may be mentioned the inclination of judges to devote their best time and thought to their private practice, the fact that partners of judges are allowed to try criminal cases before them, and the fact that they are permitted, while being judicial incumbents, to practice criminal law.

Perhaps of even greater importance than well qualified and incorruptible judges in the ordinary criminal courts is the need of eliminating political considerations from the appointment of juvenile court judges. There are encouraging instances in several cities of an effort to appoint to these courts high-minded men and women, specially fitted by both legal and extra-legal training and by temperament for this work of prime social importance. But only a few years ago a recognized authority on child welfare expressed the view that we have "hardly begun to tackle" the problem of political interference in the juvenile court.[45]

Clerks, bailiffs and other attendants are also involved in the drama of Justice. They, too, are not infrequently political in their origin. In New York

> a substantial number of these clerks were captains of election districts for the local Democratic clubs: others held offices in the clubs, or were members of their county committee. Sixteen clerks in the Magistrates' Courts in the First Judicial Department admitted upon examination that they were active politically: their appointments were rewards for service within their political organization. The great majority of them had no previous experience or actual knowledge of court procedure or any form of preparation for the duties which they were called upon to perform upon their appointment.[46]

In setting dates of trial, in the dropping of complaints, and in other manipulations of the processes of justice, these officials are highly useful henchmen to political bosses. Even petty favors, such as the disposal of complaints involving violations of municipal ordinances or licensing legislation, can be translated into substantial incomes, as can service as agents of unscrupulous lawyers and bondsmen.

Clerical work in a busy court requires high intelligence and some technical training.[47] But some of the surveys and grand jury inquiries and the Seabury investigation have disclosed that there are many incompetents among clerks and their assistants, and that even where the post of assistant clerk is subject to civil service selection, political influence is involved. One clerk examined by Judge Seabury, after pointing out that clerks are appointed from civil service lists, admitted that "there is a remarkable tendency for people who have political connections to come out at the head of the Civil Service list at times. . . . It sometimes mystifies how that happens, but it happens too often." [48]

Still another knight of Justice whose acquaintance we should make is the bail bondsman. His function is to supply, at a reasonable cost consistent with the risk involved, adequate surety for the appearance at some future stage in the criminal proceedings of a defendant who is released until his presence in court is needed. The unscrupulous bondsman has a number of valuable contacts with the criminal proceedings, in return for which he risks little or nothing. In the first place, he benefits from too many or too long postponements of the various steps. In the second place, he charges too high a rate for his services. In the third place, he not infrequently puts up inadequate security for the bail bonds; one mortgaged building in which he has but a small equity may be used to cover several bonds. In the fourth place, though these bonds are frequently forfeited, it is the rare exception rather than the rule for the state to profit from such forfeitures, relatively few proceeding to judgment and many of these not being collected. In the fifth place, the carelessness of some bail-granting authorities and the inadequacy of the examination of prospective bailees results in many offenders being forced to obtain bail bonds when their mental makeup, character, social and economic background and the surrounding circumstances of the offense are such that their failure to appear later in court is most unlikely. In a dependable analysis of a sample of unsentenced prisoners in Chicago jails it was found that at least 28 per cent. could have been allowed their freedom while awaiting trial, or at all events might have been released on much lower bail or on personal recognizance without sureties.[49] The records of any large city will show that carelessness in granting bail not only keeps in jail many defendants who might safely be at large pending trial, but also results in freeing confirmed criminals who are not averse to plying their professions anew while awaiting trial on old offenses. Finally, unscrupulous dealers in bail bonds have a tendency to tie up with police, prosecutors, professional criminal lawyers and others in an unholy alliance against Justice, for the division of the spoils of the game.

Who are the corrupt bondsmen and how do they work? The Missouri Crime Survey gives a few biographical sketches, of which we reproduce one by way of illustration:

> His police record shows twelve arrests on minor charges. . . . $30,000 in forfeitures were outstanding on September 1, 1925. . . . In spite of the foregoing facts he was on September 1, 1925, liable for $90,000 of bonds. . . . In the year covered by our investigation of misdemeanor bonds he signed $390,595 in bonds, and in the circuit court in the same year he signed $279,700. . . . Basing our estimate upon commonly known rates charged by bondsmen, this man whose real estate was valued at $24,100 with a mortgage of $31,500 was permitted to become surety in one year on bonds aggregating $670,295 and his compensation in all probability was not less than $33,000, and may have ranged as high as $100,000.[50]

The partnership in evil of unscrupulous bondsmen and other betrayers of Justice may be illustrated by a case drawn from the Seabury investigation:

> Miss A. J., a nurse in a doctor's office, was framed by a stool pigeon. She was bailed out by S., a bondsman to whom she gave her bank books as security for a bond of $500. At the time she had over $600 on deposit in the Bank. S. supplied a lawyer for a charge of $150 to cover all. S. and another man then called on Dr. X. the employer of Miss J., in an attempt to get him to make up the difference between $1,000 and Miss J.'s $600 on the misrepresentation that the charge might have very serious consequences to Miss J. and to Dr. X. himself. S., in attempting to meet this doctor's objections, reduced his first demand from $400 to $300. Dr. X. paid no money to S. S., however, took Miss J.'s entire savings of over $600.[51]

Bond commissioners and superintendents of insurance have in a number of states reduced the evils described; but the bail bond situation and the alliance of professional bondsmen with underworld characters on the one hand and unscrupulous lawyers and officials on the other are on the whole still among the unsolved problems of Justice.

What now of the knights (and ladies) of the jury? Both because of the increase in the disposal of cases before trial and the spread of legislation giving the accused the right to waive jury trial, the prominence of the jury in criminal procedure has in recent years been materially reduced. However, juries still dispose of a substantial number of criminal cases. In this process they are supposed, ideally, to sift the testimony introduced by both sides and arrive at a conclusion based on the facts. But only the most naive would insist that juries are not swayed, consciously or unconsciously, by other considerations. In a few states juries have considerable power in determining the punishment to be imposed.

The Cleveland Survey put its finger on a major cause for the inefficient operation of the jury system: "In Cleveland, as in many other large cities, most citizens of means or intelligence avoid service. This avoidance has become traditional, so that it is a kind of mild disgrace for a so-called 'respectable citizen' to allow himself to be caught for jury service — like being swindled, for instance." [52] Contrasting the jury service in two wards of largely "shifting white, foreign, and negro population, and the recognized prosperous suburbs", the Cleveland Survey disclosed that of 10,488 prospective jurors to whom letters were sent in one term, 37 per cent. of the residents in the more favorable sections of the city failed to reply to the summons, compared to 26 per cent. in the poorer wards; 9 per cent. in the favorable suburbs were away when summoned or received the letter too late, compared to 4.4. per cent. in the poorer districts. "It also seems that the exclusive suburbs are much more unhealthful than the poorer districts"; illness was "reported proportionately almost 50 per cent. more often in the most desirable residential districts." As was to be expected, disqualification on account of illiteracy or lack of language requirement was practically confined to the poorer districts.[53] Of a total of 8,747 prospective jurors recently investigated by both police officers and jury commissioners in Boston, 17.6 per cent. were eliminated as "not found", 4.7 per cent. as being public employees, 9 per cent. because of a criminal record, 3 per cent. because of physical disability, and 4.8 per cent. for other reasons.[54]

A four-week record was kept of the occupations claimed by those in Cleveland who served, indicating that 22 per cent. of the jurors were various kinds of "metal workers, repairers and laborers", 18 per cent. were clerks, 11 per cent. were employed in domestic duties, 8 per cent. were skilled workers, 7 per cent. were engineers or conductors, 6 per cent. were merchants and tradesmen, 5 per cent. were in personal service employments, and the balance were in various scattered occupations with but few in executive or professional work.[55] Unfortunately, these findings were not compared with the incidence of various occupations in the entire Cleveland population. In the Boston investigation it was found (with some qualifications) that juries are, from an economic standpoint, approximately a true cross-section of the community. The Cleveland report, while granting that the distribution of jurors "fairly represents the bulk of Cleveland's population," points out that "a system designed to select for the difficult task of administering justice 'judicious and discreet persons, competent in every respect to serve as jurors', does ill to produce even a cross-section of a great unassimilated industrial population. The qualifications for a competent juror are high."[56] Moreover, when unemployment was great, it was demonstrated that the jury box became the "haven of the unemployed", so that men out of work might earn $2 a day.

On top of the inefficient methods of original selection of jurors in various jurisdictions, there is the matter of peremptory challenges of prospective jurors at a trial.

It is here that the skill of counsel is exercised more to obtain a sympathetic hearing for the accused than to secure intelligent judges of the facts. There is more than a grain of insight into the true processes of justice in Clarence Darrow's description of what makes a good juror for the defense: "The main work of a trial lawyer," says this veteran of the criminal bar, "is to make a jury like his client, or, at least, to feel sympathy for him; facts regarding the crime are relatively unimportant. I try to get a jury with little education but with much human emotion. . . . The man who is down on his luck, who has trouble, who is more or less a failure, is much kinder to the poor and unfortunate than are the rich and selfish." [57]

Finally, there is the fact that juries can be, and sometimes for long periods are, corrupted. On October 7, 1933, the Council of the Boston Bar Association was frank to state: "The fact that during the past few years jurors in this country have been accepting bribes is established beyond peradventure." [58] Other jurisdictions have had their share of jury-fixing.

3

Consider next those knights of Justice that are concerned with the correctional and punitive processes. These are probation officers, prison workers and parole agents.

In recent years there has been a great expansion of probation — a correctional service that is in the hands of the courts. In theory, probation is sound, as is also, in our opinion, the view that the officials who determine the sentence should supervise its effective execution through agents of the court. A defendant placed on probation because his background and characteristics give promise of his surer rehabilitation in the community under oversight than in a prison, requires a type of supervision that combines the highest arts of the resourceful teacher, the wise parent, the sympathetic but firm guide. But of growing importance is a second function of probation officers: the investigation of cases and the rendering of reliable reports to the courts on the basis of which they can more intelligently determine the appropriate sentence. How do probation officers meet the high standards required for the performance of these essential duties?

In educational background and other qualifications probation officers vary, at the present stage of the movement, from a fraction comprising men and women excellently equipped for the high duties they must perform to a larger proportion who have little but political or other irrelevant contacts to bring to the work. The Wickersham Commission's Advisory Committee on Penal Institutions, Probation and Parole adequately summarized the situation as follows: "Individuals chosen as probation officers have been too often untrained, lacking in the suitable point of view or personality, and unpaid or underpaid. In many jurisdictions they are little better than political pensioners." [59] Despite the commendable efforts of the National Probation Association and local probation commissions in a number of states to place appointments under effective central control and to require high standards of education and experience, the post of probation officer is still too often regarded as the personal plum of local judges. Instances are known where the justice appointed his barber or tailor or some unemployed relative to a post that required high technical equipment. The following is an account of the background of probation officers in one state: "The previous equipment of the part-time probation officers in these counties varies widely. . . . Lawyer, teacher, insurance agent, candy manufacturer, clergyman, nurse, relief agent, jail warden, sheriff, district attorney, court clerk, county detective, constable, tipstaff, janitor, Red Cross worker, wheelwright. . . . Old men and women, even aged men and women, are found in the service. At times the appointment seems to be used as a pension or to be considered as a sinecure." [60]

The salaries of rank and file probation officers vary from small part-time compensation to $3,000 or more per annum. In 1931 the average salary throughout the country, exclusive of the directive personnel, was over $2,000, with occasional highest salaries of $4,000 and more frequent ones ranging from $3,200 to $3,600. Directors of the services in the larger cities draw substantial compensation. On the whole, therefore, salaries of probation officers have in larger centers reached a respectable standard, and ought to attract candidates of the quality, say, of competent high-school teachers.

While past investigations have here and there shown some corruption on the part of probation officers, they have a cleaner record in this respect than some of the other agents of Justice. The fault lies rather in the poor quality of the investigative and supervisory work in many a probation office than in corrupt practices. For this there is some excuse in the fact that the techniques involved in probation are relatively new and the case-load carried by each officer is often much too heavy.

Other knights of Justice perform their deeds in correctional institutions. Those engaged in tasks that might be of the highest value for society are the workers in the field of juvenile delinquency. The Children's Bureau a few years ago included in its standards of institutional care of juveniles the requirements that political control and interference be absent and that the superintendent and staff "be selected on the basis of their special qualifications for the work", and be adequately compensated, their salaries to be "comparable with those paid for other public service in the educational and social field." [61]

What is the true situation? By and large these institutions, in which so much of the destiny of children is lodged, are not staffed by a highly qualified type of worker. In fact, the most that can be said about them is that "although there is an encouraging sprinkling of cultured, well-educated men and women with the right viewpoint in institutional work, there are still many, especially among the cottage workers, who fall much below the standard of public school teachers, for example." [62] Parole officers of juvenile institutions are as a rule not trained in the pertinent disciplines.[63] Personality traits have also not been given enough attention in choosing workers with children. Superintendents constantly complain about their inability to get properly qualified staffs.[64] That the tentacles of politics have reached out toward children's institutions in many places may be inferred from the fact that within a five-year span two-thirds of the thirty-nine institutions for girls studied in 1921 changed superintendents. Some institutions have had three superintendents in one year.[65]

Of similar or lower grade is the personnel of many penal establishments for adults. The wardens and deputies of most of the prisons of the country are frankly political appointees. Often they are promoted from the post of guard, provided they can draw on political influence. Not infrequently they are former petty office-holders, police officials or sheriffs. In their own mind and that of many legislators and the public, their chief tasks are to prevent escapes at all hazard and to be more concerned with making profits for the state from the prison industries than with remaking human beings through the training in trades, adult education, mental and physical hygiene and character-training — a program which a correctional institution ought to offer its inmates but too frequently does not.

The guards as a rule have no special qualifications for their duties except that of muscle. As a rule they are chiefly concerned about their wages and working conditions, and are pessimistic about the possibility of reforming their charges. Here and there a guard is found who combines unusual intelligence with a rare intuitional understanding of the springs of human nature. Occasionally one finds guards with marked capacity for leadership. But for the most part they may be characterized as an under-paid and disillusioned crew, engaged in hazardous and thankless routine duties, spending many more hours at their tasks than is good for them or for the prisoners. They are no miracle-workers in the vineyards of reform. Many of them are as much the victims of the standard American prison routine as are the men whom they guard. The chief difference is that they are voluntary prisoners.

There is little wonder that the turnover in their jobs is very high. Their corruption usually takes the form of petty graft obtained from giving little favors, selling little luxuries; occasionally it rises to the dignity of obtaining a good sum for supplying an inmate with a weapon or conniving in his escape.

The typical personnel of jails is if anything worse. It is here that political spoils-getting has been raised to a fine art. It is a notorious fact that jails are the happy hunting grounds of minor political henchmen. The post of sheriff or keeper is a source of considerable revenue. In one county in New York, the sheriff added to his $12,000 yearly salary honoraria amounting to no less than $60,000. In a Georgia county the sheriff for some time pocketed $20,000 a year, making the Governor's salary appear small by comparison. Of twenty-two states examined a few years ago, eighteen still gave the jail administrator a fixed sum per day for feeding the prisoners,[66] a historic custom born in the days when jails were conducted as private businesses and inmates had to find their own food. Numerous instances are on record where the jailor obtains, say, 70 cents a day for the food of each inmate and manages to feed them on 50 cents or less. But even where the historic fee system has been abolished, the jail is a rich source of "legitimate graft" in the way of contracts or jobs. Nor are the evils limited to these sources. J. F. Fishman, a former inspector of jails for the Federal Government and an acknowledged authority, has recently reported that "in badly managed prisons, particularly in some of the large city-jails, where guards are selected because of political influence, the practice of permitting prisoners who pay to have sex relations with their wives or women friends is allowed to flourish untroubled by the officials." [67]

It is only in recent years that a few places have, through the establishment of special schools, translated into reality their conviction that the personnel of penal institutions should be trained. It has been well said that, "Many of the failures of American prisons can be traced to the mismanagement of officers who were selected without regard to their ability or training for the important work they are called upon to perform. A task requiring character, education, experience, and the scientific attitude has often been entrusted to novices and politicians merely in quest of a job, who were incapable of social vision and constructive work." [68] And again, "The real solution of the reformatory problem lies in personnel first, and afterwards in program. In these institutions there is need not only of high-minded and especially trained superintendents, but also of staffs that are composed of intelligent, trained men who are capable of exerting a stimulating and beneficial influence whenever they come in contact with the individual inmate. Experts are needed for the technical problems." [69]

The last representative of Justice with whom the offender usually has contact is the parole agent. Like the probation officer attached to the court, the parole agent (sometimes connected with the prison and sometimes with the board of parole) performs both investigative and supervisory duties. His chief task is to supervise the offender's transition from incarceration to freedom. Realistically interpreted, this means that the parole agent needs to know the inmate and his background thoroughly, to prepare the ex-prisoner's family for his return and to aid him in obtaining employment correlated with what the institutional industries and trade-schools have taught; that he needs to cope intelligently with emotional and conduct crises in the life of the parolee and to help him over the obstacles to reinstatement in the community; and, finally, that he must have the firmness and courage to arrest the parolee who is flagrantly violating the conditions of freedom. These tasks are, if anything, even more difficult than those of the probation officer; for the former frequently deals with first offenders or men not yet moulded by the prison matrix into sad shapes of human beings.

What kind of qualifications do parole agents bring to their tasks? In recent years, Illinois, New Jersey, New York, two or three other states and the federal parole system have set adequate standards for their appointment. In a number of states they compare favorably with probation officers of the average grade, in some they are above the norm. But in many states they are of like caliber to probation officers of the unskilled, untrained and unimaginative variety; and their compensation is low. Burdened with much too heavy a case-load, but on the whole less subject to political influence than some of the other knights of Justice, these officers are going through motions that superficially resemble parole, but are of little value except possibly as a transient deterrent.[70]

Parole is frequently administered by special and more or less independent boards. In recent years there has been some tendency to staff boards of parole with adequately qualified members. But political considerations still bring into the service men and women not particularly fitted by background and education to determine which prisoners to release on parole, when to release them and under what conditions, or to profit from their experience with parolees so as to make needed changes in administration and suggest constructive legislation.

In reflecting upon these conditions are we not justified in asking, with Anatole France, "What matter of Justice being in the Laws, if it is not in men's hearts? And if men's hearts are unjust, what gain shall it be that Equity reign in the Courts of Law?"

To be sure, there are brighter aspects of the picture. In various jurisdictions, police officers, prosecutors, judges, probation officers, prison workers and parole agents are well qualified for their duties and above suspicion of corruption; some of them would grace almost any public or private office.[71] But we are concerned in these pages with the pathology of Justice. And in diagnosing that condition, the disease-dealing servitors of the goddess must be emphasized. It is they who must be coped with and replaced if disease is not to spread further through the organism.

CHAPTER VI

THE PAWNS OF JUSTICE

1

IN THE last chapter we considered some of the officials entrusted with the highly important social business of Justice. What, now, of those with whom they deal? Who are these pawns in the game? What are the physical and mental characteristics, the social and economic backgrounds, of the many thousands of boys and young men constantly fed into and ground out of the mills of Justice? [1] We say "boys and young men" because modern crime, both in volume and in the difficulty of the issues it presents, is essentially a problem of youth and young manhood. "The age of maximum criminality lies . . . in the young-adult period of life. This maximum is not clearly defined, for delinquency or criminality increases from the age of ten to about nineteen, where it remains nearly constant until the age of twenty-seven, after which it decreases sharply with advancing age." [2] There are, of course, vast hordes of offenders of the older vagrant and alcoholic types who fill the jails and houses of correction. But at this stage they are no longer aggressively dangerous; they are the flotsam and jetsam of the social stream. The gravest concern is caused by the children, adolescents and young-adults who crowd our industrial schools, reformatories and prisons, and most of whom sooner or later commit serious offenses.

Several difficulties beset the description of criminals, and more beset the analysis of causal influences in their careers. The first difficulty is that a completely valid sample of actual criminals cannot be obtained. The human beings we subject to study — be they those arrested, or convicted, or placed on probation, or committed to one penal institution or another — are not the criminal class in general, but only a selected group of that class. For example, most of the studies on the makeup of criminals deal with *prisoners*, and it is quite possible that in some or several respects prisoners may differ — perhaps markedly — from criminals as a whole. Prisoners are, after all, those unfortunate or stupid or uninfluential enough to get caught, prosecuted, convicted and imprisoned. Besides, much that is violative of the law is done secretly and does not come to the attention of the authorities. Other crimes are winked at by public opinion and the police. Still others are the serious offenses of "higher-ups" for whom the lower-downs habitually "take the rap." As was suggested in the first chapter, anti-social attitudes and practices are far more common and pervasive than is ordinarily assumed. There are, besides, forms of anti-social behavior which, though they may have much the same motivations as recognized crimes and may indeed have far more extensive evil consequences for society, are none the less "within the law", or at most give rise to only civil remedies. For such reasons it is impossible to know exactly how many of the population of a city like Boston, for example, commit crimes during any specified period, much less to have such criminals under control for the purpose of studying their traits and the conditioning factors involved in their misconduct.[3]

Thus far we have not considered the causal problem. Even if we possessed a picture of the criminal class, we should still have to compare it with that of the general population if our object were to make significant headway in determining the probable etiologic significance of the various traits involved. Here also there are numerous difficulties. Not only must one guard against selective influences which may prevent the obtaining of a truly representative sample of the *non-criminal* population, but having secured a valid control group there would still be the difficulty of subjecting its members to the same thorough sociologic, and above all psychologic and psychiatric, examinations to which the criminal sample had been subjected. Ordinary citizens do not like to be investigated and examined solely for the unselfish object of a possible contribution to science; and volunteers are likely, by that very fact, to be atypical.

Causal studies in the field of criminology are beset by other difficulties, some of which are discussed elsewhere.[4] To illustrate the imperfection of etiologic researches thus far made, despite the numerous investigations in this field it is as yet too early to arrive at any unassailable and significant conclusion regarding the relative degree of participation of social and biologic factors.[5] As in certain other fields, the controversy between the hereditarians and environmentalists in respect to crime causation has produced more smoke than fire. Particularly in the etiology of anti-social behavior is it almost impossible as yet to differentiate completely innate from acquired tendencies.

Birth injuries or anomalies of embryologic development are confused with inherited conditions. Social inheritance is confused with biologic. Inheritance of a "criminal instinct" is confused with inheritance of physical or mental handicaps that sometimes are, but more often are not, causal of criminal conduct. The very mechanisms of human heredity are themselves as yet far from clear, especially when mental abnormalities are involved. This does not mean that a reasonable knowledge of the mental and physical characteristics and the cultural background of certain samples of offenders is as yet not at hand. It means simply that the transition from ascertaining the traits of samples of delinquents and criminals under control to arriving at specific conclusions regarding causation should not be made too readily. The history of causation theories is strewn with such easy transitions.

Some of the deleterious conditions surrounding the childhood and adolescence of delinquents and criminals may not actually have been causal of their delinquency. And even to those which appear to have played a clear role, it is impossible as yet to assign exact weights or indicate the order of influence. How, exactly, did they operate to produce delinquency? Why do not the majority of children reared in similar circumstances develop into criminals? Such questions cannot as yet be conclusively answered, but we may advance what appears to be a reasonable theory.

In the first place, a tendency to law-abidingness is not something we are born with. To be able to guide one's conduct in accordance with ethical and legal standards requires hard and ceaseless effort. All about us are the pressures and pulls and temptations of life. Some persons are relatively impervious to deleterious influences, while others are easily affected by them. Some have a porous mental skin and a resilient conscience (or, in psychoanalytic language, "super-ego"); others are mentally tough-skinned and morally well integrated. Further, human beings are not merely systems of reactive mechanisms pushed and hauled about under the whips and spurs of life. They are also striving organisms, reaching out and selecting, as it were, those elements in the environment that are constitutionally congenial to them. And human beings differ in this respect. By these two streams of influence — stimulation by the environment and selection of the environment — are the human personality and conduct realized and directed.

We now perhaps begin to get some conception of what goes on in the conditioning of delinquency. A wise clinical psychiatrist and criminologist has acutely observed that a factor in the life of the offender is not a "cause" of his delinquency unless and until it becomes a *motive*. Two boys are reared on the "sidewalks of New York"; the one takes the *via dolorosa* that leads to crime and punishment, the other advances steadily along the road to fame, fortune and the respect of his fellows. When, therefore, we speak of poverty, or the unimaginative school system, or the broken home, or ignorant parents, or the hazards of child life in the city streets, or any other component of the "environment" as being related to delinquency, we must remember that both the inert and living elements of these situational samples are not completely outside the individual. They are absorbed by each person selectively and to varying degrees, and woven into the fabric and dynamic system of his being. It is unscientific to place environmental factors on one side of an imaginary line and biologic elements on another, except for certain purposes of analysis. In life, the environmental elements are introjected into the human personality and, according to its peculiarities, become part of its vital being. One of the most necessary and crucial lines of research, not only in the causation of delinquency but in education and many other problems of life in a complex society, is a careful inquiry into the introjective processes of various types of human beings; into the why and wherefore of the conscious and unconscious acceptance or rejection by different persons of certain bits of the environment. This process of weaving of environmental elements into the fabric of personality is the key to many a problem of behavior. Long ago Samuel Butler wisely observed that "a life will be successful or not, according as the power of accommodation is equal or unequal to the strain of fusing and adjusting internal and external changes."

A second aspect of our theory remains to be presented. It is true that individuals differ in their gifts and weaknesses and in the quality of their introjective capacity. In criminal conduct, therefore, as in most other forms of human expression, every person has his own resistance-point or, if you will, breaking-point. It is difficult for all members of a society at any one time to lead a socially acceptable life, involving as this does a subordination of natural impulses to the supposed general welfare as expressed in the laws and customs of the time and place. But it is also true that most persons are able (natively, or through elaborate education, or through protection) to meet such ordinary requirements. However, if that society raises its demands, or if through social stress such as long-standing unemployment, or through social neglect, the breakdown of sources of authority and control of behavior (such as the home, the church and others) or other influences, it makes it more difficult to adhere to the rules of the social game or more inviting to break those rules, it thereby taps a deeper layer of persons who will violate its laws. For it has in one or more of these ways brought further pressure to bear on those whose resistance-capacity is *at present* stretched almost to the breaking-point. Thus the criminal act occurring at any given time is the outcome of constitutional and acquired personal and social forces. It shows that the individual's power of resistance, or self-guidance, or selective choice and introjection of bits of the environment, has been overbalanced by the strength of the other circumstances.

This does not necessarily mean that the threat of punishment plays no part. Nor is it contended that the presence of a partial cause-and-effect determinism means that human beings have not some spark of capacity for consciously and creatively guiding their conduct in conformity with legal sanctions.[6] On the contrary, it is reasonable to conceive of the whole process of education as consisting of fanning into flame this precious spark of creative self-direction despite the biologic and social ashes that are constantly tending to smother it. But both constitutionally and through the accidents of "conditioning" and education, human beings differ markedly in this capacity. The greater the pressure the more likely it is that many in whom this self-directive power is weak will succumb to their primitive and egoistic impulses.

If we look at the problem of causation from the points of view of legal theory and social responsibility, we should recall that, though our criminal law is predicated upon the conception of responsibility as flowing from freedom of will, society has not yet invented an instrument for diving into a man's mind and determining the exact capacity for self-direction, self-control and selective introjective power that he or the fictional "reasonable man" of the law possesses. We are, however, beginning to learn something about the internal and external pressures that are at work in the determination of behavior. These are concrete and can be taken into account in administering justice in the individual case, — if not through the apparatus which determines "responsibility" then at least through that which determines what shall be done with the convict at the bar. Further, considering that widespread anti-social conduct frequently means that the resistive capacity of a mass of human beings has been overcome by the pressures of a deleterious environment, our line of attack becomes clearer so far as preventive efforts are concerned. To the extent that it is feasible to raise the general standard of social life, it is possible to take immediate action likely to reduce the need and opportunity for criminalistic behavior on the part of many. But in addition to social pressures, individual impulses are involved in delinquency. Hence, to the extent that the techniques of mental hygiene enable us to place in the hands of children and adults some effective instruments for the healthy management of the impulses of the organism, both social duty and social self-protection dictate the need of making such means more generally available.

It is well to stress the distinction between researches into causation and studies of the characteristics of a special group of offenders — for example, inmates of a reformatory or prison — made for some such practical purpose of administration as classifying prisoners, establishing an educational policy, planning an industrial program or a recreational regime and the like. Whether the traits found among such prisoners have been causal of their criminality or not, it is generally regarded that improvements along lines indicated by the discovery of certain handicaps of the prisoners will make it easier for them to conform to the demands of the criminal law than it was before, when they were illiterate, unskilled industrially, deficient physically, possessed of destructive recreational habits or enslaved by faulty mental attitudes. For criminals as for others, these are bad weapons with which to fight the battle of life in a complex society. In a wholesome civilization all persons, whether in prison or out, should be given certain minimal advantages. If such social institutions as the family, the home, the school, the church, charitable agencies and the like have somehow failed to meet this responsibility in the case of some members of society, and those persons happen to be under the control of some other social institution such as a reformatory, it falls legitimately to the lot of the correctional authorities to carry out a responsibility previously neglected or poorly performed.

In varying proportions some of the conditions and traits of the prisoners may also have been causal of their original delinquency or repeated criminality. Thus, in ascertaining and acting upon the traits of offenders under control, the agents of society will in part be engaged in treating mere symptoms, in part in treating causes. This probability puts the inventive penologist in a unique position to make contributions to a greatly needed science of experimental penology. To illustrate, if he stops up the gaps of illiteracy, ill health, unhygienic mental attitudes and others suggested by the careful study of the prison population, and finds later that the conduct of his charges has perceptibly improved although community conditions have remained essentially the same, he may be justified in concluding that his program has uprooted some of the criminogenic factors, or furnished his former prisoners with additional tools adequate for enabling them to participate legitimately in the affairs of life despite the operation of criminogenic forces. Moreover, intensive preoccupation with programs of control and treatment, based even upon a dealing with symptoms alone, some of which may later turn out to be unrelated to etiology, is one of the most likely ways of getting nearer to the hitherto impregnable citadel of causation.

Even assuming that the administrator of criminal justice has serious doubts that certain traits of offenders have been causal of their criminality, he might still be justified in moulding his program to take account of them. Suppose, for illustration, it were found that, while 20 per cent. of the prison population of the country are mentally defective, a similar proportion of the general populace are likewise handicapped. That would not destroy the utility of the data regarding the prisoners so far as their trial and imprisonment or other treatment are concerned. If a fifth of the prison population is mentally defective, at least the correctional program, if not also the sentencing and parolling regime and the criminal law itself, ought to be deliberately accommodated to that finding. For our present purpose an examination of the traits of offenders who have been subjected to particularly detailed and careful study is extremely useful. It should suggest the problems that judges are faced with in any realistic sentencing program; it should also be helpful in indicating the very practical correctional tasks of classification, education, instruction in trades, mental treatment, character training and the like. But in considering the traits of the delinquents and criminals about to be described, the reader should bear in mind the qualifications and distinctions emphasized above.

In the light of these, let us now examine the outstanding characteristics of offenders as disclosed by two recent researches into the careers of 1,000 juvenile delinquents and 510 young-adult male criminals who were under control, respectively, of the Boston Juvenile Court with its related treatment agencies and the Massachusetts criminal courts with the state reformatory.[7]

2

Consider first the family background, as suggested by these samples:

Almost a third of one or both parents or of the brothers and sisters of the delinquents, and a seventh of those of the young-adult criminals, were either mentally diseased or defective.[8] These findings do not include cases of mental disease or feeblemindedness on the part of other near blood relatives of the offenders, nor many instances of undiagnosed mental peculiarities or of a strong suspicion of mental defect. Without knowing the exact incidence of such conditions in the general population, and without passing judgment on the possible hereditary influences involved, the presence of mental disease or defect in many of the families may resaonably be assumed to have been deleterious to the wholesome rearing of the children. It may also be presumed to present special correctional problems of a psychologic nature, so far as the offenders themselves are concerned.

To the conditions noted must be added the fact that large proportions of the parents of delinquents and criminals have received no formal education. In over half the families of the juvenile delinquents neither parent had ever attended school, and in more than three-fourths of the families of the adult criminals one or both parents had had no formal schooling. In almost a third of the delinquent families and over a third of the criminal, one or both parents were illiterate, these proportions comparing to but 5 per cent. of illiteracy in the general white Boston population of twenty-one or over. High-schools or college attendance by the parents of delinquents and criminals was negligible.[9]

As might be expected from such conditions, unwise parental oversight of the children was exceedingly common. In the juvenile group the discipline of the mother could be designated as sound in but 2.5 per cent. of the cases, that of the father in only 4 per cent. In the many other cases, control of the children during their formative years either was extremely erratic or ranged from great laxity to repressive and fear-inspiring domination.[10] (Data on parental discipline were unfortunately not obtained in the research involving the young-adult offenders.)

As one possible source of friction between parents and children, the differences in the nativity of the members of the family must be mentioned. Compared with the general population, the families of delinquents and criminals frequently contain a high incidence of native-born children of foreign-born parents. Such families often have higher criminality rates than those in which there are native-born children of native parents or foreign-born children of foreign parents. Among the boy delinquents, 70 per cent. of the families had native-born sons with either one or both parents born abroad, compared with but 29 per cent. in the general Boston population. Among the adult offenders the proportions were 53 per cent. in the criminal families, 22 in the general population.[11] With such differences in background, it is natural to expect some conflict of cultural, and more particularly moral, standards and attitudes between the American-born younger generation and the foreign-born elder group. A finding of this kind indicates how necessary it is to provide sympathetic child and parent education during the critical period of transition between foreign and native generations, when old-world ways, habits and attitudes are prone to be misunderstood by American-born children and when, in turn, parents are likely to fail to comprehend the outlook of their children and to adapt themselves to new-world conditions.

What were the relations between the parents? In a

fifth of the families with juvenile and over a seventh of those with adult offenders they were so disharmonious as to result in separation, desertion or divorce. In another 16 per cent. of the former, parental relations were only fair, by which is meant that although no open breach occurred, the parents were obviously incompatible. In fact, if one takes into account cases in which the parents, though present in the household, were for one reason or another not giving suitable oversight to the children, as determined by reasonable standards,[12] the total of abnormal or deleterious home situations mounts to over nine-tenths in the juvenile delinquent families and over four-fifths in the adult.[13]

Closely related to this topic is the question of broken or grossly distorted homes. In the families of the juvenile delinquents a fourth of the homes were broken because of the death of one or both parents and a fifth because of desertion, separation or divorce. In the families of the young-adult offenders, a third of all the homes were disrupted by death, a seventh by desertion, separation or divorce.[14] The seriousness of the matter is enhanced by the fact that to a marked degree these unfavorable home conditions became acute during the pubertal and adolescent years of the future delinquents and criminals.

Another condition frequent in the households of delinquents and criminals is the inebriety, immorality or criminality of parents or near relatives. In no fewer than a fifth of the juvenile delinquent families, and a fourth of the young-adult criminal families, one or both of the parents were criminalistic as determined by official records.[15] And if the brothers and sisters be included, the proportion of officially recorded criminality among members of the families of the young-adult offenders rises to 50 per cent. If, finally, delinquencies and immoralities which did not come to the attention of the officials be added, the proportion of families in the adult criminal group found to have been immoral, delinquent or criminal mounts to the very serious figures of 85 per cent.

It requires no elaborate reflection to conclude that the moral climate in such families is not conducive to the wholesome growth of children. The parents and near relatives are not likely to set an example of socially acceptable conduct to their offspring; indeed, in such households criminality may be said to be almost a tribal tradition. Contact by a boy or girl with the police and courts can therefore hardly be a novel experience which shocks the parents into a vivid realization of the precarious status of the family's moral fortunes. Hence it cannot be expected to result in any fundamental reform of attitude and behavior, even if one concedes to the utmost the deterrent effect of the fear of punishment. In fact, to rely simply on the recollection of the punishment endured as an effective curb to further wrongdoing is to indulge in extremely naive beliefs about human motivation, conceptions which the substantial figures of recidivism continually refute. Mere imprisonment, or for that matter the usual routine to which prisoners are subjected, including moral preachments, neither are founded upon a sound understanding of the mechanisms of misconduct nor penetrate deeply enough to change criminal behavior permanently.[16]

What, now, of the economic conditions of these families?

In the juvenile delinquent group 68 per cent. of the families were in marginal economic circumstances, living on daily earnings, accumulating little or nothing for the many rainy days they experienced and being constantly on the brink of dependency; and 8 per cent. more were definitely dependent, being supported almost continuously by public or private charity. In the adult criminal group, 56 per cent. of the families were in marginal circumstances, 15 per cent. dependent.[17]

Further light on the economic status of the families is obtained from analysis of their contacts with social welfare organizations. In all but an eighth of the juvenile delinquent families, one or more relief and social welfare organizations had at one time or another been active, and in over a third there had been five or more such contacts. More than half the families of the adult criminal group had been dealt with one or more times by various social agencies.[18]

The hazardous economic status of delinquent and criminal families is evident from yet another angle. In the juvenile delinquent group, 41.5 per cent. of the mothers worked outside the home in order to eke out the meager family purse, this figure comparing to but 10 per cent. of the married women in the general population who were engaged in gainful occupations. Among the young-adult criminal families, 28 per cent. of the mothers were employed.[19] Still more light is thrown on the low economic fortunes of these families by the fact that of 376 of the 1,000 Boston juvenile delinquents who had withdrawn from school and whose school status was known, two-thirds had done so because the family needed their financial aid — twice the incidence of withdrawals among Boston schoolboys generally.[20]

Closely related to all this is the fact that high percentages of the fathers of delinquents and criminals are of the kind who, even in happier economic times, are unskilled and irregular workers. Some two-fifths of the fathers in the juvenile delinquent group,[21] and a like proportion of the adult criminals, were engaged in unskilled occupations[22] — that is to say, in rough work requiring merely strength of hand or keenness of eye, without apprenticeship training. Large percentages of the remainder worked at only semi-skilled employments or those calling for merely simple processes and little learning, but some experience under guidance or study and probably the use of tools. Finally, only 1 per cent. of the fathers of the juvenile delinquents, and but 2.4 per cent. of those of the adult offenders, were engaged in the professions, compared to 6.1 per cent. in the general population.

In addition to whatever causal relation there may be between adverse economic conditions (with all the evils they bring in their train) and criminal conduct, it is a fact that the presence of poverty makes rehabilitative efforts with delinquents and criminals exceedingly difficult. All threats of punishment or kindly efforts at reform are likely to be set at naught when an ex-prisoner, after weeks of sincere effort, finds society apparently leagued against him in depriving him of an honest job. Case histories abundantly illustrate this truth.

What, now, of the household and neighborhood conditions? Only 13 per cent. of the homes of the delinquents could be regarded as wholesome; that is, having adequate space, light, ventilation and cleanliness. At the other extreme, 62 per cent. were definitely detrimental, being characterized by overcrowding, uncleanliness, and inadequate ventilation.[23] Similar data regarding the homes of the adult criminals were not obtained, but judging by their economic status an equally high proportion would probably be found to be unwholesome.

Turning now to the neighborhood conditions, only 2.8 per cent. of the juvenile delinquent families resided in regions that could fairly be called favorable; that is, localities in which there was an absence of street gangs and centers of vice or crime, together with opportunity for wholesome recreation through playgrounds, school centers, parks and the like situated within a radius of two blocks of the home. At the other extreme, over four-fifths of the homes were set in regions with the corrupting influences mentioned and a total absence of constructive agencies.[24] As in the general population, the families of delinquents and criminals are extremely mobile.

From such facts it seems clear that substantial proportions of delinquents and criminals come from families and homes that are biologically and sociologically unwholesome. Nobody can state definitely, as yet, whether like proportions of the general population that do not become delinquent or criminal are equally handicapped; because reliable comparative data on some of the points discussed are not yet available. But even if it were demonstrated that every one of the conditions noted was present to a like degree in the families of non-criminals — a remote contingency, to judge by those factors as to which comparative data do exist — the tainted family heritage of delinquents and criminals would still have to be taken into account both in a general social program and in legal and institutional provisions; unless, indeed, society is to cling stubbornly to disproved simplistic conceptions regarding some single "cause" of crime and the efficacy of traditional sentences and punishments.[25]

3

Such conclusions, suggested by a study of the family background of offenders, are even more justified with regard to delinquents and criminals themselves. To their characteristics and careers we now turn our attention.

Consider, first, their physical condition. Examination of the juvenile delinquents showed 13 per cent. of them to be in poor health, 30 per cent. in only fair health.[26] The first designation includes such serious diseases, handicaps, or deficiencies as tuberculosis, syphilis, marked defects of vision or audition, serious heart lesions, paralysis, and the like. The second signifies merely poor general physical development. Among the young-adult criminals, 7 per cent. were in poor health, 79 per cent. in only fair; 6 per cent. of the entire group had various heart lesions, 27 percent. were suffering from venereal disease. Absolutely comparable data regarding the general population are not readily available, but such as are at hand would seem to indicate that the incidence of venereal disease is not excessive.[27]

Consider, next, the mental makeup of delinquents and criminals. It should be said at the outset that the extreme claims of a high incidence of feeblemindedness among delinquents and criminals, which were made during the first two decades of the present century, are today recognized as gross exaggerations.[28] Many of the researches were conducted in the pioneer stage of intelligence-testing, when the tests had not been perfected, the testers were relatively unskilled, and the norm of mentality of the general population used in computing intelligence quotients was placed too high. Moreover, there has been considerable question of just what it is that the tests determine — whether largely innate or largely acquired intelligence, whether capacity to deal with abstract or with concrete matters, and the like. More cautious recent investigations have materially reduced the incidence of mental deficiency among delinquents, convicts and prisoners. The two Boston researches, as well as others, indicate a rather high incidence of mental deficiency among delinquents and criminals, affected in part perhaps by the fact that they were examined some years ago. But making substantial allowance for this factor, there remains a residue of evidence which cannot be ignored.

Comparison of the intelligence of juvenile delinquents with that of school children in three different cities of Massachusetts disclosed that only 41.6 per cent. of the former were of normal or supernormal intelligence, in contrast to 79 per cent. of the latter. At the other end of the scale, 13.1 per cent. of the delinquents and only 1.5 per cent. of the non-delinquents were found to be definitely feebleminded.[29] Making ample allowance for the possibility that the non-delinquent public school children include some who came from more fortunate socio-economic strata, the difference in the mental capacity of the two groups remains striking. Among the young-adult criminals, only 33 per cent. were found to be of normal intelligence, and at the other extreme, 20.6 per cent. were reported to be mentally defective.[30] These findings are pertinent not only in determining what to do with delinquents and criminals after they have become such, but more so in devising programs for warding off possible tendencies toward misbehavior. An experienced child psychiatrist, in surveying the population of an "average school", discovered "both in Minneapolis and in Cleveland that there is a correlation between behavior difficulties and intelligence in the sense that those children who on intelligence tests depart in either direction from the average present a larger number of behavior problems than does the group with average intelligence."[31]

Psychiatric study disclosed further that among the juveniles there were 137 whose temperamental and conduct tendencies suggested to trained observers a possibly pathologic mental state.[32] Three hundred and fifty more manifested to an apparently abnormal degree various deviant temperamental traits, such as marked impulsiveness, over-suggestibility, intense sensitiveness, and the like, which possibly contributed to their difficulties of adjustment in home, school and community. Finally, 70 of the boys showed "marked adolescent instability." This leaves only 443 of the thousand cases examined in which none of the foregoing conditions was specifically noted. Among 384 young-adult criminals, the reformatory psychiatrist diagnosed 17.7 per cent. as "psychopathic personalities", 3.1 per cent. as having definite major psychoses, 3.9 per cent. as either alcoholic or drug deteriorates, 2.4 per cent. as epileptics.[33]

Diagnosis of the emotional and volitional aspects of personality cannot, at the present stage, be even as accurate or definite as the testing of intelligence. For example, considerable confusion still exists as to the differentiating traits of "constitutional inferiors", "psychopathic personalities", "psychoneurotics", and certain adolescents whose emotional instability may be transient. But the general picture is one suggesting that among juvenile delinquents and adult criminals there is much emotional instability and temperamental handicap.

Consider next the educational equipment. Among 397 of the 1,000 boys who had already completed their schooling when brought before the juvenile court, 11 per cent. had stopped school at the fifth grade, 46 per cent. went as far as the sixth or seventh, 25 per cent. reached the eighth, while 17 per cent. had begun but not completed high-school work. The amount of schooling of the delinquents is clearly below that of the general school-boy population, as is indicated by the fact that while but 17 per cent. of the former entered the ninth grade, 93 per cent. of Boston school boys at a comparable period did so.[34] So also, delinquents are more backward in their studies as is shown by the fact that over four-fifths of the delinquents were retarded — usually for two or more years — while only slightly over a third of the schoolboy group were retarded.[35] In fact, proportionately seven times as many delinquents as non-delinquents withdrew from school because of inability to do the assigned tasks. The educational equipment of the adult offenders was also such as to be unlikely to carry them far in legitimate competition in the modern urban, highly industrialized community. Forty-three per cent. had never gone beyond the fifth grade or less, 46 per cent. had proceeded no farther than the sixth, seventh or eighth grade, and but 9 per cent. had gone beyond the eighth. While, during a comparable period, over half the Boston school children entered the ninth grade, only a tenth of the young-adult offenders had done so in boyhood.[36]

Since many delinquents and criminals are limited in mental capacity and educational equipment, these groups as might be expected, are not among the successful in industry and economic achievement. While it was premature to classify the boy delinquents permanently with respect to skill, since their capacities had not yet ripened when they appeared before the juvenile court, it is noteworthy that 58 per cent. of the two-thirds gainfully employed were engaged in the street trades — as newsboys, bootblacks, errand-boys or messengers; 16 per cent. worked as office-boys, bell-boys or minor clerks, 11 per cent. were factory hands, and the remainder were engaged in other unskilled occupations. Four-fifths of the group were irregular workers, changing jobs frequently without any effort or plan to advance vocationally.[37] The grade of work customarily performed by the young-adult criminals was also largely of the unskilled variety, only 14 per cent. being in the skilled category. Like the delinquent boys, they changed employments frequently, over half of them having held their longest job for less than a year. The industrial habits of the majority of them were poor, the young men being unreliable, lazy, unstable, dishonest or of the vagabond, wayward and ambitionless type, so that only a fifth of the entire group could be characterized as trustworthy and industrious.[38]

Comparable data for the general population are not available. But so far as the juvenile delinquents and young-adult offenders are concerned, we are clearly dealing with youths who, during the years of puberty and adolescence, were thrown among the hazards of street employments where the development of anti-social attitudes and the assimilation of anti-social cultural traditions by those very suggestible or otherwise inclined to such stimulation was to be expected. In such an atmosphere early peccadilloes often lead to more serious offenses — gambling, petty theft, unhealthy sex practices — and finally to dangerous crimes such as armed robberies. Forced or choosing to begin work at a very early age, such youths hardly ever make any planful industrial adjustment. They rarely seek or receive even rudimentary vocational guidance. Even in more normal times, they drift from pillar to post without definite or enduring aim, without opportunity and with but little desire to rise by legitimate means from the great army of unskilled, inefficient, unstable, unorganized and frequently unemployable classes to the more capable ones. At the same time these young men see and hear of wealth all about them; and many engage in property crimes as a short cut to the acquisition of those things that to them seem to be so easily acquired by others. In a land where "everyone has a chance to become President", where not only in the cinema but in daily life we frequently learn of the rise of millionaires from the "lower depths", it is natural for everyone to reach out for the good things about him. Those with defective equipment, who cannot compete within the framework of the accepted social and economic system, are easily tempted to break through the fences and pluck the attractive fruits of the rich orchards. Their early offenses may be mere youthful adventures, but as they mature without the capacity and habit for legitimate work their misconduct is likely to crystallize into patterns of economically motivated aggressions.

What were the spare-time activities of these delinquents and criminals? The question is important because during their formative years children have an abundance of energy which, if not guided into wholesome recreational channels, will spill over into harmful pursuits. Only 1 per cent. of the juvenile delinquents used their leisure constructively; that is, in supervised activities of boys' clubs and similar organizations, or in such outlets as attendance at night-schools. Only 6 per cent. employed their spare time in a harmless if also non-constructive way. The remaining high proportion of 93 per cent. frequented the streets, gambled and indulged in other activities likely to lead to delinquency. In fact, only 4 per cent. of the group had neither bad companions nor harmful habits, and of the remainder over a third had undesirable companions but no markedly bad persistent habits, while 60 per cent. not only had harmful associates but indulged in excessive drinking or drug addiction, gambling, or unhealthy forms of sex expression.[39] The remissness of society in the matter may be inferred from the fact that three-fourths of the boy delinquents and over four-fifths of the adult offenders had never belonged to supervised playgrounds or recreational centers, such as boys' clubs, Y.M.C.A., Boy Scout troops and settlement houses.

There is small wonder that in the fast-moving, glittering and exciting scene of the modern metropolis most of these youngsters readily found unwholesome and even dangerous channels of recreation. Analysis of case histories discloses that many delinquents and criminals, not having developed an enduring loyalty to some legitimate institution or circle — one of the strong bonds between the individual and law-abiding society — become attached to anti-social groups wherein they achieve recognition and approval. Positively deleterious outlets, such as belonging to unwholesome clubs or gangs or frequenting low resorts, dance-halls and cheap movies to excess, are indulged in. Without moorings to a wholesome circle having legitimate ideals and constructive programs, without development of a sense of "belonging", without opportunities for the healthy expenditure of energy, and deprived of a substitute for all this in an adequate home atmosphere, these youths tend to drift into companionships with others similarly deprived. Investigations have shown that substantial proportions of delinquents are likely to group into gangs ranging from the relatively harmless, undirected play circle of the streets and alleys, through roughly organized predatory groups to efficiently organized, formidable and sinister anti-social bands.[40]

Analysis of the situation discloses that rarely, in the careers of delinquents and criminals, have only one or two of the many influences referred to been operative. The usual situation is rather a clustering of deleterious traits and circumstances in a dynamic, demoralizing interplay.

Such forces, more than the mysterious and oversimplified "free will" of tradition, are likely to generate delinquency and crime.

There remain to be discussed the kind and intensity of anti-social conduct exhibited by delinquents and criminals. Criminal conduct as a rule is the gradual development of a related series of anti-social acts. Thus, among our juvenile delinquents all but forty-five had misbehaved prior to the arrest which brought them into the juvenile court, many of them more than once and in more than one respect. The high proportion of two-thirds, for example, had been truants, over half were in the habit of stealing, almost half had "bunked out" or run away from home, 13 per cent. had indulged in sex delinquencies, lesser percentages flashed other danger-signals of an unwholesome situation likely to lead to ultimate delinquency and crime.[41] Some two-thirds of the boy delinquents had been arrested one or more times prior to the arrest which brought them into the juvenile court.[42] So, also, 85 per cent. of the adult criminals had been arrested one or more times preceding the arrest that resulted in their sentence to the Massachusetts Reformatory. In fact, only four out of 480 of those offenders about whom reliable data could be obtained had committed no known delinquencies or crimes prior to the offense for which they were sent to the reformatory.[43] It should be added that intensive follow-up of the behavior of the boy and adult offenders after treatment by juvenile court, probation, industrial school, reformatory and other methods discloses that fully four-fifths of them subsequently commit crimes.

The layman does not sufficiently realize how early in

life appear many manifestations of maladjustment of the young individual to the various social groups in which he finds himself. Among 643 boys about whom the age of first or early delinquency could be ascertained, 14 per cent. showed symptoms of such maladjustment and misconduct at the early age of six or less, 23 per cent. at seven or eight, 26 per cent. at nine or ten, 21 per cent. at eleven or twelve, and only 16 per cent. at thirteen or over. The mean age for the group was but nine years and seven months.[44] A few years later we condemn and punish the very acts formerly comprising "juvenile delinquency", or others growing naturally out of them, as crimes for which the offender is regarded as unquestionably and fully "responsible"!

Such then is the disheartening picture of our delinquents and criminals. Other researches bear out most of the findings, though the incidence of some of the factors described is occasionally not quite as high, sometimes not as low, as in the two samples described.[45] A substantial proportion of poverty and dependency and all they mean in the way of unhygienic home and neighborhood situations and the taking of the mother out of the home;[46] unskilled, incompetent bread-winners;[47] illiteracy of parents;[48] unhappy relations between husband and wife and between parents and children, and unwise disciplinary practices;[49] broken homes;[50] immorality, alcoholism and criminalism of parents and brothers and sisters;[51] mental defect, disorder and distortion;[52] inadequate schooling;[53] employment of children in hazardous street trades;[54] unwholesome recreations and vicious companionships;[55] an early beginning in delinquent tendencies;[56] marked recidivism[57] — each picture is a little different in emphasis and perspective, but the composite one is a portrait of unfortunate, underprivileged biologic, social and economic status.

4

Clearly, then, the task of society in coping with delinquency and criminality is herculean. Involved in the process are not only those agencies specially set up to deal with violations of the criminal code, but practically all social institutions: the state, community, home, school, church, recreational center, welfare agency, the general economic order, the moral climate — in brief the standard of civilization which we pride ourselves upon having achieved. By the time delinquents and criminals fall into the hands of police, courts and punitive and correctional agencies they are in many respects the finished products of failure and neglect on the part of our most cherished social institutions. And since they usually return to equally bad conditions, high percentages of rehabilitation or "reform" are hardly to be expected.

How superficial, uneconomic and unjust, in the light of the complexity of the motivations and conditioning factors in crime, is the practice of treating offenders as simple mechanisms and overemphasizing the fear motive appealed to through punishment! While the appeal to fear has some socially desirable effect as a deterrent, it is a stimulus to but one constituent of the personality, and often not an enduring one. In fact, in certain pathologic cases the threat of punishment may rather be an incentive to the very wrongdoing it seems to deter.[58] For these reasons its results in most cases are disappointingly superficial and transient. To reduce recidivism on the part of offenders subjected to the blandishments of Justice, a more realistic approach is necessary: one that will face the reality of the complexity of human motivation and of the pressures and pulls that condition anti-social behavior.

CHAPTER VII

THE PROSPECT OF JUSTICE

1

It is often claimed that conditions have been greatly improved since various disclosures of the ills of Justice were made. True, here and there minor changes have occurred in response to transient reform movements. But one with historic sense should know how deep-rooted are the evils described in the foregoing pages and how slow is fundamental reform. The disclosures of the Tweed era were echoed by the more recent investigations of the New York courts and the house of correction on Welfare Island; and even as we write they are being re-echoed by further investigations of some of the personnel of Justice in New York City and elsewhere, and of penal institutions and parole practices in various parts of the country. The headlines record the appointment of special prosecutors to investigate racketeering, the putting into office of incompetents and spoilsmen as wardens of prisons, the corruption of police and prosecutors. The files of grand jury investigations and the press show vividly that evil and incompetence in public office, particularly where dealing with crime is concerned, are the most persistent dragons to slay and keep slain. As long as the soil from which Justice draws her nutriment remains essentially unchanged, it cannot be expected that minor manipulations, bits of reform legislation or the throwing out of a few rascals here and there will bring about basic improvement. Simple operations may give temporary relief, and that is highly desirable; but the patient requires more radical treatment.

What shall be done about this situation? The tasks to be performed are so vast and complex that one may well stand before them in despair. It can never be too strongly emphasized that there is no magical abracadabra of reform. The history of the criminal law and its administration is already a tale of misplaced confidences. The object of this and the succeeding chapter is merely to explore a few of the more promising remedies suggested by the diagnosis.

2

Success in any enterprise depends a good deal on the attitude with which it is approached. There are several attitudes that seem essential to any marked amelioration of the ways of Justice. The first is that despite the fact that our criminal law lags behind the progress of mechanical invention, scientific discoveries and the changes in psychologic attitudes and social customs, "conscious effort *can* reduce lag."[1] Instead, the belief of many laymen and lawyers seems to be that there can be no really fundamental change in the administration of criminal law because none is needed, or if it is, the obstacles are too great. Almost every significant reform in criminal justice has had to cope with this tradition-rooted and fear-motivated inertia. It long barred the way to the establishment of juvenile courts with equity instead of criminal jurisdiction;

it opposed the professional development of the probation movement; it ran counter to the adoption of the indeterminate sentence and parole; it interfered with the movement for simplification of civil and criminal procedure; it stands in the way of the installation of crime prevention programs in police departments; it has opposed many other changes in the conventions of the American criminal law and its administration. So, too, in England, "writing at a time when the subtlety, prolixity, and incoherence of English law were at their apex, Blackstone still conceived the system to be the 'perfection of reason.' A generation later it was torn to tatters by Jeremy Bentham."[2] The codification of criminal law was a chief item in the program of Lord Beaconsfield's government, which introduced Sir James Fitz-James Stephens' Criminal Code Bill in 1878, 1879 and 1880. Yet in 1933 an authority on the English criminal law could write that codification "seems in England to be more remote than some fifty years ago."[3] It is this conservative attitude of drift instead of direction that must be overcome before lawyers and legislators can face realities and redesign the criminal law in accordance with modern needs and knowledge. The patent-medicine approach to a pervasive social problem will have to give way to a fundamental attack before we can expect crime to be permanently reduced and the criminal law to be more effective as well as more just.

But, the question may reasonably be asked, if the deeper forces discussed in the opening chapter are so fundamental and pervasive, how can one expect even a modernized criminal code to do much good? To this it is replied that the proponent of a better administration of justice does not ignore those protean conditioning forces to which the criminal law and procedure, like other social institutions, are subject. But he recognizes that all social organisms, in their functioning, have reflex effects upon each other. Establish a more rational system of justice and it will ultimately contribute its part to erasing or counteracting, or at least more clearly defining, some of the irrationalities of other social institutions. They too need to be radically reformed — a fact that in these days of economic storm and stress can hardly be questioned. To design and establish a code of substantive law, procedure and administration more adapted to the times is but one of the pressing needs of the day.

The second attitude with which our task must be approached was long ago suggested by Mr. Justice Holmes in one of his wisest and most trenchant addresses. "An ideal system of law," he said in 1895, "should draw its postulates and its legislative justification from science. As it is now, we rely upon tradition, or vague sentiment, or the fact that we never thought of any other way of doing things, as our only warrant for rules which we enforce with as much confidence as if they embodied revealed wisdom."[4] And then he threw the gauge of battle into the teeth of the legal profession by asking the embarrassing question: "Who here can give reasons of any different kind for believing that half the criminal law does not do more harm than good?"[5] That Justice Holmes was as customarily sound in his views on social problems is evident to all who have eyes to see. When it comes to the repetition of crime by those already punished, the situation is little short of appalling. In New York, during the past two years, of 4,254 indeterminate-sentence prisoners paroled, about whose prior arrests information was available, at least 68 per cent. were found to have had previous arrests, 1,432 of them three or more.[6] In Massachusetts, during the statistical year ending in 1934, of 3,654 male offenders sentenced to jails and houses of correction, 58 per cent. were reported to have had prior commitments; of 1,675 sentenced to the state farm, 89 per cent. had served prior sentences of incarceration; of 83 sentenced to prison, 70 per cent. had previously been imprisoned; of 110 sentenced to the reformatory, 64 per cent. had served prior sentences.[7] Among 7,236 offenders committed to federal institutions during the year 1933–34, 48.5 per cent. were reported to have had prior commitments — an increase over the three preceding years; and it is pointed out that "the percentage of *known* recidivists might tend to increase from year to year, since identification records are becoming more complete."[8] Such statistics, moreover, never tell the whole story. Intensive field investigations of samples of juvenile delinquents and adult graduates of the reformatories in Massachusetts prove that the true recidivism rate is appreciably higher than that officially recorded, even in a state which has a central pool of criminal records.[9] In 1933, over 12,000 persons in the United States are reported to have been victims of homicide. The death rate of 9.6 per 100,000 population was eighteen times that of England and Wales.[10] In one recent decade (1920–29) 2,722 murders and manslaughters were committed in Chicago alone, a figure that does not include homicides due solely to criminal negligence.[11] In contemplating such facts it is difficult not to agree with

Holmes' inference that our present penal system does more harm than good. Nobody can say exactly what the deterrent effect of existing methods is on "the rest of us"; but so far as delinquents and criminals are concerned, it appears to be very low.[12] When to this fact is added the deterioration that comes from the typical jail or prison, the indictment of the system is amply justified.

Assuredly, therefore, not only an ideal system of law, but even a fairly decent one, in the twentieth century "should draw its postulates and its legislative justification from science." Pound suggests "four ways of looking at things political and legal" which "left their mark upon nineteenth-century criminal justice . . . the pioneer attitude, the natural-rights attitude, the democratic attitude, and the entrepreneur attitude."[13] It is time to insist that the criminal law of the twentieth century be characterized by the scientific attitude. Such an approach will not exclude humanitarian considerations. The sensible blending of these two elements is a major problem of contemporary reformers of criminal law, procedure and correctional policy and practice.

The third general attitude necessary to amelioration of the ills of Justice is to recognize that its problems in a complex society, functioning at a time when scientific methods can assist in the administration of law, but also when the large rewards of venality in public office are particularly tempting, unequivocally demand the talents of properly trained workers of unimpeachable integrity.

The fourth general attitude called for is one involving the soil in which both crime and the administration of law grow — recognition that there must be economic, social and political improvements beyond any thus far brought about, if we are to have a more effective and just functioning of the criminal law.

In generating such attitudes and improving the climate of Justice the church and school have obvious responsibilities. But the powerful modern weapons for informing and moulding public opinion — the press, the radio, the moving picture — can also play a great role and perform a momentous service, if those who control them be so minded. Opinion-forming agencies should devote much of their energy to improving the processes of Justice on the basis of research, and interpreting its aims and methods to the people with a view to putting public opinion behind vigorous but fair and intelligent law enforcement; to placing honest and capable men and women in office, regardless of party, religion or other irrelevant considerations; to remoulding the unfriendly or thoughtless attitude of the people toward unprotected childhood and adolescence, and toward the ex-prisoner striving to regain a legitimate foothold in society; to raising the general moral standard of business, law and other professions; to improving economic and social conditions. An immediate need is a congress of representatives of opinion-moulding agencies who will publicly pledge themselves to carry out such ethical obligations.

When one considers the havoc that has been wrought in certain parts of the world by these instruments for formulating public opinion, he must tremble before their potentialities. If any enterprises are really vested with a public interest, these are. If any instruments are capable of bringing about a better moral climate, these must be numbered among them.

3

Assuming it is possible to cultivate the necessary attitudes through a continuous, intensive campaign of education, a major task before American legal scholars today is to draft a more realistic criminal code to replace the existing tangle of legislative and judge-made law. It will take years of research and reflection for such a code to be constructed. An orderly restatement of the existing law is not enough; that is merely one of the instruments for the enterprise that is demanded — the redesigning of the criminal law to produce a code suitable to the America of our epoch and our aspirations. The present mass of law in this field is, as we have emphasized, a jumble of conflicting theories and nice technicalities many of which have long outlived the historic reasons for their birth. Over a hundred years ago Livingston, who drafted a significant code for Louisiana (which unfortunately never was enacted), called for a criminal law in which

> the incongruities which have pervaded our system will disappear; every new enactment will be impressed with the character of the original body of laws; and our penal legislation will no longer be a piece of fretwork exhibiting the passions of its several authors, their fears, their caprices, or the carelessness and inattention with which legislators in all ages and in every country have, at times, endangered the lives, the liberties, and fortunes of the people, by inconsistent provisions, cruel or disproportioned punishments, and a legislation, weak and wavering, because guided by no principle, or by one that was continually changing, and therefore could seldom be right.[14]

What Livingston said in the 1830's is even more pertinent now. For peno-correctional practices to be made substantially more effective, a major need is the critical re-examination of the underlying policies, rules, standards and instruments of the criminal law in its substantive, procedural and administrative aspects, with the aim of drafting a code that is both scientific and realistic. By "scientific" we mean one in which, in addition to the traditional legal considerations of an analytic, historic or philosophic nature, the possible contributions of such disciplines as sociology, political science, anthropology, psychiatry, psychology, education and all other pertinent bodies of science or art will be brought into play. By "realistic" we mean a code in which the cultural and physical environment in which Justice is compelled to function in different regions of the United States will be taken into account in making local adjustments of principles and policies.

A more consistent code must be predicated upon one or a few underlying social-ethical principles which will express its *raison d'être*, instead of leaving this to be implied from a mass of confusing and sometimes contradictory laws and decisions. Given a pervasive principle that will underlie the definitions of the crimes, the implementation of the code with correctional instruments and the putting of its provisions into effect by the servants of Justice should have some uniformity of purpose and plan.

In the light of the humanitarian and scientific elements that must be taken into account in the modern correctional code, it seems reasonable to found it upon some such basic principle as the following: Society should utilize every scientific instrumentality for self-protection against destructive elements in its midst, with as little interference with the free life of its members as is consistent with such protection, and with a recognition of its responsibility to aid the offending member in every way that gives reasonable promise of his reform and rehabilitation.

The employment of every available scientific instrument is a point that need not be labored. The demand for increased efficiency dictates that society should carry out its prime aim of social security by all scientific means. The very life of the social order depends upon an up-to-date administration of criminal justice. Outmoded tools, inherited from times and cultures long past cannot cope with modern problems, especially when those who attack the general security (particularly professional criminals) avail themselves of scientific devices.

But why has society, through its administration of justice, the responsibility of aiding its offending members in every way that promises their reform and their reestablishment in the community? Both humanitarianism and economy dictate such an obligation. While society has the prime right to maintain the general security, it also has the duty to use the best available means to aid its members to lead a law-abiding life. Even a socially harmful individual has a right, as a human being, to be treated by those means that will give him a reasonable chance of rehabilitation. This conclusion flows from the recognition that the conditioning factors of criminality involve, as we have seen, other biologic and social forces than the traditional and oversimplified "free will." Up to the point where the recognition of such a right becomes socially dangerous, a human being in our civilized society cannot be held to have forfeited it by a mere act of aggression. Not he alone, but in a larger sense society itself, is responsible for his condition; he therefore has the right to have his handicaps taken into account in the determination of how the courts and prisons shall deal with him.

Such a policy is also dictated by the economic principle. Our present knowledge of the bankruptcy of the existing system, so far as its failure to reform criminals is concerned and also, though perhaps to a less extent, as a general deterrent to wrongdoing,[15] dictates a fundamental reorientation of the entire process in a way which, by affording ample opportunity for the reform and rehabilitation of offenders, will give more promise of reducing crime.

But in fairness to society and in the light of this same principle of economy, there is a limit to non-interference with the free life of offenders and to reformative and rehabilitative efforts, beyond which politically organized society cannot afford to go. For example, to keep experimenting blindly by allowing a dangerous individual to be at large when a reasonable number of trials and errors on probation and parole have demonstrated his incorrigibility is no longer consistent with social self-protection. Scientific aids, such as prognostic tables, to be later described, can help to determine the methods of accommodating individual and social interests, and the degree beyond which it is dangerous to carry experiment.

Assuming the validity of some such underlying social-ethical principle, one is led to the following fundamental criterion of the proposed penal code: The legal and institutional provisions for the protection of society should be based not so much upon the gravity of the act for which the offender happens to be on trial, as upon his personality and character; that is, upon his social dangerousness, his assets and liabilities, and his probable and actual response to correctional treatment. This criterion takes account of the recognized fact that a relatively innocuous act may be, and not infrequently is, committed by one who in fact is a menace to society, while a relatively serious offense (even murder) may be committed by one who is fundamentally not dangerous. In speaking of "personality" rather than "crime" or "act", it takes account of the further fact that in the administration of justice we are dealing with a developing, dynamic organism rather than a static act, and that gravity of the crime is but one manifestation, and not always the most significant one, of the true nature of the offender.

The phrase "probable and actual responsiveness to correctional treatment" recognizes the fact that the knowledge of the offender possessed by the sentencing authority immediately after trial is less perfect than that obtainable at the later stages of the proceedings. At the point of sentence the situation of the offender can be spoken of only in terms of probability, often of but possibility; the offender has not yet been subjected to correctional treatment under scientific observation, and it is difficult to say in advance what his response will be. At some later stage, as when his case is reviewed after an experimental period of treatment or when he is being considered for transfer to a more liberal correctional regime or for release on parole, his basic traits can be more exactly determined.

So much for the need of a scientific and realistic criterion. Of course the breaking down of one or two general principles into sub-principles can only be accomplished when specific policies, definitions and other provisions of the proposed code are undertaken. A code spun completely out of one's head would have little relation to reality. The process of weighing the evidence of the peculiar problems presented by different classes of anti-social activity and different types of offenders may cause a reëxamination or even abandonment of the criterion employed at the outset. The broad principles we have suggested are not offered as final but rather as illustrative of the type of generalizations that are needed if the substantive, procedural and administrative elements of an organic criminal code are to have an underlying unity of design and aim.

The drafting of an improved criminal code involves also, among other basic problems, the following ones: A reëxamination of the philosophy of punishment, a consideration of the "limits of effective legal action", and a determination of how the sum total of society's legal power to cope with crime may be most efficiently distributed among the several agencies for administering justice. These fundamentals require consideration.

Punishment in modern criminal law still contains too much of the vindictive element.[16] True, much has been said in recent years, in treatises and judicial decisions, about the deterrent and reformative aims of punishment; but it cannot be denied that the vengeance motif is still very strong. Philosophers have rationalized it into "transcendental" theories of "just retribution" or atonement for wickedness, but its roots lie deep in human nature. Writers with psychoanalytic insight have helped to lay bare those roots in man's psychology:

> The criminal [says Dr. William A. White] thus becomes the handy scapegoat upon which [man] can transfer his feeling of his own tendency to sinfulness and thus by punishing the criminal he deludes himself into a feeling of righteous indignation, thus bolstering up his own self-respect and serving in this roundabout way, both to restrain himself from like indulgences and to keep himself upon the path of cultural progress. . . . The legal punishment of the criminal today is in its psychology, a dramatic tragic action by which society pushes off its criminal impulses upon a substitute. The principle is the same as that by which an emotion such as anger is discharged upon an inoffensive lifeless object.[17]

The transcendental retaliative-retributive theory of punishment might therefore more accurately be termed the scapegoat or lightning-rod theory. Many regard it as socially desirable to continue to found criminal law on such a basis. It is in fact strongly urged in certain quarters that if social vengeance is not allowed to express itself immediately and forcefully in extreme punishment of those who commit revolting crimes, the people will "take the law into their own hands" and lynching will occur. It is noticeable, however, that the regions which still insist most emphatically upon this theory are also the places where most lynchings occur. This suggests that very much the same motivations that determine and rationalize vengeance through law are likely also to stimulate illegal vengeance.

Official social institutions can help to dilute the vengeful element in law enforcement. If progress is to be made in civilizing man's impulses, the criminal law must be so framed as to reduce to a minimum the area of vindictive punishment. It is precisely the controlling of primitive responses and the substitution of orderly procedures that was a chief historic function of English law when early in its development it supervised forms of self-help and took over the jurisdiction in criminal affairs formerly exercised by ducal and baronial courts, under the fiction of maintaining the "king's peace." One of the tests of a civilized society is its capacity to discipline its vengeful reactions. There are very few lynchings in those older, more sophisticated communities in which education in the value of orderly and fair practices has permeated the population. This indicates that the scapegoat or lightning-rod function of the criminal law is not indispensable. Mental hygiene and education can contribute more wholesome ways of bolstering up the self-respect and restraining the anti-social impulses of a people.

Yet the framers of the criminal code of tomorrow will have to face the facts. The criminal law of a state may be too far in advance of its general culture as well as too far behind it. If in certain regions the tradition of vengeance is as yet too strongly entrenched, the criminal law will have to make compromises with it until the attitude of the public has been reformed.

Another basic problem to be solved is that involving the limits of effective legal action. It must be recognized that the criminal law cannot be expected to take over most of the former functions of the home, the school, the church, the workshop and the play-group. Attempting to control certain forms of undesirable conduct through the mechanism of the criminal law may do more harm than good, because of annoyance to the public, difficulties of administration, relative insignificance of the evils to be remedied, and existence of other social institutions than police, courts and prisons, whose responsibility it is to act as agencies of social control. The fact that these other agencies of control have been losing their authority and effectiveness is no reason for turning over their functions to the law. Attention should rather be directed to ascertaining the causes of such weakening of traditional controls and to finding means to counteract them or develop new ones. The evils of the increasing tendency to pass prohibitory laws covering conduct that should be restrained by other means, or behavior that the great majority of the people deem relatively harmless, are vividly pointed out in these words:

> Suppose, for example, that a legislator should feel himself authorized to undertake the extirpation of drunkenness and fornication by direct laws. He would have to begin by a multitude of regulations. The first inconvenience would therefore be a complexity of laws. The easier it is to conceal these vices, the more necessary it would be to resort to severity of punishment, in order to destroy by the terror of examples the constantly recurring hope of impunity. This excessive rigour of laws forms a second inconvenience not less grave than the first. The difficulty of procuring proofs would be such, that it would be necessary to encourage informers, and to entertain an army of spies. This necessity forms a third inconvenience, greater than either of the others. Let us compare the results of good and evil. Offences of this nature, if that name can be properly given to imprudences, produce no alarm; but the pretended remedy would spread a universal terror; innocent or guilty,

> every one would fear for himself or his connexions. . . . Instead of suppressing one vice, the laws would produce other vices, new and more dangerous.[18]

This was not said by a modern writer inveighing against the "noble experiment." It was said by Jeremy Bentham a century and a half ago. Clearly, principles will have to be worked out which will govern legislators in deciding whether or not to resort to penal sanctions for coping with alleged evils. Perhaps one function of the "Ministry of Justice" proposed in the concluding chapter will be to exercise guidance in this field. At all events, if social action through criminal law is necessary in some of these cases, simplified summary proceedings, specialized tribunals and pressures other than the traditional punitive mechanism of small fines and brief imprisonments are called for in a substantial segment of the expanding field of modern "crime." The persons who violate many of our petty regulatory provisions are usually not dangerous aggressors. A more elaborate procedure, focused on the makeup of offenders, is applicable to only a proportion of them, namely those who by repeated offenses of this kind indicate the need of their being treated as wards of society.

A third problem is that of determining how the sum total of society's legal power to deal with criminal aggressions shall be distributed among the agencies of Justice in order to obtain the highest efficiency in repressing crime consonant with humanitarianism and the constitutional protection of individual rights. This problem has not been sufficiently recognized or systematically coped with in American codes. What part of this power had better be embodied in the legislatively enacted substantive law which defines crimes, defenses to crimes and punishments? What part of it can safely be entrusted to the discretion of judges, and to what kind of judges? What part had better be left to administrators of penal and correctional institutions, and to what type of administrators? Even under the criminal law of the future there will be a need for some effective and fair method of separating the sheep — those whose acts are not really violative of the law or who have not committed the crimes charged, or who have some other legitimate defense — from the goats — those whose status, as determined at the trial, renders them subject to correctional treatment.

Without considerably more legal and extra-legal research, the precise mechanisms of a more realistic penal code cannot be designed. Perhaps it will be found feasible and desirable to evolve a purely objective — behavioristic — criminal law;[19] that is, one in which such psychologic elements of the legally defined crime as the "criminal intent" can be wholly eliminated, leaving them for determination by the sentencing agency. Such an approach will meet with several serious legal obstacles that may render it impossible to make so radical a modification. To cite but one illustration, the excuse from responsibility on the ground of "mistake of fact" depends upon the proof of a mental element; if true mistake existed, the offender is not liable. To hold a man guilty for taking a handbag under an honest but mistaken belief that it is his own would be undesirable, even though the body of specialists selected to pass upon the mental element and the necessary correctional treatment would promptly discharge him. This is true so long as too much of the stigma of disgrace is attached to a finding of guilt.[20]

But the radical departure of a totally objective criminal law may not be necessary. The problem presented by the fact that the courts today deal with psychologic, psychiatric and sociologic issues through an unsuitable medium might be solved by retaining much of the present technical paraphernalia of the substantive law of crimes so far as determination of status at the trial is concerned, but introducing more scientific points of view and techniques in the *sentencing* process. Analysis of the sentencing practices of the courts and of the results of the existing system has indicated that a basic improvement is called for. Whatever may ultimately be decided regarding the definition of crimes, much of the proposed criterion may be incorporated in the sentencing aspect. It will be recalled that our criterion stresses the dynamic personality rather than the static act. It is possible, without radical changes in substantive criminal law, to administer justice upon some such basis. The stages at which it may be done are when sentence is imposed, when treatment is being carried out, and when it is determined whether or not to discharge an imprisoned offender. The method proposed is the scientific yet just individualization of treatment.

"Individualization of punishment" has long been a slogan of reformers. One such evidence of attempts to fit the treatment to the case is to be found in the very definitions of crimes, such as the historic distinctions between voluntary and involuntary manslaughter, and between murder and manslaughter. These are crude legislative and judicial individualizations of types of analogous crimes, based on the idea that the classes of acts differ in degrees of blameworthiness or of the "vicious will" they are supposed to reflect, or in their social harmfulness, or in their effect in arousing fear and anger. So, too, the breaking down of crimes into detailed "degrees", so common a phenomenon in American codes and statutes in the nineteenth century and today, is a later form of legislative individualization, or more accurately categorization, in the provision of different kinds and lengths of punishment for varieties of criminal acts.[21] Such code or statutory provisions often leave the judge relatively little discretion.

But while these forms of individualization exist, they are very crude; they distinguish crimes rather than criminals; they prescribe *in advance* the length of time the patient should be kept in the hospital and then hold him there the full period or discharge him ahead of time, whether cured or not. The so-called indeterminate sentence movement, which began late in the nineteenth century as a recognition of the need of individualizing punishment, has in practice had but little effect upon these fixed provisions or upon the attitude which inspired them. For not all states have indeterminate sentences, even now; and in most jurisdictions such sentences apply only to specified types of crime or persons within certain age limits. Moreover, the aims of the proponents of the indeterminate sentence have frequently been defeated in two ways: either judges have imposed sentences which make the minimum limit virtually identical with the maximum (such as a sentence of from 24 years and 6 months to 25 years), or parole boards have blindly released prisoners after the minimum limit of the sentence has been served.

Even where indeterminate sentences provide wide zones between the minimal and maximal limits, and judges are thereby given considerable discretion in fixing the punishment or correctional treatment within such zones, their efforts, as we have seen, are likely to be erratic or mechanical, or at all events unscientific. There are judges, for example, who make up their minds in advance to impose heavy or light sentences on all offenders against certain statutes, or on all third or fourth offenders; or to place on probation only violators of some specific law, and that regardless of how often in the past the probationers have already failed to respond to such extramural treatment or of how promising of rehabilitation offenders against other laws might be.

We must conclude, then, that though crude attempts have been made to individualize correctional treatment on the basis of the type of crime and by the indeterminate sentence, the mass-treatment practice of dealing with offenders, or their erratic treatment through a haphazard and uncontrolled exercise of discretion, is still in vogue. The trouble with existing methods of separating the sheep from the goats is that they do not constitute efficient instruments of scientific individualization indispensable to an economical as well as a just administration of the law. Legislative prescription of detailed degrees of offenses is individualization of acts, not of human beings, and is therefore bound to be inefficient. Judicial individualization, without adequate instruments wielded by competent personnel, is destined to deteriorate into a mechanical or erratic process involving the application of rules of thumb, or implied or expressed prejudices, or worse practices.

How, then, shall a more scientific and just individualization be brought about? Four features of an improved system appear to be indicated by analysis of the existing sentencing practices. First, the treatment, or sentence-imposing, feature of the criminal proceedings needs to be differentiated from the guilt-finding phase in method and, to a large extent, in personnel. Second, the decision regarding the treatment necessary for each offender needs to be left to a tribunal or board specially qualified in the interpretation and evaluation of sociologic, psychiatric and psychologic, as well as legal, data. Third, the treatment program arrived at in each case needs to be modifiable in the light of periodic reports of the offender's progress, submitted to the tribunal by those entrusted with carrying out its mandates. Fourth, the rights of the individual must be safeguarded against possible arbitrariness or other unlawful action on the part of the treatment tribunal.

The first two propositions flow logically from the existing malpractices in sentencing. The two functions of the courts — to determine guilt or innocence and to impose sentence — are quite different in methodology and aim. Moreover, they involve essentially different talents. While a legally trained judge can act as an impartial referee during a technical trial, rule upon the exclusion or inclusion of evidence, give a legally adequate charge to the jury and perform other such functions, his education and habit of mind have not necessarily qualified him, acting alone, for the specialized task of determining the treatment best suited to various types of offenders. Since this requires accommodation of legal and extra-legal disciplines, a reasonable conclusion is that the sentencing function should be entrusted to a tribunal to be composed, say, of a psychiatrist or psychologist, a sociologist or educator and the trial judge.[22] Such a diagnostic body would also determine the specific plan of treatment in the light of the individual and social interests at stake.[23] After ascertaining the defendant's guilt, this tribunal, upon investigation by its probation officers and clinicians, would determine the appropriate sentence as well as its tentative duration, writing a decision in support of its action.[24]

Like so many other reforms deemed to be highly revolutionary, this call for scientifically fitting the treatment to the needs of the individual offender has long been recognized. It is at least as old as Aristotle, from one of whose most famous writings we quote:

> The knowing what is just and what unjust, men think no great instance of wisdom, because it is not hard to understand those things of which the laws speak. They forget that these are not just acts except accidentally. To be just, they must be done and distributed in a certain manner. And this is a more difficult task than knowing what things are wholesome. For in this branch of knowledge it is an easy matter to know honey, wine, hellebore, cautery, or the use of the knife; but the knowing how one should administer these with a view to health, and to whom, and at what time, amounts in fact to being a physician.[25]

The sentencing judge of the future must be a social physician.

The third principle of wise individualization — modifiability of the length and type of treatment in the light of progress of the offender — is dictated by the logic of the foregoing. For the proposed tribunal to carry out its functions more effectively than do the present criminal courts, it would be necessary to evolve methods for the observation of the delinquent's progress under the form of correction originally prescribed. If called for, the treatment might thereby be modified, much as the physician changes treatment in the light of progress. To that end, periodic reports and their review by the tribunal, would have to be provided for.

Finally, individual rights and liberties would have to be safeguarded against the possible arbitrariness of a technically skilled, yet all-too human, administrative board. This is not the place to go into detail as to the possible ways of judicialization of the administrative act that determines the appropriate treatment. Speaking generally, there are several possible safeguards. First, the statute defining and delimiting the powers of the tribunal might set down broad socio-psychiatric categories within which, as the result of a hearing, the latter would classify each offender as a basis for determining his sentence.

The present definition of "defective delinquents" in Massachusetts illustrates one such category. The statute, it will be recalled, defines a defective delinquent as one who (*a*) is "mentally defective", (*b*) has shown himself upon "examination into his record, character and personality, . . . to be an habitual delinquent or shows tendencies towards becoming such", (*c*) in whose case "such delinquency is or may become a menace to the public", and (*d*) who is not a proper subject for treatment in certain enumerated penal or correctional institutions that deal with other classes of offenders.[26] Such definitions, striking an effective balance between categorization and detail, might be worked out for various classes of offenders, such as the psychotic or psychopathic and those whose career of crime is shown to be essentially attributable to social forces largely beyond their control, and others. On appellate review of a case in which it is claimed that the sentencing board acted arbitrarily, the question of the reasonableness of its classification of an offender and the data upon which such classification was made might be gone into.

Another safeguard might be afforded the defendant by allowing him to have counsel and witnesses at the hearing, as well as by permitting the examination of psychiatric and sociologic reports filed with the tribunal. Such a hearing would of course avoid a technical, litigious procedure, hidebound by strict rules of evidence; it would be more in the nature of proceedings in juvenile courts based on principles of equity. A third safeguard would be the provision already noted for periodic — say annual — review of each person's case as a matter of right.

While judges need to have ample discretion in sentencing, discretion must not be allowed to run wild. Hence in the proposed system an appellate tribunal somewhat analogous to the English Court of Criminal Appeals, ought to be provided. Its function would be to review instances of alleged arbitrariness, and to evolve sentencing standards and principles tending to coordinate the activities of the different treatment boards of a state.[27]

To be effective the treatment tribunal would have to be empowered to impose a *wholly indeterminate* sentence, so that manifestly dangerous individuals might be kept under control within institutions and on parole for long periods — if necessary throughout life — while those rapidly rehabilitated might be released, at least experimentally, after relatively short periods of control.[28] At present many dangerous offenders must be discharged at the end of the maximum limit of the indeterminate sentence, even though all concerned know full well that such offenders will forthwith commit further crimes; and socially harmless prisoners who give every promise of a successful and law-abiding subsequent career must be detained, often for so long a time that they are of little use to themselves, their families or society upon discharge.

The treatment tribunal ought further to be implemented by appropriate clinics and means for forecasting, at least approximately, the probable subsequent behavior of various types of offenders if subjected to given methods of treatment. Recent researches have demonstrated that it is possible to classify offenders into "treatment types", and to predict their conduct.[29] In an analysis of the prognostic value of prediction tables based on such factors as mental makeup, industrial habits, economic responsibility, attitude toward the family, frequency of prior crimes, former penal experiences and the like, it has been shown that such considerations are much more significant in forecasting subsequent behavior than either the type or the seriousness of the crime for which the offender happens to be before the court.[30] Yet today sentences are based largely on the nature of the offense. To be sure, such predictive devices will have to be used with the greatest care; they are not intended to replace the judgment of trained officials but to supplement it. Their prognostic value is as yet only approximate. But as Beccaria long ago pointed out, "in political arithmetic, it is necessary to substitute a calculation of probabilities, to mathematical exactness."[31] Assuredly the use of prognostic tables is superior to the present hit-or-miss methods of imposing sentence.

Because the substantive criminal law will require long study before the definitions of crimes and defenses can be fundamentally improved, we have contented ourselves with referring to the importance of its problems and indicating a few lines of attack. It should be pointed out, however, that the establishment of a system of treatment tribunals would suggest the avenues of needed modification of the criminal law, because it would for the first time make feasible the development of a body of experience based on its actual operation. The history of the law shows that modifications in substance have not infrequently followed in the wake of procedural changes. Perhaps, eventually, the basic mode of analysis of crimes into "act" and "intent" will be radically modified.[32] One can conceive, for example, that the effective operation of the type of board described will have its influence on the tests of the irresponsibility of the insane; it might even render them superfluous. It would probably also have the effect of reducing the number and variety of degrees in the definition of homicide, robbery, rape, larceny and other crimes. Furthermore, it might influence the substantive law regarding attempts. The minute splitting up of offenses into degrees, and the distinguishing of attempts from completed criminal acts, with the scrupulous setting down of supposedly appropriate doses of punishment, based upon degrees of "vicious will" as reflected in types of crime, belong to an era when punishment was considered the only or best means of coping with anti-social behavior, and when artificially circumscribed means of individualization were set down in advance by legislatures, to be automatically applied by judges.

There remains the question whether the proposed system should be applied to all crimes and offenders, and if not, how it should be limited. A wise social policy would require it to be confined to persons committing felonies, at first excluding, perhaps, as a concession to local public opinion, two or three such felonies as first degree murder and armed robbery. We should be under no illusion that the vindictive element in punishment can be eliminated altogether in our generation, or even in several to come. The possibility of offenders who have committed passion-arousing crimes escaping execution, or being returned to society before they had served long sentences, might so seriously disturb public opinion in certain communities as to make the entire new sentencing technique extremely unpopular. One of the shrewd policies of the imperial Roman government was to enforce its laws by taking into account local differences of custom; and the fact that such a crime as rape is in different regions of the United States punishable in ways varying as widely as from a few years' imprisonment to the death penalty shows how necessary it is to take cultural differences into account in projecting reforms. Much of this need may, however, be met not by excluding certain offenses from the jurisdiction of the treatment tribunal, but by prescribing minimal limits to the indeterminate sentence in certain serious crimes, so that regardless of their reform persons committing them could be kept imprisoned for at least a definite span of years by way of punishment. Which offenders would be retained still longer would then be left to the wise discretion of the treatment tribunal.

Public opinion would probably also oppose the application of the proposed system to certain misdemeanants, since under the recommended procedure some of these might be kept under control for long periods and even throughout life, for offenses generally regarded as petty. It might be provided, however, that when a chronic offender of the misdemeanant type, such as a person habitually arrested for drunkenness or vagrancy or prostitution, has failed to respond to ordinary treatment, as judged by his having committed some stated number of offenses within a specified period, the courts should declare him to be an "habitual delinquent" and he should be turned over to the treatment tribunal for the more intensive and enduring regime applied to those who commit felonies. Although this would often mean that effective procedure would in many cases come too late, it would at least result in taking out of circulation a helpless group of people who require continuous care and whose ceaseless rearrests, retrials and recommitments are an avoidable drain on the taxpayer's purse.

As already intimated, this entire problem involves decision as to what acts or courses of anti-social behavior in a modern society ought to be included in a criminal code in the first place. It may well be that a more effective non-criminal commitment procedure could be utilized for persons committing certain offenses, with the provision of unwalled farms and medical institutions for those wishing to place themselves under care. Some compromises with the basic institution of a separate, scientifically staffed treatment tribunal will doubtless have to be made in every state. But if the board performs its functions properly, its jurisdiction may later be extended to embrace crimes not originally included. The jurisdictional limits suggested for the proposed system, though somewhat arbitrary, seem feasible and necessary in the meantime.

Would a more scientific system of criminal law and correction remove the deterrent effect of the threat of punishment? Hardly; anti-social persons would still be deprived of their liberty. Moreover, since the length of incarceration would not be determinable in advance by them and might endure throughout life, and since, as is not the case under the present practice, they would not be released at the end of a stated time regardless of whether they were still social menaces, the proposed regime would probably have greater deterrent effect than the present one. Under the former the length and kind of punishment would not be based on a single criminal act or even a few isolated ones, but upon a continuous course of conduct, upon typical attitudes of the offender and upon his character and personality and the chief motives of his wrongdoing.

It may be maintained that the proposed system would be too expensive; but there is good reason to assume the contrary. When one considers the frequent rearrests, retrials, resentences and recommitments to penal institutions of the vast hordes of criminals, and realizes that many of them, under the new system, would not be allowed at large for long stretches of time to continue their social depredations, the saving seems obvious. Another objection that may be raised is that of paternalism; but it has been shown that substantial proportions of offenders thus far studied are precisely those who need a societal parent as a substitute for self-management; throughout their lives — in industry, in family relations, in meeting the demands of politically organized society as embraced in criminal law — they usually require the oversight of a social nurse. The need of such supervision has long been recognized in the case of many of the mentally ill or defective, who are committed to special institutions or placed under guardianship.

In the foregoing analysis we have not included the juvenile court; not because it is unimportant — on the contrary, it is of vital significance, considering that so many adult criminals begin their anti-social careers in childhood — but because the topic has been gone into recently elsewhere.[33]

4

In addition to a fundamental examination of the underlying suppositions, aims, principles and methods of the law that defines crimes, criminal responsibility and punishments, far-reaching changes in criminal procedure and administrative practices may be found necessary. The Code of Criminal Procedure prepared by the American Law Institute several years ago contains some excellent features. But it is predicated upon the assumption of the continuance of the existing criminal law and administrative practices. If and when a penetrating examination of basic principles of the criminal law is made in the light of related disciplines, the resulting code will unquestionably affect procedural and administrative provisions. The criminal law defining crimes, the bases of responsibility and exemptions from responsibility and peno-correctional practices ought properly to be an organic part of a comprehensive code which will include not only substantive law but procedural, administrative and correctional provisions. But the framing of such a code is a task of the future. In the meantime, certain administrative and procedural improvements are patently called for.

Consider, first, the weaknesses of police administration. Details cannot be gone into here, but several fundamentals stand out. One of these is the need of introducing the best modern scientific methods in the detection and apprehension of offenders and in the patrolling of beats. A fund of valuable technique has been assembled both in foreign police agencies and, more recently, in American. The scientific crime detection laboratories of the Northwestern University School of Law, the federal Bureau of Investigation and a few others are gradually proving their worth; and we may hope that other police systems, which still lack basic technical equipment and competent personnel for photographic, ballistic and chemical investigations useful in crime detection, will be compelled by an informed public and professional opinion to adapt their activities to the needs of the time. We may reasonably expect that with the increasing use of scientific method and professional personnel the resort to illegal means of law enforcement will be reduced.

Another major need which a few police departments

are beginning to bring home to others is the development of a preventive attitude and program. A shift of point of view is more than ever called for — one that will not regard the threat of the "cop on the beat" as the beginning and end of police work, but will focus attention on helping children to avoid the pitfalls of city life, turning their energies into constructive channels and aiding former prisoners to regain a foothold in the community. The experience of a few police departments both here and abroad proves that it is not inconsistent for a police agency to be efficient in the direct repression and detection of crime committed by ripened criminals and at the same time to offer intelligent and sympathetic leadership in preventing the making of future criminals.

A third element of improved policing has to do with the problem of administrative efficiency. Since contemporary crime knows no political boundaries, this involves questions of the advisability of establishing metropolitan police systems or state-wide police organizations, as well as interstate coöperation. A significant beginning in such coöperation has been made by the National Conference of Commissioners on Uniform State Laws, the New York Law Revision Commission and, very recently, the Interstate Commission on Crime sponsored by the state of New Jersey. The bills respecting police functions which have thus far been approved by the commissioners and law professors engaged in the New Jersey enterprise make uniform and expand the procedure on interstate extradition, provide for the securing of the attendance of witnesses from outside the state and authorize officers engaged in "close pursuit" of an offender to cross state lines and arrest him with the authority enjoyed by officers in the out-of-state jurisdiction.[34]

Improvements in criminal procedure beyond the point of arrest are also urgently required. In order to make the work of police and prosecutor more effective and at the same time protect the right of the accused against unfair methods like the third degree, it has been proposed by the Wickersham Commission, and previously by Pound, that legal provision be made for taking the arrested person forthwith before a magistrate, for his being there advised of the complaint against him in the presence of counsel charged with safeguarding his rights and for his interrogation by the magistrate, the answers to be taken down to insure accuracy. These recorded answers would then be admissible in evidence at the subsequent proceedings. "If he choose not to answer, it should be permissible for counsel for the prosecution and for the defense, as well as the trial judge, to comment on his refusal."

Such a recommendation is designed to "satisfy the reasonable demands of the police and the prosecutors for an interrogation of suspected persons and thus do away with the excuse for extra-legal questionings."[35] It is a provision that deserves to be tried, provided the quality of many magistrates can be raised. It ought, if adopted, to go far to reduce resort to illegal methods of interrogation. It may also help to discourage unlawful methods of search and seizure. Further, in many instances legalized interrogation would make the traditional "preliminary hearing" unnecessary, since the facts brought out in the questioning of the accused before a magistrate might show that there was no cause to go further.

In discussing the preliminary hearing and grand jury in Chapter III we suggested that one or the other of these sifting agencies might well be done away with, at least as a compulsory procedure.[36] To eliminate the preliminary hearing in all cases and have no grand jury would give the prosecutor, who already enjoys too great an unsupervised authority in starting and stopping the mills of Justice, too great a power; on the other hand, it has been found that in all except a very small percentage of cases the grand jury serves no useful purpose. What is needed is a more careful sifting of cases by magistrates, through employment of more formal and penetrating proceedings. The conclusion seems inescapable that in order to improve preliminary hearings the first requirement is to raise the quality of the lower court judges. The problem of personnel is reserved for the concluding chapter; its mention here is pertinent to show that with the betterment of the preliminary inquiry the grand jury step may in almost all instances be done away with. However, improvements in the preliminary hearing are not dependent solely on the efforts of magistrates. They involve also the question of a sounder police policy in making arrests, and a more careful preparation of the proof by police and prosecutor; this illustrates the unavoidable effect of one process of justice upon the others.

Turning now to the trial stage of the proceedings, the question may be asked whether the contentious, adversary methods of trial should not be remoulded to resemble the gathering of facts in the better juvenile courts and administrative tribunals. Under such a system, procedural formalities and rules of evidence would still play their part,[37] but they would be simplified and brought into greater harmony with the problems presented by contemporary crime and with modern psychologic and sociologic considerations. It is doubtful, however, whether the time has arrived for such a radical transformation of traditional proceedings, and they are not without danger of abuse.[38] The immediate task, therefore, is improvement of the existing adversary procedure.

Reasons were given in Chapter III for extending the practice of trial by a judge (or bench) without a jury. Not only are the advantages already noted to be expected, but through a reduction in jury trials the need of overly technical rules of evidence would be lessened.[39] Where jury trials are retained, greater authority of judges in guiding the proceedings has frequently been recommended; it is provided for in the American Law Institute's Code of Criminal Procedure. At present, in most states, the judge is not permitted to comment on the weight and credibility of the evidence and is in other ways little more than a figurehead, being swayed here and there by opposing counsel.[40] The recommendation that he be given real authority is of much deeper significance than appears at first glance. Its general adoption should go far to restore "the true character of the trial as a proceeding for the ascertainment of truth."[41] Proof exists that where the judge has such power, time and expense are saved in the bringing in of "quicker verdicts, reducing the number of disagreements, and diminishing the number of new trials and applications for new trials";[42] that the practice raises the position of the judge from that of mere moderator, in which role he is inclined to neglect his duties during the conduct of the trial, to that of an alert superintendent; that it reduces the chances of miscarriage of justice by the accidental superiority of counsel on one side; and that it gives the jury "the benefit of the opinion of the only impartial expert engaged in the trial."[43]

Here, too, however, a basic need is that of raising the quality of the knights of Justice. How important this is may be gathered from the sad truth that a chief objection raised by many experienced lawyers to giving trial judges the power to comment on the credibility of witnesses and the weight of the evidence is their poor average quality.[44]

Another aspect of criminal procedure that has not as yet been adequately explored is the discovery of means of controlling the wide discretion of prosecutors in determining which defendants to proceed against, which cases to nol pros, when to accept pleas of guilt to lesser offenses than those originally charged, and the like. Making prosecutors appointive would probably improve proceedings, especially if they were kept in office during good behavior regardless of changes in the governorship, and thus had few political obligations to fulfill. But even then the problem would partially persist. This reflects one of the central issues of justice — the disciplining of discretion by rules, standards, oversight and other devices, so that flexibility of administration may be retained while abuse and inefficiency are prevented. No organization has as yet drafted a code of administration, within the province of which this problem would largely fall, to supplement the American Law Institute's code of procedure. Here one can of course do no more than point to the need of such a code.[45] In the final chapter we recommend control of the work of the prosecutor by a Ministry of Justice. Here we remind the reader that administrative aspects of law enforcement cannot fully be divorced from substantive problems involved in a fundamental reëxamination of the definitions of crimes and defenses, the aims of punishment and correction and the instruments for achieving those aims.

Closely related to the problem of prosecution is that of defense. Aside from the question of the unethical methods of certain practitioners, there is that of more adequate defense of a large proportion of those accused of crime. The governmentally financed public defender and privately endowed voluntary defender for indigent defendants have done considerable good. But they have been provided for in only a fraction of the cities, and deal with but a small proportion of the criminal clientele. Wider extension of these services to poor persons accused of crime is a crying need.

If more systematic and rigorous control of the activities of unethical criminal lawyers does not bring expected results, and if inequality of the poor before the law in large measure persists, it will be necessary to consider whether criminal defense should not be recognized as a public function; whether counsel for *all* defendants in criminal cases should not be employed by the state from public funds. There are many arguments in favor of so radical a move, and they seem to overbalance its undesirable aspects. It cannot be denied that "equality before the law" is more figurative than real so long as moneyed offenders are enabled to employ the best counsel, while the poor must rely on no lawyers at all, unscrupulous shysters, or largely incompetent assigned counsel. A socialized criminal bar, a panel of publicly compensated counsel, would place defendants on a more uniform basis before the law. It ought to drive out the shyster and banish the professional criminal lawyer who is retained at large fees by gangsters and racketeers to ensnare and betray Justice. It ought virtually to eliminate unethical means of influencing prosecutors and juries. It would reduce the "framing" of innocent persons, unlawful searches and seizures and the third degree, and the suppression of evidence favorable to the accused. It would tend to dignify and simplify the trial, reducing motions, continuances and haggling over the impaneling of jurors and admissibility of evidence. It would limit the influence of unscrupulous bail bondsmen. It would enable defendants to employ all of the state's facilities, including the police, for bringing out their side of the case and for making witnesses available. Indeed, compulsory public defense ought to have a very sobering effect on the whole prosecutory process. The state is not interested in whether a defendant is able, by the employment of clever or tricky or corrupt counsel, to procure acquittal; its concern is to determine the truth of the issue. It should give the accused every facility for establishing his innocence, just as it furnishes every means for determining his guilt. The proposed system would make for a greater respect for law and government than exists at present, by reducing the "sporting" element in the trial.[46]

Finally, a career as counsel in a general system of public defense would attract a higher type of lawyer than many of those who now customarily practice at the criminal bar, and provide a panel of trained persons from which public prosecutors and criminal court judges might be selected. The appointment and promotion of members of the public panel of defense counsel would of course have to be governed by strict civil service regulations; and tenure would have to be protected against political interference in order to insure independence.[47]

5

A remaining topic for discussion here is the improvement of correctional practices. This has in recent years received detailed consideration in several intensive researches, and we shall therefore mention but a few fundamentals. The best of treatment tribunals would not get very far if the facilities for carrying out its recommendations for dealing with offenders did not achieve a high standard of efficiency. With notable though relatively few exceptions, probation, various forms of incarceration, parole and other treatment facilities are not as yet adequately developed. Excluding the small number that meet reasonable standards, the remainder range in inadequacy from the probation and parole systems in which one or two politically appointed agents are supposed to supervise hundreds of offenders, or from the most insanitary and corrupting jails, to supervisory systems with poorly qualified probation and parole officers, or to institutions that are compelled to struggle along with unsuitable penal structures.

But a more serious characteristic of the existing regime is the fact that sufficient ingenuity has not been expended in inventing new forms of correctional treatment. For example, the possibilities of psychoanalysis in treating psychoneurotic offenders have been little explored. That the analytic method meets special difficulties in the case of criminals [48] is no reason for not experimenting with it systematically or at least utilizing the insights that study of psychoanalysis gives into the intricacies of personality maladjustment. So, too, a modernized transportation system has as yet untapped possibilities. That the eighteenth and nineteenth century transportation of prisoners to isolated colonies may have been a failure under past conditions is no indication of its uselessness today, for communication facilities and correctional practices have improved. There are many thousands of acres of unused land to which active young offenders could be transported, and where they could be maintained under a disciplined but just oversight that might aid in building body and mind. Such a procedure would remove them from the overcrowded prisons and city slums, and might be the beginning of settlements of socially useful individuals. If, for example, a prisoner were rewarded with an acre of land for every ten reclaimed through his efforts, the incentive to industry might be strong enough for many to practice it. Several states could combine in the purchase of land for such a purpose.

Again, there has been little or no experimentation in allowing prisoners to visit their families on periodic vacations. Many of the disciplinary difficulties of correctional institutions, as well as their sexual problems, might thereby be reduced. Selected prisoners released for a brief vacation every few months could readily be supervised as special parolees, and some might be placed on bail if necessary.[49] There has also been very little experimentation with a scheme for allowing various classes of prisoners to go to work in shops or on farms away from the institution, returning at night. Such a system is feasible for selected offenders. It would reduce the expense of their maintenance and help them to support their families; while keeping them under restraint for certain purposes, it would allow them sufficient contact with the outside world to prevent their being transformed into vindictive robots by the hope-destroying routine of institutional life.

The responsibility of correctional institutions for an adult education program is also evident; yet it is still only the exceptional institution that has coped adequately with this problem.[50] So also various constructive recreational outlets, such as music, drama, handicrafts and corrective athletics are still to be introduced in many institutions.

These and other reforms will be possible when the state decides that the chief business of correctional institutions is to make men rather than profits. When that time comes, prison industry will be limited to the manufacture of goods needed in state and local institutions, and will take up only half the time of the prisoners at a speed and efficiency comparable to that achieved outside. The remainder of the time will be devoted to well-planned efforts to return prisoners to society better than when they came in. The fact that correctional administrators have here and there been able to break away from traditional methods without the dire consequences predicted shows that daring experimentation in correctional regimes is feasible. Here again, however, we are led to the crucial problem of a more adequate personnel of Justice.

The practitioners of probation and parole have also

not been as inventive as they might have been. In many regions officers have failed to call into play the community facilities — employment offices, recreational centers, clinics, hospitals and the like — which are indispensable to the improvement of their charges. Again, means have not been found for continuing in freedom many probationers and parolees who must today be returned to institutions because they are troublesome. There is need for a stricter extramural regime to supplement more liberal probation and parole oversight. Where police administration is forward-looking, parole and probation offices might coöperate with a branch of the police department for the stricter supervision of those requiring it. Such a system could be planned so as not to result in a hounding of offenders, furnishing at the same time an element of immediate deterrence as one ingredient in the rehabilitative process.

These suggestions are not put forward as exhaustive, nor have they been developed in detail. They are made merely as illustrations of possibilities that deserve exploration if correctional programs are to be humanized and made more effective.

We have not discussed the various improvements required in the treatment of juvenile delinquents, as this is a vast topic in itself and has been partially considered elsewhere.[51] In the care of youthful offenders, however, even more than in the treatment of mature ones, creative ingenuity is called for. Much vital work remains to be done in improving foster-home placement of delinquent children, raising the standards of probation and parole in juvenile courts and institutions, and above all experimenting with intensive treatment of conduct problems through various psychologic and educational approaches.[52]

The basic problems that remain for consideration are these: a means of integrating the various disconnected processes of law enforcement; a method of bettering the personnel of Justice, upon whom, in the last analysis, more efficient enforcement largely depends; determination of the essential elements of a crime prevention program; and the development of a more healthy moral climate for Justice. To these topics we next turn our attention.

CHAPTER VIII

THE HORIZON OF JUSTICE

1

THROUGHOUT these pages we have presented evidence of the lack of integration in what ought to be a unified, centrally directed system of justice. The atomism of the existing procedures is reflected in the absence of a centralized statistical service; in the frequent lack of a clearinghouse for criminal records and other elements of a continuous and thorough case history of each offender; in the multiplicity and local jealousies of police administrations within the state; in the dispersion of prosecution; in the persistence of petty independent county jails and district courts; and in the decentralization of probation and other services.[1] Functionally, the system is marked by an absence of general plan from beginning to end. The right hand not only knoweth not what the left is doing but too frequently tendeth to undo what the left hath done.[2] Most of this localism and disjointedness has valid historic reasons going back to Colonial times and England.[3] The excessive emphasis on "local rights" did little harm in a largely rural and static society. Today, not only the great mobility of the population but general considerations of efficiency call for a systematic interrelation of all services connected with the control of crime.

Other major weaknesses, partly related to the lack of a centralized, businesslike superintendence of the entire system of justice, are the slowness, awkwardness and other defects of procedure; the anachronisms, conflicts and confusions in the substantive law; inexpertness in dealing with problems requiring special technical equipment, such as the sentencing and paroling functions; failure to profit by the experience of the law in action, that is, to study its actual operations and results through continuous investigation, and to make needed adaptations and improvements; the vast output of the legislative mills and the undesirable quality of some of the product with respect to poor draftsmanship, its lack of organic relation to the preëxisting body of legislative and judge-made law, its employment in fields that had better be left to other agencies of social control; and the mediocre or lower qualifications of many of the servants of Justice.

In respect to all these fundamental problems a well-planned, expertly staffed Ministry of Justice might bring about considerable improvement.[4] "Departments of Justice" have very recently been established in a few states, and many others are considering their creation. But such departments are not entrusted with all the functions and authority necessary to an effective integration of the processes of law enforcement and to taking remedial measures for the other ills enumerated. They deal largely with partial centralization of police or prosecutory functions; and the power entrusted even over these services is usually very limited.[5]

Study of the Belgian Ministry of Justice on the ground has impressed us with the great value of a more comprehensive organ for the control of justice, particularly in integrating the processes of law enforcement, in exercising a general superintendence of them, and in maintaining a high standard of personnel. In addition to various services not pertinent to our situation, the Belgian office contains bureaus and sections charged with supervising such far-flung yet interrelated enterprises as the state police; a school of criminology and scientific police work for the training of officials; a criminal investigation and correctional laboratory; the prosecutory service; certain aspects of the work of courts; prison establishments and related psychiatric facilities; offices analogous to our probation and parole departments; a bureau charged with the drafting of penal and other legislation, and with critical attention to the course of judicial decision.[6] Examination, appointment, promotion and discipline of officials concerned with law enforcement are centralized in the Ministry.[7]

In American polity, such a department would be in a strategic position to standardize processes, integrate procedure and administration from the point of arrest to the point of the return of the offender to the community, centralize records and statistics, eliminate waste and overlapping, and inspect functions at every step — such as, for example, the exercise of the power of *nolle prosequi*, the operation of the bail system, the sentencing practices, the administration of the various correctional devices.[8] In all these fields it would be in a position to define standards of efficiency and to develop, on the basis of studies of the law in action, the principles and safeguards needed for a wise exercise of discretion at the various stages of the procedure. In brief, the proposed department might well serve as the endocrine system in the organism of Justice, regulating its health and growth.

The proposed Department of Justice within the states would be headed by a changing chief executive who would carry out the general policy of the party put in office by the electoral mandate; but it should be permanently staffed with a group of competent civil servants, performing technical services as follows:

(1) A bureau of police administration would integrate the work of various police units, and maintain central criminal identification laboratories and other services. Regional police organizations might be permitted to operate independently to some extent in respect to such services as local traffic regulation and simple patrol work. But the general duties connected with a scientific attack upon modern criminality are too difficult and expensive for local action; they embrace state-wide problems and hence require centralized control. However, in the statute providing for the Department of Justice, careful protection against undesirable employment of the centralized police force, as, for example, its use as an oppressive instrument in quelling strikes and other lawful incidents of labor-capital disputes, would have to be provided for. Oppression is too high a price to pay even for the utmost efficiency of police administration.

(2) A bureau of public prosecution would standardize and supervise the work of district attorneys, who would be appointed by the head of the Department of Justice under civil service regulation.

(3) If socialized criminal defence is ever established,

the Department might contain a bureau of public criminal defense lawyers, chosen on the merit system.

(4) A bureau of court administration would bring about greater coöperation between lower and upper courts, recommend to the legislature changes in court jurisdiction, aid in the drafting of rules of court, standardize records and administrative practices, and in general superintend the mechanics of court administration — without, of course, interfering with the independence of the judiciary as to purely judicial functions.

(5) A bureau of correctional facilities would be entrusted with central control of all penal and correctional agencies and institutions. It would gradually eliminate local jails, substituting modernized state-managed farms and houses of correction for short-term offenders and decent houses of detention for persons awaiting trial; it would also have oversight of probation and parole. In these services the Department of Justice would work in close collaboration with the various treatment tribunals of the state.

(6) Services of a less specialized nature have to do with keeping abreast of needed changes in legislative and judge-made law. A bureau would continuously study existing legislation and judicial decisions with a view to suggesting the elimination of anachronisms and sponsoring improvements. It might serve as an impartial agency for social and civic organizations desiring to present problems in their legal aspects to those with a mastery of the law and at the same time open-minded as to reform. It might serve as an expert body in aid of the legislature in organizing its efforts along lines of law reform, collaborating with or

replacing legislative reference bureaus. It might be a reservoir of information gathered from such sources as reports of judges and prosecutors, survey investigations, and studies of legal scholars in the restatement of branches of the law. It might help to systematize the complex and confused mass of laws ground out annually by our legislative mills, suggesting to the legislature how proposed innovations can be brought into organic relationship with existing law. It might exercise a tactful advisory power looking to the reduction of penal laws in fields which would be better supervised by other agencies of social control.

(7) Finally, a bureau of personnel would be charged with setting up and maintaining standards of appointment, promotion, discipline and retirement of the various officers of Justice, and their transfer from service to service to give them rounded experience and enable them to see the processes of the criminal law in their entirety. In this work the Department would have to be in close collaboration with a greatly improved civil service office. To this subject, so vital to the success of the entire enterprise, we next turn our attention.

2

While fundamental improvements in substantive law, procedure and administration are needed, it must by now be apparent that all roads of reform lead ultimately to the Rome of a greatly improved personnel. Competent, honest and socially minded administrators of the law can do much even with antiquated processes, for there is enough play in the system for them to exercise discretion all along the line, and to mould historic legal materials towards socially desirable ends. An incompetent or corrupt personnel will soon find ways to manipulate the best of social institutions to their advantage. How to get well-trained officials, devoted to the public weal, is the crucial question.

The recently published report of the Commission of Inquiry on Public Service Personnel of the Social Science Research Council begins with the widely recognized and significant view that

> our governmental units, federal, state, and local, do not generally offer the more capable men and women a fair chance, in any way comparable with that offered by private business, industry, or the professions, for a lifetime of honorable work affording opportunity for advancement based on merit and accomplishment. The spoils system, the use of the public payroll for charity, undiscriminating criticism of public employees, and the failure to adjust our ideas, our governmental institutions, and our public personnel policies to the social and economic changes since the Civil War, are primarily responsible for this condition.[9]

The Commission admirably analyzes and exposes the major fallacies with respect to governmental personnel. There is the historically entrenched and even sanctified notion of the victor's right to the spoils. The Commission points out that this virus, introduced into the body politic between 1810 and 1824, "is of no value to government nor, in the long run, to political parties, and has been abandoned in many parts of the United States, and in most of the democracies of the world."[10] There is the naive Jacksonian doctrine that the tasks of government are "so plain and simple that men of intelligence may readily qualify themselves for their performance."[11] Professor Frankfurter has jarred us out of this bucolic complacency by his reminder that "there never was a more pathetic misapprehension of responsibility than Harding's touching statement that 'Government after all is a very simple thing.' "[12] There is "the false idea that charity begins on the payroll",[13] a saccharine sentiment that in many regions throughout the country substitutes the loss of a leg, a husband or a job for the more relevant qualifications for public service. Charity via the civil service is a triple waste, involving the payment of salaries to incompetents, inefficient service, and dissatisfaction on the part of well qualified employees whose superior work is not recognized. There is the fallacy that "patronage is the price of democracy", which, in the view of the Commission, "is responsible for the hopeless, defeatist attitude of good citizens, deterring them from advancing to the annihilation of the spoils system."[14] The Commission points out that "in great sections of the United States, and in other democracies, . . . parties thrive, without the spoliation of the appointive administrative services. The truth is, as Theodore Roosevelt once observed, that patronage is the curse of politics. It is the selling-out price of democracy, because of itself it turns the political party into a job brokerage machine, creating a mercenary army of occupation, which, under the guise of democracy, robs us of self-government."[15] To this we may add the not unreasonable expectation that when the spoils system is markedly reduced, an indirect effect will be the improvement of democracy through concentration of voters on questions of policy rather than on possible spoils or the selling of their votes.

Another common fallacy pointed out by the Commission is that the first-rate public servant is not desirable because "he eats holes in our liberties." Thinking men will concede that protection against the entrenched authority of permanent civil servants is necessary, even if they are technically trained. But this would be supplied through the liability of policy-making heads of departments to be replaced by the mandate of the people, expressed in elections, as well as by other safeguards. Frankfurter has pointed out that no "new type of oligarchy" is called for by the introduction of capable, permanent civil servants into government. "To call the administrative *régime* of the British Civil Service 'the new despotism'," he says, "is to use the language of lurid journalism. But the power which must more and more be lodged in administrative experts, like all power, is prone to abuse unless its exercise is properly circumscribed and zealously scrutinized." [16] He reminds us of a fact that cannot be too often stressed: "Undoubtedly ultimate protection is to be found in ourselves, our zeal for liberty, our respect for one another and for the common good — a truth so obviously accepted that its demands in practice are usually overlooked"; but wisely adds that, "safeguards must also be institutionalized through machinery and processes. These safeguards largely depend on very high standards of professional service, an effective procedure (remembering that 'in the development of our liberty insistence upon procedural regularity has been a large factor'), easy access to public scrutiny and a constant play of alert public criticism, especially by an informed and spirited bar."[17]

Still another common fallacy that stands in the way of a prompt and vigorous raising of the standards of public service is the superficial civil service reform conception that mere permanence of tenure will do away with the evils of the spoils system. Yet protected tenure of office is a double-edged knife: it maintains in the service not only many capable officials but also much deadwood. Evidence presented to the Commission indicates that "tenure should not be established except as a part of a merit system which selects with care those who are to be given tenure, establishes a definite retirement system, and sets up the method of getting rid of deadwood."[18]

Other obstacles to a basic attack on this most fundamental of all problems of government are the fallacies that the proper approach is to eradicate the spoils system in the minor clerical grades of employment instead of the directive posts; that "home town jobs" should be confined to "home town boys", a view that is detrimental to the service in limiting the choice of the best available personnel to some small geographic unit; that public service is always and necessarily "less capable and efficient than private enterprise"; and "the erroneous idea that the spoils system, the eleemosynary system, and the other corrosive influences can be driven out of the public service through the prohibition of specific abuses"[19] by petty legislative tinkering, instead of through basic reconstruction.

In the light of the permeation of the system of justice with so many incompetent and politically sired spoilsmen, the conclusion of the Commission that "the establishment of CAREER SERVICE is . . . the required next step in the history of American government"[20] must be heartily concurred in. It would take us too far afield to describe in detail the procedure necessary for this to be consummated. But the branch of such a service which embraces the functions of criminal law enforcement may, without charge of bias or exaggeration, be called one of the two or three most pressing contemporary needs.

All of the halls of Justice need to be staffed with men and women who combine a broad cultural education with the technical training required. Police administrators and officers coping with modern crime need to possess a general knowledge of the social, economic and ethnic conditions of their communities; those who deal with detection need to have at their disposal the means for utilizing the latest discoveries of the physical and the chemical laboratory; those who deal with crime prevention must have special training in individual and social psychology and social case work. Prosecutors, in addition to their required legal training, need also to have an educational background that will aid them in the exercise of discretion. Judges in trial and appellate tribunals need to utilize their special technical equipment in law in the light of a thorough grounding in social, economic and governmental studies, as well as in the psychology of judicial decision. Sentencing judges need to know enough of the specialties of psychiatry, psychology, education and sociology to be able to weigh individual and social interests in a realistic and just individualization. Correctional administrators also need such equipment. As a recent prophet of the future of legal education and activity hopefully puts it, "The lawyer who has been in this country somewhat of a rigid doctrinaire in the eyes of others will be a much more flexible and facile personality. The law will rejoin its old companions, literature, history and the arts." [21]

This is not the place to go into detail regarding the many special problems that must be solved in connection with the classification of the services concerned with justice. But general references to some of them are in order.

The question will have to be faced whether our law schools should not prepare a separate curriculum, perhaps in collaboration with other university departments, for the training of young men and women who intend to engage in the administration of criminal justice. At present, in the better law schools, few students except those in the lowest grades expect or desire to do so. In the nineteenth century the general practitioner not infrequently made his greatest reputation in criminal cases. Today the abler young lawyers shun the criminal courts as they would the plague: not without some justification, they regard criminal law as a "dirty business." Given the possibilities of honorable careers as public defenders, prosecutors, criminal court judges and correctional administrators — with rewards not as rich, to be sure, as those gained in private practice but adequate for decent comfort — many young men and women of talent would unquestionably be attracted to the public service.

There is a good deal of disgust with "government jobs", and this will of course have to be overcome.

> Only in America [says a recent commentator] is government service regarded as an inferior occupation, as tantamount to a

> confession of failure, or of lack of ambition, at least. Where other peoples are proud to serve their country by accepting government employment, America shows her deep-seated indifference to the state by rendering such employment both socially and financially unattractive. . . . Very adroitly the sense of collective duty is branded as a preference for "supervision", while the slow, onerous, and frequently subservient stages of a business career are glowingly described as "independence." [22]

This view of the supposed superiority of the businessman to the public servant must be replaced with one of eagerness to express the "sense of collective duty" in a public career.

The second question to be touched upon is more specialized. The Commission of Inquiry on Public Service Personnel apparently exempts judges from the "general service" which is to be placed on a career basis.[23] In various parts of the country judges, including those of the supreme court, are elected; in some they are appointed for life. It is a mistake to conclude that the regions having the elective system necessarily get worse judges than those with the appointive.[24] New York, with its largely elective system, has in its Court of Appeals one of the best supreme tribunals in the country. At the same time not a few of its appointed magistrates in the lower courts have detracted from the fair name of Justice. Whether all judgeships should be placed in the permanent, civil service career branch or all should be exempt from its operation, or only the chief justice of the entire system should be exempt, are questions to be answered on the basis of local experiment. We see no compelling reason why judges as well as other law officials should not be part of a career panel subject to civil service regulation, promotion, discipline and tenure. But some would doubtless deem this an interference with the desirable independence of the judiciary, even though civil service employees protected in tenure would, so it seems, be more independent than either politically appointed or popularly elected judges.

Another problem is suggested by our analysis of the functions of both lower court magistrates and upper court judges. Would it not be wise to provide for a single bench for criminal cases, composed of judges of equally high caliber, dignity, emolument, and tenure? Such a roster should attract a higher type of judicial intellect. From the pool of "correctional judges" — to venture a name for the proposed bench — those with special gifts in the sifting of cases at preliminary hearings would be assigned to that task, those most suited to the trial of felonies would specialize in it, those particularly acquainted with the methods of extra-legal disciplines and interested in correctional problems would be placed in juvenile courts or sentencing tribunals, and those whose chief talent is in questions of law would be assigned to the court of criminal appeals. Only in some such fashion can the misnamed "petty courts" be raised to a much higher level and their work be recognized by the public as of equal social value to that of appellate tribunals. To maintain the invidious distinction between juvenile court judges or trial justices and appellate court justices, or between those in the district courts and those in the superior, is to continue to foster an unjustified conception of the relative social value of the different enterprises of Justice.

Length of service and special competence should be rewarded by salary increases in the special judicial field in which the incumbent has demonstrated competence, rather than by appointment to a so-called higher court which may require different talents or by bringing about the increased emolument indirectly through transfer to such court merely because the salaries there paid are better.

Clearly, the need for trained public servants presents a challenge to our high schools, colleges and professional schools which they have not yet fully accepted. Yet there are hopeful signs on the horizon. In the first place, a definite educational ferment is today apparent in the leading universities. One great institution of learning has just announced a plan to establish a special school for training future government servants; a few of the chief law schools are beginning to be seriously concerned with basic questions of curriculum and a redefinition of aims. Influential elements at the bar are themselves awaking to the need of a rigorous housecleaning and a return to the great traditions and the grand manner of an old and cultivated profession. The recent heated attacks on the bench and bar, particularly from the angle of maladministration of criminal law, may yet turn out to be the kiss that will wake the Sleeping Beauty.

At the same time, the people are becoming aware of the seriousness of the problem of adequate public service. In the view of the Commission of Inquiry on Public Service Personnel, the call for fundamental improvement in selection and appointment is the overwhelming mandate of the American people in so far as the Commission . . . is able to judge from the . . . testimony which it has taken in public and private hearings in all sections of the United States. In the East and in the West, in the North and in the South, throughout the States, the cities, the counties, and the innumerable minor public jurisdictions, it is generally agreed by public officials and employees, by business and civic leaders, by labor officials, and [God save the mark!] by politicians, that the time has come for a new nation-wide program for the improvement of the quality of the personnel of government.[25]

3

The third problem left for discussion is so fundamental and so pervasive that we cannot do more than suggest a few of its implications. In the opening chapter and in those dealing with the servants and subjects of Justice, it was shown how important is the culture medium in which the dramas of law enforcement are enacted. It is, after all, shortsighted statecraft for society to expend most of its energies and income in tinkering with the processes that deal with criminals and incapable or dishonest public servants, while doing little to change the soil which continues to produce them. It is not the function of the criminologist to explore new byways to Utopia; we cannot avoid indicating, however, some implications for an improved economic and social order, of the materials dealt with in criminologic research.

We have seen that the families from which a good many delinquents and criminals spring are in numerous respects not healthy components of a vigorous society. The spreading social sores of broken and twisted homes, divorce and desertion present tremendous problems in themselves. The high incidence of vice and crime in the families of the parents of offenders, as well as in those they themselves establish, is another challenging situation. Bound up with the disrupted home life of many criminals, entangled in the vice, crime, bad companionship and poor industrial habits of their parents, siblings and themselves, are lack of education, inadequate preparation for industry, unemployment and unemployability, dependency and poverty, poor housing conditions, slums and other evils. Some of this is doubtless due to uneugenic mating; but much of the sorrowful social brew is fermented by the yeast of modern industrialism and the ailments and injustices of the existing economic regime.

It is too early to assign relative weights to these interacting influences. But while no one can as yet say with precision which of the handicaps of mental defect, psychopathy, neuroticism, and poor physical health customarily found among criminals are largely innate and which or how many are largely acquired,[26] they are all unquestionably serious handicaps to a legitimate struggle for survival in a highly competitive, complex society. Hence, in the long run a fundamental probing to the roots of anti-social conduct depends both on the raising of the status of the economically underprivileged and on the better control of the biologically unfit. It cannot be proved by the most ardent exponent of economic determinism that biologic handicaps are caused exclusively by economic forces.

It is not absolutely necessary to assign relative responsibility to these interacting influences before taking effective action. In both the biologic and economic fields there is so much to be done in the way of immediate amelioration that determination of the respective influences of heredity and environment in the final product of crime and corruption can be left to the future. At all events, here is a complex of interacting evils which must convince the most skeptical that far-reaching and deep-probing attacks are necessary along the entire front of social pathology if one is to expect any marked reduction in delinquency and crime.

In attacking this problem, we must bear in mind the implications and mechanisms of criminal conduct as a whole. It is possible to range wrong-doers along a scale beginning with those who are so constituted that disciplined life in society is too difficult for them, and ending with those who, with good biologic and social heritage and ability to compete in legitimate enterprise, have more deliberately embarked on a career of crime. At the first end of the scale, as the history of crime shows, there are very probably some persons who would be found in the criminal classes in almost any social system; to that extent, at least, the Lombrosian theory seems justified. Such persons find it difficult to mould their behavior in conformity with the requirements of even a simple, savage civilization, much less those of modern complex and dynamic society. "In every community are to be found intractable, rebellious, and unadaptable persons who are sure to react against any form of social control. . . . Consequently, while the personnel of the criminal class at any time and place is determined in part . . . by the kinds of acts which are criminal, it is also determined in part . . .

by the traits" which enter into the composition of the class of persons who find it difficult, sometimes impossible, to become "socialized." [27] This is one reason why it is naive to assume that either crime or a "class struggle" would completely disappear in a socialistic state. If there were not one motive for the struggle of man against man, there would be another in its place. If classes were no longer deeply divided along economic lines, other cleavages would occur. If property crimes would be reduced, they would not wholly be eliminated and other crimes would in large measure still be committed. In addition to assaults, certain sexual offenses, homicides and the like, there would be the new crimes called into being by the new social order. As long as the springs of human nature spurt forth anger, hatred, fear, jealousy, envy and like emotions, we may expect aggressions by some members of society against their fellows.

But a good deal of crime can unquestionably be eliminated through intelligent study and social control. Thus, when more is known of the laws of human heredity it will be the task of society to reduce the reproduction of the extreme types that would probably be criminalistic in almost any society, or at any rate would be a drag upon its development. Even now, the biologic handicaps of the parents and children in criminalistic families cannot be ignored, though their relative participation in the total of crime-generating factors is difficult to determine.

Many states have enacted sterilization laws [28] on the assumption of a far greater accuracy of knowledge regarding human heredity than in fact as yet exists.[29] The attitude that heredity is a chief reason for sterilization still has to be justified by much unbiassed research. At the same time, the evidence is overwhelming that persons of the kind so largely represented in criminal classes are often unfit to care properly for children. Nor can it be gainsaid that a large proportion of them are irresponsible in their sexual relations and that the women in such families, as well as female offenders themselves, are prolific breeders.[30]

The widespread dissemination of birth control techniques through legitimate medical channels is obviously called for. But in deciding upon a social policy that will involve more drastic measures, it must not be forgotten that while compulsory sterilization laws have on the whole not been abused in American jurisdictions, and while legal and administrative safeguards are thrown around such laws, they always present the danger of being transformed into instruments of oppression. Moreover, it is difficult to enforce them. Voluntary sterilization, by which is meant prior consent of the patient or his guardian to the necessary surgical treatment, is a different matter. In a field full of prejudices and queries concerning which mental abnormalities are hereditary and which acquired, what degree of mental defect or disease will be necessary in the individual case and how and by whom the sterilization laws shall be administered, it is best to err on the side of caution. Practically, therefore, at the present juncture voluntary sterilization laws are preferable to compulsory ones. The former can be made to yield highly desirable social results if a wise educational program regarding the harmlessness of sterilization operations, except in preventing childbirth, precedes and accompanies its adoption. In the meantime, it is a chief duty of society to discover the mentally handicapped early in life, aid them if possible through the best scientific personnel and equipment, and segregate those incapable of self-management.

At the other end of the scale are those offenders with adequate mental and emotional equipment, and capacity to earn an honest living, who make a career of crime because of greed, cynicism or other such major motive. It is in such cases, probably, that the weapon of deterrence, efficiently applied through prompter and more systematic law enforcement, would play the greatest role.

But a vast proportion of modern criminals fall between the extremes noted; to them society owes a major duty, and from them it can expect the most valuable returns. Many of this army of citizens might, given a more privileged and secure status, lead sober and law-abiding lives.

Crime prevention so far as such persons are concerned involves several spheres of influence. The first is the community or neighborhood, whose influences percolate into the family and in part shape its behavior. The second is the municipality, which must be called upon to furnish necessary tax-supported services. The third is the state, which must supply legislation and state-wide institutions. The fourth is the Federal Government, which has the basic responsibility of raising the status of the underprivileged.

The community has first and foremost the duty to improve family life. As has been abundantly indicated in a number of recent researches, there is strong evidence of a tragically casual entrance upon marriage on the part of parents of delinquents; of a very high rate of desertion, non-support and unhappy marital relations; of anti-social home standards, including an amazingly high incidence of criminality among parents, sisters and brothers of delinquents and criminals. In addition there is much evidence of such danger signals as frequent running away from home, bunking out and like indications of childhood dissatisfactions or unwholesome relations between children and parents. There are abundant signs, also, of parental ignorance of even the rudiments of adequate child care; of unsound disciplinary practices; of broken homes; of conflict between those of different generations.

Obviously, these families need help. A civilized community should give it to them. Facts of the kind enumerated call for the establishment in each community of some such agency as a marital and family guidance clinic. It would give professional advice on questions of the choice of spouses, birth control and kindred problems. It would assist parents unable to cope with the personality and behavior difficulties of their children and of themselves, teaching them the fundamentals of wholesome parent-child relationships and of proper disciplinary practices. More important because more preventive, such clinics would carry on educational campaigns in schools, men's and women's clubs, factories and welfare agencies with a view to warding off family difficulties. In brief, the clinics would have the essential program of finding means to counteract one of the most serious phenomena of modern times, — family disintegration. Private funds for their support should be supplemented by public subsidies, since the obligations involved are those of society as a whole. The eager response of parents to crime-preventive bureaus, even when these are part of the police system, proves that puzzled parents would gladly seek out the services of such clinics. Professionally staffed, they would draw into their sphere of influence intelligent aid from medical, educational and religious agencies.

Another valuable service to be rendered by the community is that of supplying recreational facilities to take children and adults off the streets and out of poolrooms, saloons and dancehalls. The constructive use of leisure is a basic problem of our highly industrialized regime. With a decrease in hours of labor dictated by the machine, its importance is bound to grow.

These and other activities of the community, calculated to salvage the wholesome values and practices and exclude the vicious influences, require close collaboration. Yet too often today churches are separated from schools, schools from social agencies, social agencies from courts. As a consequence, the average neighborhood of the large city fails to bring to bear all its resources concertedly upon individual and communal problems. Some cities, such as Los Angeles and Berkeley, have pointed the way to a practical instrument for community organization. Community ("coördinating") councils, made up of representatives of various civic, welfare and social activities, are tending to bring about this much needed integration and to counteract the destructive forces that readily invade the cracks of a disorganized neighborhood.

The municipality can help to prevent or reduce delinquency by establishing a crime-prevention unit in the police or public welfare department, to work in harmony with community agencies. It can establish child-guidance clinics in the school system to collaborate with privately supported ones. It can counteract mass-treatment in schools and provide special classes where children dissatisfied with the typical curricula and unable to compete academically with their fellows may find self-expression and training in more interesting and practical pursuits. It can expand its system of visiting teachers in order to cope with personality and behavior problems of children before these become serious or chronic. It can coöperate with private enterprise in the extension of children's clubs, playgrounds, community centers and other recreational means. Finally, the modern municipality, with state and federal aid, has the duty of razing slums, eradicating bad housing conditions and providing decent, low-priced dwellings for the underprivileged.

The state can help to prevent delinquency by establishing proper schools for mentally defective children and adequate hospitals and colonies for the mentally ill. It can set up a children's bureau analogous to the federal office, to serve as a clearing-house and center of encouragement for child-welfare enterprises. It can reëxamine its methods for dealing with delinquent children and modernize the juvenile court practices throughout its jurisdiction. It can redesign its law enforcement agencies along lines of greater efficiency, and adopt an adequate career-service system that will attract a higher personnel of Justice.

But how society is to meet its obligations by raising the level of economic security, is the basic question to be answered. In this, the Federal Government must continue to carry the heaviest burden of obligation. An authoritative survey of economic conditions among the underprivileged shows how vital is the issue involved:

> Today [says Miss Katharine F. Lenroot, Chief of the Children's Bureau, speaking in December, 1934] approximately 18,000,000 people are dependent upon relief for the barest necessities of life, suffering not only from physical want but from want of most of the avenues for self-expression and achievement which make life worth while. Of these about 7,400,000 are children under the age of 16 years and 1,800,000 are youths between the ages of 16 and 21. Millions of boys and girls are entering upon the period of manhood and womanhood without jobs or prospects, and tens of thousands of young people are escaping from intolerable conditions at home and leading a nomadic existence or receiving care in transient shelters or camps. The wonder is, not that crime challenges our attention, but rather that the vast majority of boys and girls, men and women, are so law-abiding. It is impossible to predict, however, the extent to which the damage suffered during these depression years will yield a future harvest of social inadequacy, vagrancy, and criminality.[31]

There are two approaches to this problem. The first and immediately feasible one deals with what can be done in a meliorative way and within the framework and ideology of the existing American economic system and governmental tradition. Even this approach involves fundamental readjustments of the competitive, private-profit regime in the direction of evening up economic advantages. The question how far this shall go is ultimately dependent on two even more fundamental ones: to what degree can rampant materialism and profit-greed be controlled, and how far can the capitalistic system stand radical manipulations without being dangerously weakened?

The second approach involves the replacement of the

capitalistic regime by some other form. This is in the lap of the gods; but it is not altogether irrelevant to consider briefly some of the implications of the first approach as suggested by the problems of crime and justice.

Some authorities insist that basic amelioration of the socio-economic conditions related to delinquency and criminality, and improvement of the status of former prisoners, cannot be brought about without a complete substitution of a new economic order. But intelligent and just reorientation of the present system has not yet been given a fair and full trial. There is ample scope within it for lifting the life, labor and comfort of the people to a much higher level, and reducing depressions, especially in so rich and self-contained a country as ours.

This might be accomplished by a fairer distribution of the joint product of capital, labor and management, through higher wage standards; by providing decent security against unemployment, sickness, old age and other hazards, through ample social insurance reserves; by razing slums and furnishing wholesome low-rent places of living for the mass of the people.

Economic housecleaning involves an attack upon lawless and unjust competitive practices and limitless greed. To appreciate this, one need only be reminded of real-estate racketeers who demand grossly unreasonable profits from housing and slum-clearance projects; of those who make blood-money out of vice; [32] of the lobbies maintained for the uncontrolled manufacture and sale of firearms and harmful foods and drugs; of the betrayals and frauds by manipulators of investment trusts and other financial racketeers; and of those who insist that unreasonably large incomes shall not be taxed for the general welfare. Without a radical change of attitude and practice on the part of all such citizens, there is little hope of any very effective yet humane treatment of the crime situation and related social ills.

What stands in the way? From time to time the President is accustomed to report to Congress on "the state of the Nation." These messages hardly ever allude to the ethical tone of the Nation. Yet the moral climate and the social psychology of a people have much to do with its well-being, and specifically with crime and its effective control. Now a pervasive element of contemporary psychology is an exaggerated materialism:

> To me it seems clearer every day [says John Maynard Keynes] that the moral problem of our age is concerned with the Love of Money, with the habitual appeal to the Money Motive in nine-tenths of the activities of life, with the universal striving after individual economic security as the prime object of endeavor, with the social approbation of Money as the measure of constructive success, and with the social appeal to the hoarding instinct as the foundation of the necessary provision for the family and for the future. The decaying religions around us, which have less and less interest for most people unless it be an agreeable form of magical ceremonial or of social observance, have lost their moral significance just because — unlike some of their earlier versions — they do not touch in the least degree on these essential matters. A revolution in our ways of thinking and feeling about money may become the growing purpose of contemporary embodiments of the ideal.[33]

Cannot the energies and talents of a democracy counteract this excessive addiction to the drug of wealth, secured by hook or crook? Cannot our businessmen adopt a set of ethical principles in harmony with the poignant cry for greater social justice, and adhere to them in their relations with each other, their employees and the public? Will they, can they, do these things voluntarily, or will governmental compulsion be necessary? Only time can give the answers to such vital questions upon which the momentous issues of our day depend.

So, also, the problem of political corruption is chiefly an instance of the unrestrained worship of the golden calf. And again, a chief remedy is a less materialistic and more far-sighted outlook on life. Ruthless dissolution of gangster-politician partnerships is indispensable; but without a fundamental change in the moral temper of the country such repression is inadequate, as is proved by the short life of typical "reform" or "fusion" movements in government. The line between large-scale, pervasive and subtle corruption by political machines and the out-and-out alliance of manipulators of criminal justice with thugs is a hazy one. The absurdity of "legitimate graft" is apparent to all but the morally distorted.

If a wide program of physical and mental hygiene is today deemed indispensable to a civilized state, a program of moral hygiene is equally so. Both religious and educational guidance are helpful; but the basic requirement is a rebirth of idealism in those who control the destinies of millions through their control of wealth and the instruments of production.

To some observers the signs of the times define the major issue thus: Can voluntary self-discipline be relied upon to transform society, or must dictatorial discipline be imposed? The question involves the very life of democracy. Four score years ago Lord Macaulay expressed his disdain of the American form of government in a well known colorful passage:

> I have long been convinced that institutions purely democratic must, sooner or later, destroy liberty or civilization, or both. . . . Your Constitution is all sail and no anchor. Either some Caesar or Napoleon will seize the reigns of government with a strong hand, or your republic will be as fearfully plundered and laid waste by barbarians in the twentieth century as the Roman Empire was in the fifth; with this difference, that the Huns and Vandals who ravaged the Roman Empire came from without, and that your Huns and Vandals will have been engendered within your own country by your own institutions.[34]

Some may regard this as a painfully perfect prophecy. Too many have been insisting that fundamental reforms cannot be brought about through voluntary action but require the iron hand and heel of a dictator. But reform by tyranny is fortunately foreign to the American scene, temper and history. "The frontier [President Graham reminds us] has left its deep mark upon our ideas, character, manners, and procedures. The diversity of our economic life, our wide regionalisms with their deep conflicts of interests, their farflung centers of diverse opinions, their newspapers and universities, all with a traditional set against political dictatorship, combine to make improbable, though not impossible, any despotism that relies on military force rather than on the constitutional forms and methods of liberal democracy." [35]

What will it profit us if we gain some improvement in our economic life and some decrease in crime, when we must pay for them with the most precious of all human possessions — freedom of thought, speech, worship and action? Is it not better to cultivate the ennobling possibilities of well informed democratic action and mutual aid to the problems that confront us, than to seek liberty through slavery? The way of planned and just democracy is the way of free men. De Tocqueville, a more penetrating seer than Macaulay, concluded his classic study, *Democracy in America*, on a more hopeful note: "I perceive [he wrote in 1835] mighty dangers which it is possible to ward off, — mighty evils which may be avoided or alleviated; and I cling with a firmer hold to the belief, that, for democratic nations to be virtuous and prosperous, they require but to will it." [36]

Side by side with the virulent elements in our modern culture are hope-inspiring ones. Professor Dewey has wisely warned against judging our civilization only by its outer or public forms. He finds vital contradictions between "the externally organized side of our life" and its inner manifestations.[37] Looking at the outer shell of our civilization, one sees "everywhere a hardness, a tightness, a clamping down of the lid, a regimentation and standardization, a devotion to efficiency and prosperity of a mechanical and quantitative sort." Probing into the heart, however, one discovers in the activities of not a few individuals and voluntary groups "a scene of immense vitality that is stimulating to the point of inspiration." As opposed to corruption in high places and a public that seemingly remains apathetic and cynical, there is a great deal of "investigation and exposure having a genuine scientific quality", together with "a feeling, as yet inarticulate and groping, that the real needs of the American people must be met by means more fundamental than our traditional political institutions put at our disposal." Even the efforts of certain public utility companies to pollute the fountains of learning by biasing teachers and textbooks writers in their favor have their cheerier side in proving that "our democracy is at least far enough advanced so that there is a premium put on the control of popular opinion and beliefs." Professor Dewey reminds us that "there was a time in history when the few did not have to go through the form of consulting the opinion of many." He makes out a convincing case for the view that the American "situation taken at its worst is that of the overt and public phase of our life, while the things that may be set forth on the other side of the account have to do with forces that are as yet unorganized and inchoate."

It is well to recall some of the more encouraging elements in our culture. By intelligent and patient planning these can be turned to good account in reducing the ills of our civilization and creating positive influences for the control of crime and the improvement of justice.

In the first place, ours is still a country of vast natural resources and generous opportunity; and our people are on the whole enterprising and inventive. Second, they are a humanitarian folk; their sympathies can readily be appealed to. Few countries can boast of a citizenry as responsive to appeals for financial aid to less fortunate brothers and even distant cousins in the world family. Vast sums flow into community chests; facilities for improving health and recreation are constantly increasing. Third, there is a growing respect for learning, and educational opportunities are both numerous and on the rise. The beginning of a dangerous tendency to political regimentation of teachers is being indignantly exposed and opposed. Fourth, there is increasing evidence that the leaders of American economic life are aware of their responsibilities for the general welfare and of the fact that their own interest lies in multiplying the consumptive power of the people through higher wages and sound forms of social insurance. Fifth, as we have noted, the public is awaking to the need of well-trained and politically non-dependent civil servants in all departments of government, particularly in that of its vital organ, Justice. Sixth, the bar associations have in the last few years attacked the problem of eliminating unethical practice, and raising the standards for admission to the bar.[38] Finally, the past two or three years have witnessed an unprecedented interest on the part of civic groups, governors and legislatures in the problems of crime, its prevention and improved law enforcement.[39]

It is impossible to assign relative weights to these influences as opposed to the alarming aspects of the culture medium of Justice discussed in the opening chapter. We are largely in the realm of immeasurables and imponderables; and only time can tell which main direction the stream of culture will take. But increased awareness of our problems is in itself a good thing, — the first step toward their solution.

"For democratic nations to be virtuous and prosperous, they require but to will it." How to motivate and guide that volition and make it endure is the cardinal problem. It may help us in embarking upon the task to bear in mind the reflection of one of the nobler of the ancient Romans, the stoic yet humanitarian emperor-philosopher, Marcus Aurelius. Meditating in the groves of the Eternal City almost two thousand years ago, he bade us "think on this doctrine, — that reasoning beings were created for one another's sake; that to be patient is a branch of justice, and that men sin without intending it."

NOTES

NOTES

CHAPTER I

1. See pp. 207–208, and notes therein cited.

2. In this discussion no attempt has been made to compare English with American conditions. There are too many variables in such a comparison for which even a relatively exact allowance cannot be made. To cite but a few conditions in England which render comparison difficult, there is first the social stratification in the former as opposed to the strongly individualistic, democratic dogma in the United States; England has long been a settled country, the United States only a short time ago a pioneer land; England, in comparison with the United States, has very little of the complex problems presented by recently arrived ethnic groups of varying cultures. The participation of the populace in the products of our mechanical age, such as the automobile, is much more widespread in the United States than in England. England's territory is small, America's is large and far-flung. There is not in England that multiplicity of local sovereignties artificially defined by state and county lines that we have. Many other differences might be mentioned.

3. Recent Social Trends in the United States, Report of the President's Research Committee on Social Trends, New York, 1933, Vol. I, pp. lxvii, xxi.

4. "Although this difficulty may be solved by the automatic working of economic forces and considerations of comfort, the delay and costs may prove great. There is evidence that factories have been moving from large cities to smaller places where land and labor are cheaper and living conditions are more favorable." *Id.*, p. lxvii.

5. Tufts, J. H., America's Social Morality, New York, 1933, p. 60.

6. Information communicated by Sampson and Murdock, publishers of city directories.

7. Recent Social Trends, *op. cit.*, p. lii.

8. "That the *World* and the *New York Journal* of the nineties had not plumbed all the possibilities of yellow journalism was demonstrated by another phenomenon of the age: the picture tabloid of the nineteen twenties. Sensing that there was a large group in the populace that cared neither for the complete news accounts nor for the rather intellectualized features of the standard papers, the publishers of the Chicago *Tribune* appeared in New York City, in 1919, with their *Daily News* — a smaller newspaper, made up of a maximum of photographs and a minimum of reading matter and devoted almost entirely to recitals of local sensations. The *Daily News* became at once successful and was quickly followed by competitors, they ranged even lower in an effort to gain the patronage of the illiterate and filled their pages with faked or so-called composite photographs, the confessions of notorious persons, the histories of gunmen, and scandal columns given over to the doings of the demi-monde and the underworld. . . . The American newspaper of the Machine Age surrendered its time-honored function of moulding public opinion for the less exciting pursuit of financial profits." — Hacker, L. M., and Kendrick, B. B. The United States Since 1865, New York, 1932, pp. 693–694.

9. National Commission on Law Observance and Enforcement, Report on the Causes of Crime, Vol VI, No. 13, 1931, separate report of Henry W. Anderson, pp. xxxvii–xxxviii.

10. "How the National Committee for Mental Hygiene is Saving Minds", pamphlet issued by the National Committee for Mental Hygiene, 1935; Glueck, B., "Mental Hygiene", Encyclopædia of the Social Sciences, Vol. X, p. 320.

11. "How the National Committee," etc., *op. cit.* See also Komora, P. O., and Clark, M. A., "Mental Disease in the Crisis", Mental Hygiene, Vol. XIX, 1935, pp. 289–301.

12. Bureau of the Census, Marriage and Divorce, 1929, p. 15.

13. Bureau of the Census, "Preliminary Report on Marriage and Divorce for the United States: 1932", p. 3 (mimeographed).

14. Recent Social Trends, 1933, Vol. I, p. 692.

15. Folsom, J. K., The Family, Its Sociology and Social Psychology, New York, 1934, p. 391, and references therein cited. The figures above are crude rates; they are modified when changes in age distribution and in the number of marriages are taken into account. See Cahen, A., Statistical Analysis of American Divorce, New York, Columbia University Press, 1932, p. 19. Taking account of marriages, "the rate

of divorce increase advanced about five times as rapidly as the proportion of married population in the United States over a period of 63 years." — Cahen, p. 21.

16. Cahen, *op. cit.*, p. 140; Folsom, *op. cit.*, p. 383. Compare Marriage and Divorce, *op. cit.*, pp. 31, 33–34.

17. See, for example, Glueck, B., "Some of the Sources of Marital Discontent", The Family, March, 1935, pp. 3–9, for the point of view of dynamic psychiatry. See also Cahen, *op. cit.*, pp. 138 *et seq.* Hankins, F., "Divorce", Encyclopædia of the Social Sciences, Vol. V, pp. 177, 183–184, gives an excellent analysis of the probable causes for the rising divorce rate.

18. Faulkner, H. U., The Quest for Social Justice 1898–1914, Vol. XI, A History of American Life, Edited by A. M. Schlesinger and D. R. Fox, New York, (1931), p. 168.

19. Folsom, *op. cit.*, p. 382.

20. Glueck, S. and E. T., Five Hundred Delinquent Women, New York, 1934. Folsom, *op. cit.*, p. 398, has tabulated the various studies regarding college men and women and other "normal" classes.

21. A recent valuable work on modern sex problems is The Sex Life of the Unmarried Adult, An Inquiry into and an Interpretation of Current Sex Practices, edited by Ira S. Wile, New York, 1934.

22. Tufts, *op. cit.*, pp. 92–93.

23. Johnson, B., and Kinsie, P. M., "Prostitution in the United States", reprinted from the Journal of Social Hygiene, Vol. XIX, No. 9 (December, 1933), p. 467.

24. Tufts, *op. cit.*, Chap. VI, gives a convincing diagnosis of the "sex obsession" of modern American life.

25. See the well known works of C. Shaw and his colleagues, and The Slum and Crime, by I. W. Halpern, J. N. Stanislaus and B. Botein, Published for the New York Housing Authority, New York, 1934.

26. Recent Social Trends, *op. cit.*, p. xlviii.

27. The differences in the attitudes of various religious sects should be taken into account in reflecting on the above generalization.

28. Faulkner, *op. cit.*, pp. 91–92, and authorities therein cited.

29. This is the title of the well known work by Lincoln Steffens.

30. Faulkner, *op. cit.*, pp. 81–82.

31. Landesco has greatly illuminated the natural history of gangsterism and its relation to politics. Describing the domain of the colorful robber-baron, Al Capone, Landesco says: "I later learned that by the

percentage any gambling house owner paid he could know whether he was privileged both by the local police of Cicero and the County authorities, or by the local police of Cicero alone. In other words, then, Capone could grant the concession to the individual place, which was given him at large for the town or towns; he would collect that share of the gross which was due the local suburban authorities and the county authorities, his own share, and leave to the owner the remainder. In return for that he would man the 'joint' and with his own gunmen who kept the place in security and order." — Landesco, J., "The Story of the Gang", Address before the Attorney General's Crime Conference, December 13, 1934 (mimeographed), p. 5. See also his revealing report, Organized Crime in Chicago, in The Illinois Crime Survey, Chicago, 1929.

32. Every thinking citizen should read and ponder the report of Judge Samuel Seabury: Supreme Court Appellate Division First Judicial Department, In the matter of The Investigation of the Magistrates' Courts in the First Judicial Department and the Magistrates thereof, and of Attorneys-at-Law Practicing in said Courts, Final Report of Samuel Seabury, Referee, New York, March 28, 1932. This volume might be used as a valuable case-study in the pathology of contemporary city life as reflected in its politico-legal institutions, particularly the police, prosecutors and judicial agencies.

33. New York Legislature, Report of the Joint Committee on the Government of the City of New York, Vol. II, p. 15.

34. See Mooney, M., Crime, Incorporated, New York, 1935.

35. Address by Hon. John J. Bennett, Jr., Attorney General of the State of New York, before the National Crime Conference, Washington, D. C., December, 1934 (mimeographed), pp. 4–6.

36. Recent Social Trends, *op. cit.*, pp. lxv–lxvi.

37. Smith, R. H., and Ehrmann, H. B., The Criminal Courts, in Criminal Justice in Cleveland, Directed and Edited by Roscoe Pound and Felix Frankfurter, Cleveland, 1922, Part III, pp. 259–260.

38. Merriam, C. E., "Government and Society", in Recent Social Trends, Vol. II, p. 1536.

39. Sutherland, E. H., and Gehlke, C. E., "Crime and Punishment", in Recent Social Trends, Vol. II, p. 1114; Frankfurter, F., The Public and its Government, New Haven, 1930, pp. 10 *et seq.*

40. Recent Social Trends, Vol. II, pp. 1120–1121.

41. Bentham, J., Traités de Législation civile et pénale, edited

by Ét. Dumont, Tome I, 1802, pp. 102–103, translated and edited as The Theory of Legislation by C. K. Ogden, London, 1931, pp. 62–63.

42. Summaries of the testimony before the Federal Trade Commission and statements of some of its implications are to be found in Gruening, E., The Public Pays, New York, 1931, and Levin, J., Power Ethics, 1931.

43. Faulkner, *op. cit.*

44. For a convincing analysis of this tendency, see Allport, F. E., Institutional Behavior, Chapel Hill, N. C., 1933, particularly the Foreword, Chap. I and pp. 118–119, 124–125.

CHAPTER II

1. Chicago Police Problems, by the Citizens' Police Committee, Bruce Smith, Director, Chicago, 1931, p. 30. See also Puttkammer, E. W., "Recent Developments in the Chicago Police Department", Journal of Criminal Law and Criminology, Vol. XXV (1935), pp. 902, 906.

2. Harrison, L. V., Police Administration in Boston, Survey of Crime and Criminal Justice in Boston Conducted by the Harvard Law School, Vol. III (1934), pp. 110–111.

3. Kaltenborn, H. V., "Radio and Crime", address delivered at the Attorney General's Conference on Crime, Washington, December, 1934, p. 1.

4. Harrison, *op. cit.*, p. 95. "While there is a very marked preponderance in the number of these offenses (murders, burglaries, robberies, and auto thefts) between 6:00 P.M. and midnight, the density of patrol has not been made to accommodate itself to this condition." — Missouri Crime Survey, New York, 1926, p. 42.

5. Smith, B., "Police", Encyclopædia of the Social Sciences, Vol. XII, p. 184.

6. Bettman, A., assisted by Burns, H. F., "Prosecution", in Criminal Justice in Cleveland, 1922, p. 118.

7. *Id.*, p. 120. See also Willoughby, W. F., Principles of Judicial Administration, Washington, 1929, pp. 136–137, and Blackburn, W. J., The Administration of Criminal Justice, Baltimore, 1935, pp. 47–48.

8. Criminal Justice in Cleveland, *op. cit.*, p. 169.

9. Baker, N. F., and De Long, E. H., "The Prosecuting Attorney: Powers and Duties in Criminal Prosecution", Journal of Criminal Law and Criminology, Vol. XXIV (1933–34), p. 1064.

10. Baker, N. F., and De Long, E. H., "The Prosecuting Attorney: The Process of Prosecution", Journal of Criminal Law and Criminology, Vol. XXVI (1935), p. 194; The Missouri Crime Survey, New York, 1926, pp. 145–146.

11. This is the title of a revealing little volume (New Haven, 1932) by Raymond Moley, who has had long and varied experience in investigating many of the problems herein discussed.

12. Howard, P., Criminal Justice in England, A Study in Law Administration, New York, 1931, p. 403.

13. Cleveland Crime Survey, *op. cit.*, pp. 97–98.

14. *Id.*, pp. 100–109, See also Blackburn, *op. cit.*, pp. 71 *et seq.*, 117 *et seq.*, and contrast *Id.*, pp. 178 *et seq.*

15. Final Report of Samuel Seabury, Referee, In the Matter of the Investigation of the Magistrates' Courts in the First Judicial Department and the Magistrates thereof, and of Attorneys-at-Law Practicing in said Courts, New York, 1932.

16. The Illinois Crime Survey, 1929, p. 308.

17. *Id.*, p. 405.

18. Ervin, S., The Magistrates' Courts of Philadelphia, Thomas Skelton Harrison Foundation, Philadelphia, 1931, pp. 82, 85.

19. Baltimore Criminal Justice Commission, First Annual Report for the year 1923, Baltimore, 1924, pp. 14, 16, 17. This organization has greatly helped to improve conditions in Baltimore.

20. *Id.*, p. 17.

21. For an informal but highly revealing analysis of the judicial function of the lower courts in the large American City of today, see Goldstein, J. J., The Family in Court, New York, 1934, and Moley, R., Tribunes of the People, *op. cit.*

22. The percentage ranged widely, however — from 17.3 to 78. See Report of the Crime Commission, State of New York, Albany, 1928, p. 57 (in New York City 58.7% of the felony cases were eliminated at the preliminary hearing, in the state 52.6%); Illinois Crime Survey, Chicago, 1929, pp. 35–36 (48.8%); Missouri Crime Survey, New York, 1926, p. 276 (27.9%); Cleveland Association for Criminal Justice, Fourth Quarterly Bulletin, for quarter ending December, 1927, p. 2, table 3 (for 1926, 37.3%); Illinois Crime

Survey, pp. 35–36 (giving 17.3% as the figure for Milwaukee). For the Philadelphia figure, see Moley, R., Our Criminal Courts, 1930, p. 26.

23. Cleveland Crime Survey, *op. cit.*, p. 298.

24. Children's Bureau, U. S. Department of Labor: Juvenile Court Standards, Publication No. 121, Washington, 1923. "Since five-sixths of the Courts of the United States do not come up to the minimum standards of the United States Children's Bureau . . . it is evident that most of our juvenile courts are such in name only." — Gillin, J., Criminology and Penology, the Century Social Science Series, New York, 1926, p. 795. The proportion is probably lower today.

The frequently expressed view that "juvenile courts or courts having juvenile sessions are chancery courts separate and distinct from the spirit and practice of the criminal courts", is, with certain exceptions, "an observation at absolute variance with the facts." — Murphy, J. P., "The Juvenile Court at the Bar, A National Challenge", in Law and Social Welfare, The Annals of the American Academy of Political and Social Science, Vol. CXLV, No. 234 (September, 1929), p. 80.

"The Juvenile Court has suffered in the house of its friends. They have too often been satisfied with only part of the necessary equipment and have stupidly vaunted themselves in the thought that they had a juvenile court but the name has no virtue in it unless it is attached to an institution of substance. It is for this reason that the Juvenile court is still on the defensive in many communities — for it is making bricks without straw." — Murphy, *op. cit.*, p. 81, quoting Carstens, a recognized authority on child welfare. See also Thomas, W. I. and D. S., The Child in America, New York, 1927, pp. 130–131, and Glueck, S. and E. T., One Thousand Juvenile Delinquents, Survey of Crime and Criminal Justice in Boston Conducted by the Harvard Law School, Vol. I, Second Edition, Cambridge, 1934.

25. "The Juvenile Court at the Bar", *op. cit.*, p. 80.

26. De Beaumont, G., and De Tocqueville, A., On the Penitentiary System in the United States, and its Application in France, translation by F. Lieber, Philadelphia, 1833.

27. Institutional Treatment of Delinquent Boys, Part 1. Treatment Programs of Five State Institutions, U. S. Department of Labor, Children's Bureau Publication No. 228, 1935, pp. 249, 251–253.

28. *Id.*, pp. 259–262.

29. Kirchway, G. W., "Institutions for Juvenile Delinquents", in

The Child, the Clinic and the Court, by Jane Addams and others, New York, 1925, pp. 332, 334.

30. *Id.*, p. 337.

31. Juvenile Court Standards, *op. cit.*, p. 6. See also Institutional Treatment of Delinquent Boys, *op. cit.*, pp. 1–4.

32. Glueck, S. and E. T., 500 Criminal Careers, New York, 1930.

33. For an instructive account of this modern form of imprisonment for debt, see Stern, M., "Treatment of Petty Offenders in Chicago", Journal of Criminal Law and Criminology, Vol. XXIV (1933–34), pp. 938–947.

34. This is the title of Fishman's well known work. See also S. A. Queen's authoritative but optimistically-entitled The Passing of the County Jail, Menasha, Wis., 1920; and the remarks of a judge of the federal Circuit Court of Appeals, "The Local Jail", address by Joseph C. Hutcheson, delivered at the Attorney General's Conference on Crime, Washington, December, 1934; and Hoffer, F. W., Mann, D. M., and House, F. N., The Jails of Virginia, New York, 1933.

35. "The County Jails", Bureau of Prisons, U. S. Department of Justice (mimeographed). See also Kinsella, N., "County Jails and the Federal Government", Journal of Criminal Law and Criminology, Vol. XXIV (1933–34), pp. 428 *et seq.*, and Sellin, T., "A Quarter Century's Progress in Penal Institutions for Adults in the United States", *Id.*, pp. 148–149. Hon. Sanford Bates, Chief of the federal Bureau of Prisons, deserves high commendation for the vigor with which he has attacked the jail problem.

36. Warner, F. M., Juvenile Detention in the United States, Chicago, 1933, pp. 16, 24–25. In addition, 77,809 were in public detention homes; 354 in almshouses and infirmaries.

"In 11 areas most of the children are kept with the women, chiefly prostitutes and very bad companions for children. In 9 communities, the unfortunate policy of placing the children in cells has been adopted; and in 10 others certain types of children are kept in cells. In some cases boys are put in the same cells with adult male offenders. Children are frequently put in the last of an open tier of cells, where they can hear everything that goes on in the cell block. The guard or signal-room is used in 7 communities for many children. For certain types of children the influence will be bad, for it is a more or less exciting experience to spend several hours at the center where all of the police calls are taken. In 13 areas, all of the children are kept in separate rooms, and in 4 others some of the children are cared for in this manner. This method is open to some question since the children are likely to be unsupervised, and consequently minor offenders and lost children may be contaminated by older, more serious offenders. The detective bureau is used in 6 communities for all children and for some children in 6 others. The assumption is that most of these children are held for questioning. In a few of the communities it was the opinion that some of the children were quite severely dealt with at the bureau, and that some of the methods of questioning were perilously near to the 'third degree' type." — Warner, *op. cit.*, pp. 24–25.

37. "The present detention home has every appearance of being a jail, with its barred windows and locked doors. . . . Its attendants do not understand the psychology of childhood. . . . The whole atmosphere of the place is wrong." — Bowen, Mrs. J. T., "The Early Days of the Juvenile Court", in The Child, the Clinic and the Court, *op. cit.*, p. 309.

38. National Commission on Law Observance and Enforcement, Report of the Advisory Committee on Penal Institutions, Probation and Parole, Vol. III, No. 9, p. 235.

39. Recent Social Trends in the United States, Report of the President's Research Committee on Social Trends, New York, 1933, Vol. II, pp. 1160–1161.

40. By the Executive Order of the President, a "Prison Industries Reorganization Administration" has recently been established under the chairmanship of Judge Joseph N. Ulman, to coöperate with the proper authorities of the several states and the District of Columbia in conducting surveys of "industrial operations and allied activities" of the penal and correctional institutions of both the states and their subdivisions, and of the "actual and potential markets for their products"; to initiate, draft and recommend for presidential approval a "program of projects with respect to replanning and reorganizing the existing prison industries systems and allied prison activities", in order to reorganize operations in a way "to relieve private industry and labor of any undue burden of competition between the products of private industry" and "products of such institutions", and "to eliminate idleness and to provide an adequate and humane system of rehabilitation for the inmates of such institutions"; and to recommend for presidential approval loans or grants or both to states and subdivisions for the carrying out of these objectives. Appropriate financial allotment for these purposes has been made. —

Executive Order No. 7194, September 26, 1935, and Executive Order No. 7202, September 28, 1935.

41. For example, some persons of high intelligence and many of the "psychopathic delinquents" have been committed to such institutions. For a competent discussion of these establishments, see Robinson, L. N., "Institutions for Defective Delinquents", Journal of Criminal Law and Criminology, Vol. XXIV (1933–34), pp. 352 *et seq.*, and Papurt, M. J., "The Classification of Defective Delinquents", Journal of Criminal Law and Criminology, Vol. XXVI (1935), pp. 421 *et seq.* For discussion of the concept of "treatment types", see Glueck, S. and E. T., Five Hundred Delinquent Women, New York, 1934.

42. A notable exception is the work of Dr. Walter N. Thayer at Napanoch, N. Y. See his "Institutions for Defective Delinquents", in Penal Affairs, Issued by the Pennsylvania Committee on Penal Affairs, Philadelphia, No. 22 (May, 1930), p. 4, and his annual reports. See also, Garrett, P. W., and MacCormick, A. H., Handbook of American Prisons and Reformatories, New York, 1929, pp. xxi–xxii.

43. Consult Classification Handbook and Statistical Guide, Osborne Association, New York, 1933, and "The Classification of the Prison Inmates of New York State", Commission to Investigate Prison Administration and Construction, State of New York, 1931. New Jersey, under the guidance of Commissioner William J. Ellis, has long recognized the value of classification. Massachusetts and the federal system under Director Sanford Bates have also been active in this field, together with a few other jurisdictions.

44. For an audit of the progress in the field of penology during the last quarter of a century, see Sellin, T., "A Quarter Century's Progress in Penal Institutions for Adults in the United States", Journal of Criminal Law and Criminology, Vol. XXIV (1933–34), pp. 140 *et seq.* Other contributions in the same volume appraise progress in other pertinent fields.

CHAPTER III

1. The Report on Lawlessness in Law Enforcement, Vol. IV, No. 11, of the Reports of the National Commission on Law Observance and Enforcement, Washington, 1931, particularly "The Third Degree", by Z. Chafee, Jr., W. H. Pollak and C. S. Stern, gives an interesting

and authoritative survey of many of the problems involved, together with suggestions for reform.

2. Including such devices as tapping wires. The majority and dissenting opinions in Olmstead v. U. S. 277 U. S. 438 (1928) present the chief arguments for and against the legality of this method.

3. "Breaking into a house and opening boxes and drawers are circumstances of aggravation; but any forcible and compulsory extortion of a man's own testimony or of his private papers to be used as evidence to convict him of crime or to forfeit his goods, is within the condemnation of that judgment." [Lord Camden's judgment in Entick v. Carrington, 19 Howell's State Trials, 1029 (1765)], — Boyd v. U. S. 116 U. S. 616, 630 (1885). See also Gouled v. U. S. 255 U. S. 298, 306 (1921). Lord Camden evidently tied up unreasonable searches and seizures with enforced self-incrimination by his condemnation of general warrants on the ground that they are issued to hunt for evidence: "It is very certain, that the law obligeth no man to accuse himself; because the necessary means of compelling self-accusation, falling upon the innocent as well as the guilty, would be both cruel and unjust; and it should seem, that search for evidence is disallowed upon the same principle." Entick v. Carrington, *op. cit.*, 1073. On the other hand, Wigmore, the distinguished authority on the law of evidence, believes that the "historical assertions" in the "ill-starred majority opinion of Boyd v. United States, in 1885", are "thoroughly incorrect." — Evidence, Vol. IV, Second Edition, Boston, 1923, Sec. 2184. In his scholarly treatise (Sec. 2264) he makes out a convincing case for the view that the historic roots of the Fourth and Fifth Amendments are quite different. The origin of the privilege against self-incrimination was a revolt against inquisitorial procedures and compulsory examination in such unpopular courts as the English Star Chamber and the High Commission. See also Wickersham IV, pp. 25–26, citing Wigmore, Evidence, Vol. IV, Sec. 2252, note 3, and Mrs. J. M. Maguire (M. Hume), whose additional historical material is mentioned in Harvard Law Review, Vol. XXXVII (1923), p. 520.

4. Exemption from compulsory self-incrimination in the state courts is not guaranteed by the federal Constitution. It is neither an abridgment of the "privileges and immunities" of citizens of the United States nor a deprivation of "life, liberty or property without due process of law." — Twining v. New Jersey, 211 U. S. 78, 114 (1908). But see Justice Harlan's dissenting opinion, *op. cit.*, 114, 124.

5. An excellent and succinct account of this chapter in the drama of human liberty is to be found in U. S. v. 3 Tons of Coal, Fed. Cas. No. 16515, 6 Biss. (U. S.) 379 (1875). See also U. S. v. Innelli *et al.*, 286 Fed. 731 (1923). The reader may be interested to consult the eloquent plea of James Otis, in the Superior Court of Boston, February, 1761, which resulted in the Writs of Assistance being declared illegal. See the learned Appendix I to Reports of Cases Argued and Adjudicated in the Superior Court of Judicature of the Province of Massachusetts Bay, between 1761 and 1772, by Josiah Quincy, Junior, Boston, 1865. See also Entick v. Carrington, the classic English opinion cited above.

6. Fraenkel, O. K., "Concerning Searches and Seizures", Harvard Law Review, Vol. XXXIV (1920–21), pp. 361, 370, and cases therein cited.

7. Gouled v. U. S. 255 U. S. 298 (1921). See also Boyd v. U. S. cited above.

8. Originally, it was held that articles wrongfully seized must be returned to the defendant or excluded from evidence upon a "seasonable application" to compel their return, made before trial. — Weeks v. U. S. 232 U. S. 383 (1913); however, in the Gouled Case and in Amos v. U. S. 255 U. S. 313 (1920) it was held that if the defendant did not know of the unlawful seizure until the trial, petition for their return at that time was enough to compel restoration of the articles. See also Agnello v. U. S. 269 U. S. 20, 34 (1925).

9. "At the time the Constitution was adopted, stolen or forfeited property, or property liable to duties and concealed to avoid payment of them, excisable articles and books required by law to be kept with respect to them, counterfeit coin, burglars' tools and weapons, implements of gambling 'and many other things of like character' might be searched for in home or office and if found might be seized, under search warrants, lawfully applied for, issued and executed." — Gouled v. U. S., *op. cit.*, p. 308.

10. Chafee, Z., Jr., "The Progress of the Law, 1919–1922, Evidence III", Harvard Law Review, Vol. XXXV (1921), pp. 673, 699.

11. Weeks v. U. S., *op. cit.*, 393; Silverthorn Lumber Co. v. U. S., 251 U. S. 385, 392 (1920).

12. Youman v. Commonwealth, 189 Ky. 152, 165–166 (1920); People v. Marxhausen, 204 Mich. 559, 567 (1919).

13. See the eloquent dissenting opinion of Mr. Justice Brandeis in Olmstead v. U. S. 277 U. S. 438, 471 (1928).

14. Cornelius, A. L., The Law of Search and Seizure, Second Edition, Indianapolis, 1930, pp. 54–55.

15. Olmstead v. U. S., *op. cit.*, 485.

16. People v. Mayen, 188 Cal. 237, 252–253 (1922).

17. Williams v. State, 100 Ga. 511, 520 (1897); Commonwealth v. Wilkins, 243 Mass. 356, 361–362 (1923); Hall v. Commonwealth, 138 Va. 727, 732–733 (1924).

18. People v. Defore, 242 N. Y. 13, 23 (1926); Massantonio v. People, 77 Cal. 392, 395 (1925).

19. Dissenting in Olmstead v. U. S., *op. cit.*, 470.

20. Waite, J. B., Criminal Law in Action, New York, 1934, pp. 92–93.

21. In addition to this aspect of the problem, there ought to be information on two others: (*a*) the effect on law enforcement officials of the exclusionary rule to induce them to invent more legitimate methods of obtaining evidence or, contrariwise, to resort to more indirect and subtle illegal methods in order to evade the rule; (*b*) the effect on the general public attitude toward law and the courts, of condoning or appearing to condone illegal methods on the part of the police by allowing unlawfully obtained evidence to be used to convict persons. Researches into these problems will meet with many obstacles, but perhaps the obtaining of statistics as to the percentage of different crimes (in all or many of the jurisdictions which have the exclusionary rule) that are thrown out because of it would give light on the first element of the problem discussed in the text. The second question (*a*) might also be partially solved by careful investigation into police methods, and a comparison of them in jurisdictions which have the exclusionary rule and in those which do not. It is almost impossible to obtain even partially conclusive proof on (*b*) the third aspect — the effect on the general public attitude toward law enforcement — owing to the many variables involved.

22. People v. Defore, 242 N. Y. 13, 23–24 (1926), opinion by Mr. Justice Benjamin Cardozo.

23. Wigmore, J., A Supplement 1923–1933 to the Second Edition (1923) of a Treatise on the System of Evidence in Trials at Common Law, Boston, 1934, p. 940. Wigmore, *op. cit.*, p. 941, cites other modifications of the general principle. The constitutional protections are against *governmental* action. "For private trespasses the law afforded adequate redress; for governmental intrusion it did not. The people

were therefore more afraid of the government than they were of themselves. For this reason, a search and seizure, however unreasonable, by a private person has no bearing on the constitutions." — Wood, J. E. F., "The Scope of the Constitutional Immunity Against Searches and Seizures", West Virginia Law Quarterly, Vol. XXXIV (1927), pp. 1, 11. See Burdeau v. McDowell, 256 U. S. 465 (1921). Also, it has been held by the Circuit Court of Appeals (Fourth Circuit) that if the property was unlawfully seized by a *state* officer, it is admissible in evidence against its owner charged with a crime in the United States courts, provided there is no evidence of an arrangement between state and federal officers. — Kanellos v. U. S. 282 Fed. 461 (1922), Youngblood v. U. S. 266 Fed. 795 (1920), C. C. A. 8th Circuit. The proviso is important in preventing indirect evasion of the exclusionary practice in the federal courts. A like proviso should govern in criminal trials in the state courts, where the evidence was obtained by *federal* officials and turned over to state officers in a jurisdiction in which the exclusionary rule prevails. But even with such judicially enunciated provisos, it must be admitted that secret arrangements are possible. For a criticism of this federal exception to the exclusionary rule, see People v. Defore, *op. cit.*, p. 22.

24. Kerr v. Illinois, 119 U. S. 436 (1886); *Ex parte* Lamar, 274 Fed. 160 (1921), C. C. A. 2nd Circuit; Mathews v. State, 19 Okla. Cr. 153 (1921); Ward v. State, 102 Tenn. 724 (1899); State v. Brewster, 7 Vt. 118 (1835); State v. McAninch, 95 W. Va. 362 (1924); Baker v. State, 88 Wis. 140 (1894); Kingen v. Kelley, 3 Wyo. 566 (1891).

25. Indictment, guaranty against double jeopardy, privilege against self-incrimination, copy of charge and names of witnesses, confrontation of witnesses (which usually means that there is no way of using evidence of absent witnesses), guaranty against excessive bail, trial by jury, guaranties against unreasonable search and seizure. — National Commission on Law Observance and Enforcement Reports, Vol. 1, No. 4, pp. 23–24. These reports are hereinafter referred to as "Wickersham" by volume and number.

26. See Waite, *op. cit.*, pp. 101–102; Scott, J. A., The Law of Interstate Rendition Erroneously Referred to as Interstate Extradition, Chicago, 1917. For an able discussion of the questions of social policy as well as legal problems involved, see Wechsler, H., "The Simplification of Interstate Rendition", in Proceedings of Interstate Conference on Crime, New Jersey, October, 1935 (mimeographed).

27. "No arrest of a person by an officer for a felony is lawful save pursuant to a warrant issued by a magistrate, upon evidence of probable cause, or without a warrant when the offense has been committed in his presence, or when he has reasonable ground to believe that a felony has been or is being committed or attempted and that the person arrested is guilty thereof." — Wickersham IV, No. 11, p. 2.

28. "It is clearly the law that while it may be true that the mere aiding of one in the commission of a criminal act by a government officer, or agent, does not preclude the conviction of the party committing the crime, yet, where the officers of the law have incited or induced the commitment of the crime, and lured the defendant on to its commission, the law will not authorize a verdict of guilty. This case presents a more flagrant violation of that rule. Here the defendant, while in a state of partial intoxication, was accosted by a military police officer, who, in return for the friendly salutation of the defendant, asked the defendant to procure him a drink, and this with the purpose and design on the part of the officer that a crime should be committed, in order that he might arrest the defendant therefor." — U. S. v. Echols, 253 Fed. 862 (1918). See also Woo Wai v. U. S., 223 Fed. 412, 137 C. C. A. 607 (1915).

29. Wickersham IV, No. 11, pp. 3–4. See also Keedy, E. R., Cases on the Administration of the Criminal Law, Indianapolis, 1928, pp. 38–43.

30. Wickersham IV, No. 11, p. 5.

31. Quoted by Keedy, *op. cit.*, note pp. 42–43.

32. In some jurisdictions the opening statement of defense counsel immediately follows that of the prosecutor.

33. Evidently the only state allowing an appeal from a verdict of acquittal is Connecticut. Conn. Gen. Stat., 1918, Sec. 6648. Under this, if the defendant's acquittal is reversed on appeal, the state may try him anew. See State v. Lee, 65 Conn. 265 (1894). See also J. Miller's instructive article on this too neglected branch of criminal procedure, "Appeals by the State in Criminal Cases", Yale Law Journal, Vol. XXXVI (1927), pp. 486 *et seq*. There are some statutes allowing appeals after acquittal merely to settle the law without affecting the status of the acquitted defendant; and others allowing appeals from preliminary orders before the case has gone to the jury. I am indebted to my colleague, Prof. L. Hall, for calling this legislation to my attention.

34. Wickersham I, No. 4, pp. 21–23.

35. See "Restating Criminal Law and Improving Criminal Pro-

cedure", Address by W. D. Lewis, the Attorney General's Conference on Crime, Washington, December, 1934, pp. 5–6 (mimeographed).

36. Incidentally, the failure to record the testimony in the magistrates' courts makes it difficult to prevent perjury at the trial by witnesses who change the testimony they have already given at the preliminary hearing.

Early in March, 1936, Governor Lehman of New York signed a bill requiring "that when magistrates discharge persons charged with felonies who have previously been arrested for or convicted of a felony, they must state in writing the reasons for the discharge. The statements of the magistrates will then become part of the accused person's criminal record." — New York Times, March 7.

37. Illinois Crime Survey, Chicago, 1929, p. 305.

38. Cleveland Crime Survey, Cleveland, 1922, pp. 94, 104, 114; Ervin, S., The Magistrates Courts of Philadelphia, 1931, Chaps. III and IV; Crime in Philadelphia, Annual Report, 1933, Philadelphia Criminal Justice Association, p. 6.

39. Illinois Crime Survey, *op. cit.*, p. 36; Missouri Crime Survey, New York, 1926, p. 275; State of New York, Fourth Annual Report of the Commissioner of Correction on Crime Statistics for the Year 1933, Legislative Document (1934) No. 85B, Table No. 8, pp. 56–57.

40. Illinois Crime Survey, *op. cit.*, p. 35; computed from tables on pages 58–59 and 66 of State of New York Annual Report for 1933, *op. cit.* The computation is based on a total of 25,528 major offenses appearing in the preliminary courts, of which 11,486 (45 per cent) were held for the action of the grand jury, the balance of 14,042 (55 per cent) were otherwise disposed of below (Table No. 9, pp. 58–59). If to the total be added 4,598 cases originating in the grand jury (Table No. 10, p. 66), the percentage of 12 mentioned in the text is even lowered. Missouri Crime Survey, *op. cit.*, pp. 274–275; see also Crime in Philadelphia, *op. cit.*, p. 6. But see the critique of recent studies of the grand jury by J. Hall, "Analysis of Criticism of the Grand Jury", Journal of Criminal Law and Criminology, Vol. XXII (1931–32), pp. 692, 698.

41. Lieck, A., "Abolition of the Grand Jury in England", Journal of Criminal Law and Criminology, Vol. XXV (1934), p. 623.

42. As to the question of expense, any redundant agency is needlessly costly. With an improved sifting of cases at the preliminary

hearing, the additional grand jury step would in the great majority of cases be superfluous. That the grand jury is a vermiform appendix in the body of Justice may be inferred from the fact that some twenty states today have wholly eliminated its unconditional requirement as a basis for prosecution, substituting the prosecutor's information for the grand jury's indictment; seven or eight more have eliminated it in all but the most serious offenses. Various crime surveys and other inquiries indicate "abundantly that prosecution by information has uniformly proved most satisfactory in practice and that none of the bad results feared by those who would retain the old system have been realized." — Wickersham I, No. 4, p. 35. That the grand jury adds to delay is also clear. Thus, in Illinois, cases that progressed to the grand jury stage took more than twice the time from the filing of the complaints to their disposal than those eliminated at the preliminary hearing. — Illinois Crime Survey, p. 94. That the grand jury inconveniences witnesses is self-evident. In most cases they have already appeared at the preliminary hearing before the magistrate and in the prosecutor's office, and in many cases they must be present at the trial.

That the grand jury adds to the opportunities for bedeviling Justice by technicalities is shown by the reversals of convictions by appellate tribunals on excessively technical grounds. This evil has been markedly reduced during the past decade. But within the recent past these tribunals have reversed findings of guilt in an arson case where ownership of the burned property was stated in the alternative, although the grand jurors alleged that "a more perfect description of the property was unknown" to them; in a case involving the violation of a minimum-wage statute, because the indictment failed to give the names of the underpaid workmen; in a prosecution for practicing law without a license, because it failed to state that the practitioner was doing so for money; in a prosecution for rape, because though the indictment charged that the defendant "raped or ravished" the girl it did not contain the technical allegations, "forcibly and without her consent", or "against her will", the fact that the indictment had been amended to include the terms "unlawfully" and "forcibly against her will" not being deemed sufficient to cure the defect. — West v. State, 152 So. (Miss.) 888 (1934); State v. Lassotovitch, 159 Atl. (Md.) 362 (1932); State v. Adair, 156 Atl. (Del.) 358 (1922); Iannaci v. State, 184 N. E. (Ohio) 843 (1933). These are but a few samples of a technicality which in this day seems excessive. In such instances it is hard to see how the defendant was materially harmed by the technical imperfection of the indictment. See Dunn, F. K., "Delay in Courts of Review in Criminal Cases", Journal of Criminal Law and Criminology, Vol. II (1911–1912), p. 843. See also: Compton v. State, 170 N. E. (Ind.) 325 (1930); Privett v. Commonwealth, 26 S. W. (2d) (Ky.) 3 (1930); Acree v. Commonwealth, 47 S. W. (2nd) (Ky.) 1051 (1932); Parker v. State, 147 So. (Ala.) 649 (1933); State v. Walker, 54 S. W. (2nd) (Tenn.) 966 (1932).

The illustrations of course indicate some improvement over the oft-cited instance in which the Supreme Court of Missouri in 1908 reversed a conviction because the indictment happened to omit the word "the" before "State", and that only in the merely formal conclusion of the instrument which closes with the clause, "against the peace and dignity of the State." — State v. Campbell, 210 Mo. 202, 223 (1908). But they illustrate the pitfalls which threaten prosecution by indictment, unless indictments are greatly simplified. Commenting not so long ago on the technicality of indictments, the experts of the American Law Institute said: "No part of English and American criminal procedure has been so burdened with artificial rules as that relating to indictments. Many of these rules, formulated at a time when all pleading was highly artificial, have persisted to the present time, and seriously hamper the due administration of the criminal law." — The American Law Institute Code of Criminal Procedure, Tentative Draft No. 1, April 9, 1928, p. 68. The code formulated by the American Law Institute has stripped the indictment of most of its technicalities by providing for a short and simple statement of the offense and for facilities for free amendment of imperfect indictments. But some states still operate under the older common law forms. On the whole, the prosecutor's information is not attended with as much technicality or as many reversals as is the indictment. It has the added advantage of not presenting the opportunities for miscarriage of justice connected with the provisions regarding the impaneling of the grand jury and proceedings before that body.

43. The American Law Institute Code of Criminal Procedure, Tentative Draft No. 1, p. 57.

44. The work of the New York County Grand Jury in studying the weaknesses in the administration of justice is particularly commendable. See the various reports of the Association of Grand Jurors issued in recent years, in "The Panel."

45. The "vanishing jury" has been convincingly described by R. Moley in various publications, particularly Politics and Criminal Prosecution, New York, 1929, Chap. VII.

46. Wickersham, Vol. I, No. 4, Report on Prosecution, "Criminal Justice Surveys Analysis," by A. Bettman, p. 64; Blackburn, Jr., W. J., The Administration of Criminal Justice in Franklin County, Ohio, Baltimore, 1935, p. 249. Sixth Report of the Judicial Council of New Jersey, 1935, prepared by L. V. Harrison and M. Ploscowe, p. 21.

47. Illinois Crime Survey, *op. cit.*, p. 241.

48. See also Waite, *op. cit.*, pp. 298–299.

49. The American Law Institute's Code of Criminal Procedure provides that the court shall examine jurors as to their qualifications. — Code of Criminal Procedure Official Draft, June 15, 1930, sec. 275.

50. Borchard, E. M., Convicting the Innocent, New Haven, 1932, and Hays, A. G., Trial by Prejudice, New York, 1933.

51. It is true that few lawyers expect the jury to be a coldly scientific evidence-sifting agency. This is not even expected of the trained judge. It may be undesirable that feelings and sentiments should be ruled out entirely in the trial of a case, even if this were humanly possible. But when all this is conceded, there remains the fact that the primary aim of the trial is to determine as accurately as possible the truth of the issue as it is formulated in modern practice; namely, whether the defendant is guilty or innocent, and not whether for some extraneous reason, vague or clear, he "deserves punishment." That this is true must be concluded from the very existence of strictly technical rules of evidence. But see my Mental Disorder and the Criminal Law, Boston, 1925, pp. 465–466.

52. Pound has shown what sways juries when they have the authority to fix punishments. See his Introduction to Saleilles, R., The Individualization of Punishment, translated by R. S. Jastrow, Modern Criminal Science Series No. 4, Boston, 1913.

53. Wickersham, Vol I, No. 4, p. 65; Sixth Report of Judicial Council of New Jersey, *op. cit.*, p. 24. In Baltimore, where offenders may elect to be tried by a judge without a jury and where such trials amount to over 90 per cent of the total, judges in 1929 had 28 per cent of acquittals, juries 38 per cent; but these proportions were practically reversed in 1934. — Baltimore Criminal Justice Commission, Quarterly Bulletin for the quarter ending September 30, 1934, J. M. Hepbron, Managing Director, Baltimore, 1934, p. 4. In Ohio, however, "the

proportion of convictions is higher in court trials than in jury trials." — Martin, K. J., The Waiver of Jury Trial in Criminal Cases in Ohio, Baltimore, 1933, p. 64.

54. The Institute's Code contains the qualification that "in any state where the constitution and judicial organization permit several judges to sit in the trial of the cause, it is recommended that the above section be amended by omitting the clause, 'except where a sentence of death may be imposed' ", and by adding a provision that "the trial of a cause where a sentence of death may be imposed shall take place before three judges, as is the practice in Connecticut and Maryland." The Connecticut statute provides that a majority of the judges "shall have power to decide all questions of law and fact arising upon the trial and render judgment accordingly."

55. The provisions are collected in Chapter 12, Official Draft, The American Law Institute Code of Criminal Procedure, Philadelphia, June 15, 1930.

56. Wigmore, Supplement, *op. cit.*, pp. 379 *et seq.*, 392 *et seq.*, 432 *et seq.*, and authorities therein cited.

57. Inbau, F. E., "The Admissibility of Scientific Evidence in Criminal Cases", in "Expert Testimony", Law and Contemporary Problems, Duke University School of Law, Vol. II (1935), pp. 495, 499.

58. Inbau, *op. cit.*, p. 500. The case in question was People v. Jennings, 252 Ill. 534 (1911). Recently some proof that fingerprints can be forged or "planted" has been advanced. — Cummings, H., "Counterfeit Finger Prints", and Lee, C. D., "Finger Prints Can Be Forged", Journal of Criminal Law and Criminology, Vol. XXV (1935), pp. 666 *et seq.* and 671 *et seq.*

59. Flacks, W. L., "Evidential Value of Blood Tests to Prove Non-Paternity", American Bar Association Journal, Vol. XXI (1935), p. 680.

60. In State v. Damm, 252 N. W. (S. D.) 7, 10, 12 (1934), on a prosecution for second degree rape on accused's foster-daughter, the trial court refused to order a blood test to establish that the accused was not the father of the child of the prosecutrix. "It was not the contention of this witness [the medical expert called by the defendant] that paternity could in any case be affirmatively proved by such blood test, but he did contend that in quite a percentage of cases the impossibility of claimed paternity could be demonstrated by blood test." On appeal the court held that no abuse of discretion was involved in the trial

court's refusal, because "it does not sufficiently appear from the record in this case that modern medical science is agreed upon the transmissibility of blood characteristics to such an extent that it can be accepted as an unqualified scientific fact that, if the blood groupings of the parents are known, the blood group of the offspring can be necessarily determined, or that, if the blood groupings of the mother and child are known, it can be accepted as a positively established scientific fact that the blood group of the father could not have been a certain specific characteristic group. In other words, we think it insufficiently appears that the validity of the proposed test meets with such generally accepted recognition as a scientific fact among medical men as to say that it constituted a basis of discrimination for a court of justice to take cognizance thereof, as would undoubtedly be the case if a court to-day should refuse to take cognizance of the accepted scientific fact that the finger prints of no two individuals are in all respects identical."

Yet a recent writer on the problem, reviewing the literature, says: "In general it may be asserted with considerable confidence backed by ample medical authority that, as for the certainty of the results obtained by the examination of human blood groups, while such an examination does not furnish an absolutely sure basis for the affirmation of a given filial relationship, it constitutes unquestionable evidence for the exclusion of such a relationship when the blood group of the child does not harmonize, in accordance with a determined system, with that of the supposed parent. Moreover, the universal concurrence of medical opinion so impressively apparent from any brief study of the work done in the field cannot but force the conclusion that American courts may act without hesitation upon their findings to the inestimable enhancement of justice." — Flacks, *op. cit.*, pp. 680–681.

61. See Inbau, *op. cit.*, and Keeler, L., "Debunking the 'Lie-Detector' ", Journal of Criminal Law and Criminology, Vol. XXV (1934), pp. 153 *et seq.* "A number of instruments are combined into one. The cardiograph records the pulse wave, the sphygmograph records the blood-pressure, the galvanograph records the galvanic reflex (which closely follows the activity of the sweat pores), and the pneumograph records the respiratory movements. The whole is technically referred to as a pneumo-cardio-sphygmo-galvanograph, more commonly called a 'lie-detector.' Various instruments of this type have been devised and used for medical, experimental and diagnostic purposes. Some have included two recording units of one combination or another, and others

three or four units." — Keeler, *op. cit.*, p. 157. Dr. Keeler's article is a commendably cautious and fair presentation of the role of this instrument, the limitations of its use and the indispensability of confining it, like all delicate instruments, to skilled hands.

62. State v. Bohner, 210 Wis. 651, 656 (1933). The chief source of abuse is one that attends all expert testimony, namely, the possibility of incompetent or quack "experts" betraying Justice. In State v. Loniello and Grignano, tried in February 1935, the Circuit Court of Columbia County, Wisconsin, admitted lie-detector records and expert testimony in regard to the procedure, after approving a stipulation or agreement of counsel for both sides "that the results and the expert's interpretation thereof are to be admitted without objection and regardless of whether they favor the cause of prosecution or defense." — Inbau, *op. cit.*, p. 503. Neutrality of expert witnesses is the goal to be sought in all cases where opinion evidence is involved.

63. When Harry Pierpont, Charles Makley and Russell Clark, members of the Dillinger gang were tried at Lima, Ohio, for the murder of Sheriff Garber, the value of an "alibi law" was illustrated. "The Ohio alibi law requires notice three days before trial, giving specific information of the place where the defendant claims he was at the time of the alleged crime. Clark stated he was at his brother's birthday party in Detroit. Investigation proved that his brother did not attend the birthday party, and the alibi, supported principally by Clark's brother-in-law, developed into an exposure of the brother-in-law. The alibis of Pierpont and Makley were proven equally false and they received death sentences while Clark was given life imprisonment." — "The Lawyer's Part in Improving Criminal Law Enforcement", Address by W. Shaffroth, delivered at The Attorney General's Conference on Crime, Washington, December, 1934, p. 8 (mimeographed).

64. Wigmore, Treatise, *op. cit.*, pp. 128 *et seq.* "Why not let the trial judge correct the possible misimpression by a few words at the trial? In hundreds of instances this can be done with entire effect and safety. Take the Opinion rule, for example. A policeman, on a murder trial, telling about the bloody hatchet he found, is asked, 'Was it human blood?' and the answer gets in, 'Yes, it looked to me like human blood.' Instead of ordering a new trial because the jury *might* give to this layman's guess a value which it does not have, why not let the trial judge say to the jury in his charge: 'You must not pay any attention, gentlemen, to the policeman's notion about the blood being

human. He knows nothing about the difference between different kinds of blood. He is no expert in blood. You heard chemists here, on both sides, testify from their analyses and give their reasons and scientific processes. Decide from their testimony. Do not mind what the policeman thought.'

"Hundreds of petty slips could be amply corrected in this way. But not under our present system. No; the ponderous machine of a new trial must be laboriously set going again from the beginning; all the complicated levers, cranks, cogs, and wheels must turn once more; and vast effort and tedious time again be consumed, — all to do what could as well be done by merely removing the gag from the trial judge's mouth." — *Id.*, p. 123.

65. See, for example, Lehman, I., "Technical Rules of Evidence", Columbia Law Review, Vol. XXVI (1926), p. 509; Hand, L., "The Deficiencies of Trials to Reach the Heart of the Matter", in Lectures on Legal Topics (delivered before the Association of the Bar of the City of New York), 1921–1922, New York, 1926, pp. 89 *et seq.*; Ulman, J. N., A Judge Takes the Stand, New York, 1933, Chap. 8, "I Object"; Chafee, *op. cit.*, pp. 710. *et seq.*

66. *Op. cit.*, p. 96. See aslo Proskauer, J. M., "A New Professional Psychology Essential for Law Reform", American Bar Association Journal, Vol. XIV (1928), pp. 121 *et seq.*

67. Wigmore, Treatise, *op. cit.*, Vol. I, p. 128.

68. Pound, R., Introduction to Sayre, F. B., Cases on Criminal Law, 1927, pp. xxxvi–xxxvii.

69. See Cardozo, B. N., "What Medicine Can Do for Law", in Law and Literature and Other Essays and Addresses, New York, 1930, p. 88; Glueck, S., Mental Disorder and the Criminal Law, Boston, 1925, pp. 444–445.

70. See the stimulating essays by Sir Arthur Eddington, New Pathways in Science, Messenger Lectures, New York, 1935, particularly Chaps. IV, V and VI.

71. Prof. M. Cohen reminds us that freedom of will need not necessarily be the basis of responsibility. He points out that the most fatalistic peoples "have not hesitated to hold men responsible for their acts. Nor is sin in the primitive consciousness always an act of free will." — Cohen, M., Reason and Nature, An Essay on the Meaning of Scientific Method, New York, 1931, p. 327.

72. The law has long recognized the extremes of such conditions

and the question of age as factors in responsibility. But the fact that hard and fast lines between the mentally ill and the mentally sound cannot be drawn has bedeviled the administration of justice in insanity cases and led to the disgraceful spectacle of partisan mental experts. — Glueck, *op. cit.*, and "Insanity, Criminal Law", Encyclopædia of the Social Sciences, Vol. VIII, pp. 64 *et seq.*

73. Consider, for example, the excessively lazy individual who, because of this trait, is found guilty of "criminal negligence", but whose laziness is, in turn, the result of endocrine disorder. — See Campbell, C. M., Personality and Environment, New York, 1934, p. 46.

74. Glueck, Mental Disorder and the Criminal Law, *op. cit.;* Weihofen, H., Insanity as a Defense in Criminal Law, New York, 1933.

75. 10 Clark and Fin. 200. See also Hansard's Debates, Vol. LXVII, pp. 714 *et seq.*

76. State v. Jones, 50 N. H. 369, 382 (1871).

77. One reason for this view is, as Kenny has said, that "lunatics are usually capable of being influenced by ordinary motives, such as the prospect of punishment; hence they usually plan their crimes with care, and take means to avoid detection." — Outlines of Criminal Law, Cambridge, Eng., 1926, p. 52. But such an argument would apply equally to the "lunatics" who supposedly do not know right from wrong; it overlooks the fact that the criminal law has other aims in addition to deterring prospective offenders. A historical review of the subject indicates that the tests themselves, while remaining unchanged in general theory, have in practice gradually undergone modification not only to meet changing attitudes toward the objectives of punishment but to take account of refinements in medical knowledge.

78. Cardozo, *op. cit.*, pp. 99–100.

79. Hall, J., Theft, Law and Society, Boston, 1935, pp. 55–56.

80. The May, 1934 grand jury of New York County made a valuable investigation of the administration of parole, and among its recommendations is one to abolish the distinction between indeterminate and fixed or definite sentences, excepting certain more serious crimes. See the Fifth Annual Report of the Division of Parole of the Executive Department, for the Year January 1, 1934 to December 31, 1934, Legislative Document (1935) No. 10, Albany, 1935, p. 88.

After this note had been printed in galley proof, The New York Times of March 7, 1936 carried the statement that a bill which "makes all sentences to State prisons indeterminate" had just become law in

New York. The statute "is designed to give parole officials broader jurisdiction in dealing with individual cases of prisoners."

81. A painstaking analysis of "conflicting penal theories" in modern criminal legislation summarizes the legislative development from the turn of the century to 1927, in these words: "The conflict between the classical and positive theories in penology is reflected in the divergent tendencies within the law itself. On the one hand the laws authorize a high degree of individualization of punishment, that is, punishment based on the nature of the offender. This is evidenced by the increase in legislation providing for juvenile courts, probation, parole, the indeterminate sentence, mental examinations, and the like. At the same time drastic measures have been introduced increasing the penalties for certain types of offenses and prescribing extremely severe or life sentences for the habitual offender." — Elliott, M. A., Conflicting Penal Theories in Statutory Criminal Law, Chicago, 1931, p. 219. See also H. von Hentig's excellent treatise, *Die Strafe Ursprung, Zweck, Psychologie*, Stuttgart-Berlin, 1932, particularly pp. 154 *et. seq.*; and N. Cantor's thoughtful "Conflicts in Penal Theory and Practice", Journal of Criminal Law and Criminology, Vol. XXVI (1935), pp. 330 *et seq.*

82. This seems to be suggested by President A. Lawrence Lowell in his Conflict of Principles, Cambridge, 1932, particulary Chaps. VII and VIII.

83. Lewis, *op. cit.*, 8–12.

CHAPTER IV

1. Holmes, O. W., "The Path of the Law", address delivered Jan. 8, 1897, in Collected Legal Papers (edited by H. J. Laski), New York, 1920, p. 188.

2. See note 5, Chap. VI.

3. Warner, S. B. Crime and Criminal Statistics in Boston, Survey of Crime and Criminal Justice in Boston Conducted by the Harvard Law School, Vol. II, Cambridge, 1934, pp. 9 *et seq.* "Measuring the amount of crime in Boston or any other city is not a task similar to that of determining the number of inhabitants or the amount of bank deposits. It resembles rather the problem of guessing the number of pins or other small objects in a huge jar at a county fair." — *Id.*, p. 10.

4. Sellin, T., "Importance of Criminal Statistics", address delivered at The Attorney General's Conference on Crime, Washington, 1934, p. 2 (mimeographed): "In 1933 there were probably a minimum of 1,300,000 serious crimes known to the police of this country. In three-fourths of these crimes no one was brought to justice; in one-fourth, at least 360,000 were held by the police for prosecution. In addition, at least 120,000 persons were held for prosecution for offenses such as simple assault, narcotic drug violations, offenses against family and children, and the illegal commerce in and ownership of dangerous weapons. Another one and a half million were charged with minor offenses like prostitution, vagrancy, gambling, drunkenness and disorderly conduct, while a minimum of 2,000,000 were charged with violations of liquor and motor vehicle laws. We have noted that in the case of serious offenses the ratio of crimes known to the police to the number of persons held for prosecution was as four to one. In the case of minor offenses the corresponding ratio (excluding liquor and motor vehicle offenses) may conservatively be placed at ten to one, which would mean that at least 15,000,000 such offenses must have been known to the police. A minimum of 1,300,000 major crimes, over 15,000,000 minor ones, not to mention those which never came to the attention of the authorities! These are almost unbelievable figures. Were we to translate them into terms of human values — ruined families, misdirected energies, misery, parasitism — we might well be appalled at our criminal crime budget."

5. Marshall, L. C., "Progress in Criminal Statistics", Journal of Criminal Law and Criminology, Vol. XXIII (1932–33), p. 1057 (note).

6. See the chapters on "Method" in 500 Criminal Careers, New York, 1930; One Thousand Juvenile Delinquents, Cambridge, 1934; and 500 Delinquent Women, New York, 1934, by S. and E. T. Glueck.

7. I believe that Mr. Alfred Bettman of the Cincinnati Bar is to be credited with the first systematic conception of the mortality table idea. See the Cleveland Crime Survey, 1922, and his Criminal Justice Surveys Analysis, in the Report on Prosecution, Vol. 1, No. 4, of the reports of the National Commission on Law Observance and Enforcement, 1931. Prof. C. E. Gehlke deserves great credit for his illuminating statistical constructions of mortality tables in a number of the surveys including the pioneer Cleveland investigation. See also the valuable critique by Jerome Hall, "Analysis of Criticism of the Grand Jury",

Journal of Criminal Law and Criminology, Vol. XXII (1931–32), p. 693, in which he rightly stresses the fundamental importance of defining *standards* of efficiency in the various steps of criminal procedure.

8. So far as I know, Massachusetts, in its Board of Probation, is the only state in the Union in which the prior criminal records of all offenders appearing in the various courts of the state are centralized.

9. Dr. Emil Frankel, a statistician of wide experience and sound judgment, has suggested some of the desiderata in this whole field in a note, "Some Suggestions for State Action in Securing Standardized Criminal Statistics", Journal of Criminal Law and Criminology, Vol. XIX (1928–29), pp. 99–100. See also the reports of Gehlke, Marshall, Sellin and Warner in the various professional journals and crime surveys.

10. Missouri Crime Survey, *op. cit.*, p. 377.

11. *Id.*, p. 358.

12. The Reminiscences of Sir Henry Hawkins Baron Brampton, Edited by Richard Harris, K. C., London, 1904, Vol. II, pp. 285–287.

13. Annual Report, City Magistrates' Court, City of New York, 1915, p. 67.

14. P. 20 (speaking of the Night Court for Women).

15. P. 7 of Commission's report.

16. Figures assembled in connection with the Harvard Crime Survey. Corresponding variations exist as to percentages of cases "filed." To simplify presentation, they have been omitted. In each instance the balance between the figures given and 100 is the percentage of cases filed.

17. Gaudet, F. J., Harris, G. S., and St. John, C. W., "Individual Differences in the Sentencing Tendencies of Judges", Journal of Criminal Law and Criminology, Vol. XXIII (1932–33), pp. 811, 814, 816.

18. Gaudet, Harris and St. John, *op. cit.*, p. 813.

19. General Laws of Massachusetts, Tercentenary Edition, 1932, Chap. 123, Sec. 113.

20. "A Critique of The Defective Delinquent Law", by C. S. Ricker, reprinted from the May 1934 issue of the Law Society Journal, Massachusetts, p. 97.

21. Stevens, E. R., "Crime and Criminal Justice", Journal of Criminal Law and Criminology, Vol. XXI (1930–31), p. 326.

22. Glueck, S. and E. T., Five Hundred Delinquent Women, New York, 1934, p. 319.

23. Gaudet, et al., *op. cit.*, p. 814.

24. Romilly, Sir S., Observations on the Criminal Law of England, as it Relates to Capital Punishments, and on the Mode in which it is Administered, London, 1810, p. 17.

25. Ehrlich, E., Judicial Freedom of Decision: Its Principles and Objects, translated from his *Freie Rechtsfindung und Freie Rechtswissenschaft*", Leipzig, 1903, by Ernest Bruncken, in Science of Legal Method, Modern Legal Philosophy Series. Vol. IX, Boston, 1917, p. 74.

26. Criminal Appeal Act, 7 Edw. VII, Chap. 23, 1907.

27. Final Report of the Judicature Commission, Massachusetts, 1921, p. 93.

28. Cleveland Crime Survey, *op. cit.*, p. 308, Table 20, Chart II.

29. For a notable exception, see the opinion of Judge Joseph N. Ulman, of the Criminal Court of Baltimore City, in State of Maryland v. Herman Webb Duker and Dale Lambert, Daily Record, Baltimore, Nov. 4, 1931. This opinion stimulated considerable constructive discussion about sentencing practices. See also Judge Ulman's instructive work, A Judge Takes the Stand, New York, 1934.

30. "Remarks on some of the Provisions of the Laws of Massachusetts affecting Poverty, Vice, and Crime; being the General Topic of a Charge to the Grand Jury of the County of Suffolk in March Term, 1822", by Josiah Quincy, Judge of the Municipal Court for the Town of Boston, Cambridge, 1822, pp. 15–16.

31. See the thought-provoking work, Crime, Law and Social Science, by Jerome Michael and Mortimer J. Adler, New York, 1933.

32. The reader's attention is invited to an illuminating article on the operations of the influential "Briggs Law" of Massachusetts: "The Briggs Law in Massachusetts", by Winfred Overholser, Journal of Criminal Law and Criminology, Vol. XXV (1935), pp. 859 *et seq.*

33. See the recent suggestive volume, Law and the Lawyers, by Edward S. Robinson, New York, 1935.

CHAPTER V

1. Harrison, L. V., Police Administration in Boston, Survey of Crime and Criminal Justice in Boston conducted by the Harvard Law

School, Vol. III, Cambridge, 1934, p. 28. See also, Police Conditions in the United States, in Vol. IV of the Reports of the National Commission on Law Observance and Enforcement, Washington, 1931, pp. 54–56, hereinafter referred to as "Wickersham IV."

2. Wickersham IV, pp. 20–22.

3. *Id.*, p. 57.

4. "The Civil Service Commission is not to be viewed here as an agency remote from political considerations which has been set up as a kind of civic watchdog over a mayor-controlled police commissioner. That has long been, and still may be, the popular opinion, but it has no solid basis in fact. Rather the Commission is a special personnel agency, which is quite as vulnerable as any police commissioner to political and other selfish influences." — Chicago Police Problems, by the Citizens' Police Committee, Staff directed by Bruce Smith, Chicago, 1931, p. 49.

5. See the informative analysis by L. J. O'Rourke, "The Use of Scientific Tests in the Selection and Promotion of Police", in The Police and the Crime Problem, The Annals, Vol. CXLVI (1929), pp. 147 *et seq.*

6. See D. C. Culver, "Training of Police: Bibliography", Journal of Criminal Law and Criminology, Vol. XXVI (1935), pp. 444 *et seq.*

7. Harrison, *op. cit.*, p. 32.

8. Consult the very suggestive article, "A Police Service Rating Scale", by A. Bellman, Journal of Criminal Law and Criminology, Vol. XXVI (1935), pp. 74 *et seq.*

9. Harrison, *op. cit.*, p. 36.

10. Chicago Police Problems, *op. cit.*, p. 58. Criminal Justice in Cleveland, hereinafter referred to as "Cleveland Crime Survey", directed and edited by R. Pound and F. Frankfurter, Cleveland, 1922, p. 25.

11. Chicago Police Problems, *op. cit.*, p. 58.

12. Bellman, *op. cit.*

13. Harrison, *op. cit.*, p. 42.

14. Wickersham IV, p. 58.

15. Cleveland Crime Survey, p. 688. The psychologic findings must, however, be considered in the light of the imperfections of psychologic tests. See Chapter VI, note 28.

16. Wickersham IV, p. 61.

17. *Id.*, p. 60. The figures for the Cleveland group reflect the results of a later test than the Cleveland Crime Survey.

18. *Id.*, p. 70.

19. State of New York, Report of the Crime Commission, 1927, Legislative Document No. 94, Report of the Sub-Commission on Police, p. 27.

20. Culver, *op. cit.*

21. Wickersham IV, pp. 71–72.

22. Beyer, W. C., and Toerring, H. C., "The Policeman's Hire", The Annals, *op. cit.*, pp. 138 *et seq.*; Blackburn, W. J., The Administration of Criminal Justice in Franklin County, Ohio, Baltimore, 1935, pp. 216 *et seq.*

23. See Merriam, C. E., "The Police, Crime and Politics." The Annals, *op. cit.*, pp. 115 *et seq.*

24. Moley, R., in Politics and Criminal Prosecution, New York, 1929, Chapter VII, "The Vanishing Jury", gives a convincing account of the shriveling of this arm of justice. See also The Illinois Crime Survey, Chicago, 1929, p. 301.

25. Moley, R., *op. cit.*, p. 152, citing Cleveland Association for Criminal Justice, 4th Quarterly Bulletin, December 31, 1925, Table No. 4, p. 6; The Missouri Crime Survey, p. 285, Table IV; Minnesota Biennial Report of the Attorney General, 1926; "Crime and the Georgia Courts", Journal of Criminal Law and Criminology, Vol. XVI (1925–26), p. 168. See also Blackburn, *op. cit.*, p. 80; Goldberg, W. A., "Optional Waiver of Jury in Felony Trials in Recorder's Court, Detroit, Michigan", Journal of Criminal Law and Criminology, Vol. XXI (1930–31), p. 55; and "Felony Trials in Michigan Counties", *Id.*, Vol. XXII (1931–32), p. 568. Sixth Report of the New Jersey Judicial Council, 1935 (drafted by L. V. Harrison and M. Ploscowe), Table IX, p. 14.

26. State of New York, Report of the Crime Commission, 1927, Legislative Document (1927) No. 94, "Report to the Commission of the Sub-Commission on Statistics", p. 103; Sixth Annual Report of the New Jersey Judicial Council, *op. cit.*, Table XV and XVI.

27. Baker, N. F., "The Prosecutor — Initiation of Prosecution", Journal of Criminal Law and Criminology, Vol. XXIII (1932–33), p. 771.

28. The Missouri Crime Survey, New York, 1926, p. 131. See also Blackburn, *op. cit.*, p. 44.

29. Moley, *op. cit.*, pp. 78–79.

30. In Cleveland 244 lawyers appeared in a total of 363 criminal

cases, none in more than three in a single year, as against a group of 89 specialists, most of them politicians, who appeared in 842 cases, not one fewer than three times. An examination of 982 "untried prisoners" recently made in Philadelphia showed that "a small group of sixteen attorneys handled from 5 to 17 cases each, while a large group of eighty-five attorneys handled only an occasional case or two." — The Cleveland Survey, *op. cit.*, p. 234; The Untried Prisoner and his Defense by L. Stern, in the Prison Journal, Philadelphia, Vol. XIII, No. 3, Supplement to October, 1933, p. 16.

31. American Bar Association Journal, Vol. XXI (1935), p. 307.

32. Cummings, H. S., "The Lawyer Criminal", American Bar Association Journal, Vol. XX (1934), p. 82. See also Martin, F., "Address to Newly Admitted Members of the Bar", Vital Speeches of the Day, Vol. I (March, 1935), pp. 410 *et seq.*

33. In a few places a system of counsel for the poor is maintained not as a branch of government financed by public funds, but as a form of social service subsidized by private donations; the New York Voluntary Defenders' organization is an example.

34. Pp. 41, 81.

35. See Supreme Court, Appellate Division — First Judicial Department, In the Matter of The Investigation of The Magistrates' Courts in the First Judicial Department and the Magistrates thereof, and of Attorneys-at-Law Practicing in said Courts, Final Report of Samuel Seabury, Referee, New York, March 28, 1932.

36. *Id.*, pp. 30–48.

37. *Id.*, p. 32.

38. *Id.*, p. 34.

39. *Id.*, pp. 13–48.

40. *Id.*, p. 48.

41. Livingston, E., A System of Penal Law for the State of Louisiana, Philadelphia, 1833, pp. 41–42.

42. Order of the Appellate Division Removing Jesse Silberman from the Office of City Magistrate of the City of New York, July 2, 1931, and Order of the Appellate Division Removing Jean H. Norris from the Office of City Magistrate of the City of New York, dated June 25, 1931, and Seabury Report, *op. cit.*, pp. 49 *et seq.*

43. The Law of Evidence — Some Proposals for its Reform, by E. M. Morgan and others, New Haven, 1927, pp. 16–17. "The answers to the questionnaire regarding the right of the judge to com-

ment upon the weight and credibility of evidence revealed the most amazing and widespread lack of confidence of the bar in the trial bench." — *Id.*, p. 67.

44. Illinois Crime Survey, 1929, pp. 402, 404. See also The Magistrates' Courts of Philadelphia, by S. Ervin, Philadelphia, 1931.

45. Murphy, J. P., "The Juvenile Court at the Bar: A National Challenge", in Law and Social Welfare, The Annals, Vol. CXLV, (September, 1929), p. 88. "How far does the general public know of the extent to which political forces throughout our cities and counties are aware of the assets which result to them through a political handling of the work of the court?" — *Id.*

46. Seabury, *op. cit.*, pp. 58–59.

47. In England the clerk has many essential functions in addition to those exercised by the clerk in an American court; and commentators stress the high quality of this "state's man of all work", in Maitland's accurately descriptive phrase. — Maitland, F. W., Justice and Police, London, 1885, p. 92; Howard, P., Criminal Justice in England, New York, 1931, p. 252.

48. Seabury, *op. cit.*, p. 64.

49. Beeley, A. L., The Bail System in Chicago, Social Service Monograph No. 1, Chicago, 1927, p. 159.

50. The Missouri Crime Survey, pp. 211–212.

51. Seabury, *op. cit.*, pp. 107–108.

52. The Cleveland Crime Survey, p. 344.

53. *Id.*, pp. 344–348.

54. "The Selection of Jurors in Boston." Supplement to Bar Bulletin No. 93, January, 1935. Report with Recommendations of Special Committee on Methods of Selecting Jurors, by B. W. Warren and others, pp. 15–16.

55. The Cleveland Crime Survey, pp. 350–351.

56. The Cleveland Crime Survey, p. 352.

57. Cited by Sutherland, E. H., Principles of Criminology, Chicago, 1934, p. 258.

58. "The Selection", etc., *op. cit.*, p. 1.

59. Wickersham III, p. 195.

60. *Id.*, p. 196.

61. Community Resources for Dealing with Conduct Problems of Children (mimeographed), U. S. Children's Bureau, May, 1928 (cited by Lenroot, K. F., Juvenile Delinquency, A Summary Mem-

orandum of Available Material on Extent, Causes, Treatment and Prevention, Prepared for the use of the National Commission on Law Observance and Enforcement, Children's Bureau, Washington, 1929, p. 137).

62. *Id.*, pp. 137–138.

63. Institutional Treatment of Delinquent Boys, Part 1 — Treatment Programs of Five State Institutions, U. S. Department of Labor, Children's Bureau Publication No. 228, 1935, p. 228.

64. See Reeves, M., Training Schools for Delinquent Girls, New York, Russell Sage Foundation, 1929, p. 65.

65. Lenroot, *op. cit.*, p. 138.

66. Robinson, L. N., "The Relation of Jails to County and State", Journal of Criminal Law and Criminology, Vol. XX (1929–30), p. 413.

67. Fishman, J. F., Sex in Prison, New York, 1934, pp. 51–52.

68. Wickersham III, Report of the Advisory Committee on Penal Institutions, Probation and Parole, pp. 249–250.

69. Handbook of American Prisons and Reformatories, 1929, P. W. Garrett and A. H. MacCormick, Editors, New York, National Society of Penal Information, Inc., pp. xxix–xxx.

70. For an authoritative analysis of the parole situation, see Wilcox, C., "Parole: Principles and Practice", Journal of Criminal Law and Criminology, Vol. XX (1929–30), pp. 348 *et seq.*

71. Such names as Sanford Bates, William J. Ellis, Lewis Lawes, Joseph N. Ullman, August Vollmer and others come to mind.

CHAPTER VI

1. Though female delinquents and criminals resemble male ones in a surprising number of traits and in their socio-economic background, we need not go into their characteristics. Much of the anti-social expression of women is related to the sex impulse, and to some extent presents special problems in law, procedure and correctional treatment. See Glueck, S. and E. T., Five Hundred Delinquent Women, New York, 1934.

2. Sutherland, E. H., Principles of Criminology, Chicago, 1934, pp. 87–88. See also The Slum and Crime, by I. W. Halpern, J. N. Stanislaus and B. Botein, Published for the New York City

Housing Authority, New York, 1934, p. 35; and the careful critical analysis in "Crime", by T. Sellin, Encyclopædia of the Social Sciences, Vol. IV, p. 568; Crime in Philadelphia, Annual Report 1933, p. 8.

3. It may be possible, however, to approach accuracy more nearly than has thus far been done by some such method as the following: the aim is to obtain as true a picture of *criminals* as we can, rather than of arrestees, those prosecuted, those convicted, those imprisoned, those paroled, or any other special group. The investigator of offenders at any one of these levels must grant at the outset that each source of figures is biased and that, roughly speaking, these biases multiply progressively in passing through the procedural steps from arrest to parole. But suppose it were feasible to obtain samples from some or all of these various levels, in different parts of the country each of which, owing to cultural and political peculiarities, has somewhat different selective mechanisms operative. Suppose, in addition, that these samples could be drawn at different times. It would seem, then, that the multiplicity of the procedural levels, cultural sources and periods of time from which the samples were taken would furnish at least some corrective to the difficulties indicated. For example, highly placed or politically influential or clever offenders are not always and in all places exempt from arrest, or being arrested do not have their cases always thrown out by servile grand juries, or influence the discretion of the prosecutor, or escape from the net through some other hole. If the samples of criminals obtained from a great variety of chronologic, procedural and geographic levels were found to possess certain characteristics in common, it might be possible to build up at least a rough approximation of the physiognomy of that very heterogeneous group known as the "criminal class" or to detect significant differences between its various constituents. But such a research still remains to be made. In the meantime we must content ourselves with less perfect data.

4. See Glueck, S., "On the Causes of Crime", American Mercury, Vol. XXXIX (August, 1933), pp. 430 *et seq.*, and pp. 13–19 of the chapter on "Housing and Delinquency", written by a committee under the chairmanship of C. Shaw, in "Housing and the Community", edited by J. M. Gries and J. Ford, The President's Conference on Home Building and Home Ownership, Washington, 1932.

5. There is no need to enter here into the historic conflict between the Lombrosians and the environmentalists, except to call the reader's attention to recent authoritative anthropologic investigations by Prof.

Earnest Hooton, involving some 16,000 inmates of the penal institutions in various states and a large sample of the general population, which essentially seems to confirm that part of Lombroso's general thesis having to do with crude morphologic differences between criminals and non-criminals. — See Hooton, E. A., "Preliminary Remarks on the Anthropology of the American Criminal", Proceedings of the American Philosophical Society, Vol. lxxi, No. 6 (1932), pp. 349 *et seq;* also "Calipers and Criminals", in Harvard Alumni Bulletin, December 11, 1930, pp. 344 *et seq.* No serious student of crime can afford to overlook Hooton's contribution when it is fully published. See also Lange, J., *Verbrechen als Schicksal*, Leipzig, 1929, translated as Crime and Destiny by C. Haldane, New York, 1930.

6. This point is developed in my Mental Disorder and the Criminal Law, Boston, 1925, p. 444. See also Cardozo, B., "What Medicine Can do for Law", in Law and Literature, New York, 1931.

7. Details and description of the research methods involved will be found in One Thousand Juvenile Delinquents, Second Edition, 1934; and 500 Criminal Careers, 1930, Cambridge and New York, by S. and E. T. Glueck, hereinafter referred to as "1,000" and "500."

8. 1,000, p. 78; 500, p. 121.

9. 1,000, p. 68; 500, pp. 115–116.

10. 1,000, p. 74.

11. 1,000, p. 85; 500, p. 118.

12. See 500, pp. 363–364.

13. 1,000, p. 75; 500, pp. 116–117.

14. 1,000, p. 75; 500, p. 116.

15. 1,000, p. 75; 500, p. 112.

16. For illuminating insight into the superficiality of punishment technique in many instances, see Aichhorn, A., Wayward Youth, New York, 1935.

17. 1,000, p. 69; 500, p. 113.

18. 1,000, p. 69; 500, p. 114.

19. 1,000, p. 71; 500, p. 117.

20. 1,000, p. 88. The reasons why the adult criminals had withdrawn from school could not be obtained.

21. Computation based on 1,000, p. 70.

22. 500, p. 114.

23. 1,000, p. 71.

24. 1,000, p. 72.

25. See pp. 207–208.

26. 1,000, p. 101.

27. 500, p. 154.

28. See the careful suggestive analysis of this subject by Sutherland, E. H., "Mental Deficiency and Crime", Chap. XV in Young, K. (Editor), Social Attitudes, New York, 1931, pp. 357–375.

29. 1,000, p. 102.

30. 500, p. 156. For the significance of mental defect in the criminogenic complex of factors, see Glueck, E. T., "Mental Retardation and Juvenile Delinquency", Mental Hygiene, Vol. XIX (1935), pp. 549 *et seq.*

31. Lowrey, L. G., "The Relationship of Feeblemindedness to Behavior Disorders", Proceedings of the American Association for the Study of the Feebleminded, 1928, p. 97. He cites other studies to like effect.

32. "Question of mental abnormality", 47 cases; definite psychosis, 3; "constitutionally inferior", 39; "psychopathic personalities", 19; "peculiar personalities", 13; psychoneurotics, 5; epileptic mental traits, 10, traumatic constitution 1. — 1,000, pp. 102–103.

33. 500, pp. 156–157.

34. 1,000, p. 86–87.

35. *Id.*, pp. 87–88.

36. 500, pp. 132–133.

37. 1,000, p. 89.

38. 500, pp. 134–135. Compare a Study of Environmental Factors in Juvenile Delinquency, Report of the Crime Commission, Legislative Document (1928) No. 23, State of New York, 1928, pp. 629 *et seq.* (separate pagination, 53 *et seq.*).

39. 1,000, p. 93.

40. See, Puffer, J. A., The Boy and His Gang, Boston, 1912; Thrasher, F. M., The Gang, A Study of 1,313 Gangs in Chicago, Chicago, 1927; Elmer, M. C., The Juvenile Delinquent in St. Paul, Minn., St. Paul, 1926; Breckinridge, S. P., and Abbott, E., The Delinquent Child and the Home, New York, 1912.

41. 1,000, p. 95.

42. *Id.*, p. 96.

43. 500, pp. 140, 142.

44. 1,000, p. 95.

45. For informative summaries of the literature, see Lenroot,

K. F., Juvenile Delinquency, A Summary Memorandum of Available Material on Extent, Causes, Treatment and Prevention, prepared for the National Commission on Law Observance and Enforcement, October, 1929 (mimeographed), pp. 90 *et seq.*, and Ploscowe, M., Some Causative Factors in Criminality, Report on the Causes of Crime, National Commission on Law Observance and Enforcement, Vol. VI, No. 13.

46. Among 2,000 juvenile delinquency cases appearing in clinics in Chicago over a series of years, poverty, roughly defined as "the constant struggle to make ends meet", was found in 20 per cent of the families. — Healy, W. and Bronner, A. F., Delinquents and Criminals: Their Making and Unmaking, New York, 1926, pp. 118–121.

Most of these studies do not compare the incidence of unfavorable economic status in delinquent families with that of the general population, and it may well be, also, that the findings are affected by the fact that delinquents and criminals from well-to-do homes are specially protected and thereby largely kept out of juvenile courts.

Regarding the work of social welfare organizations in the families of delinquents, see Bailey, W. B., Children before the Courts in Connecticut, U. S. Children's Bureau Publication 43, 1918, p. 80; and From Truancy to Crime — A Study of 251 Adolescents, by the Subcommission on Causes and Effects of Crime, State of New York, Report of the Crime Commission, 1928, Legislative Document (1928) No. 23, pp. 485–486 (separate pagination 49–50); Burke, D. W., Youth and Crime, U. S. Children's Bureau Publication No. 196, 1930, p. 91.

For data regarding occupation of mothers of delinquents outside the home, see the New York Report, pp. 449, 482 (separate pagination 13, 46); Sixteenth Annual Report of the Chief of the Children's Bureau, 1928, p. 15; Thirteenth Annual Report of the Municipal Court of Philadelphia for the year 1926, p. 89.

47. Slawson, J., The Delinquent Boy, Boston, 1926, pp. 393–398; Channing, A., "Alcoholism among Parents of Juvenile Delinquents", Social Service Review, Vol. I (1927), pp. 359, 363.

48. There is little in the publications on the illiteracy of parents of offenders; this may, however, be inferred from their low occupational status described in many investigations.

49. *Desertion, separation, divorce:* Breckinridge, S. P., and Abbott, E., The Delinquent Child and the Home, New York, 1912, pp. 91–92;

Lenroot, K. F., and Lundberg, E. O., Juvenile Courts at Work, A Study of the Organization and Methods of Ten Courts, U. S. Children's Bureau Publication No. 141, 1925, pp. 225, 236; Cooley, E. J., Probation and Delinquency, New York, 1927, p. 87; Report of Crime Commission, 1928, *op. cit.*, Individual Studies of 145 Offenders, by the Subcommission on Causes and Effects of Crime, pp. 324, 353 (separate pagination 16, 45).

Poor disciplinary practices: Burt, C., The Young Delinquent, New York, 1925, pp. 96–99; Healy and Bronner, *op. cit.*, pp. 125–126.

50. See prior note, references to desertion, separation, divorce; Burke, *op. cit.*, p. 89; Juvenile Court Statistics 1927, U. S. Children's Bureau Publication No. 195, 1929, p. 9.

51. Healy and Bronner, *op. cit.*, pp. 126–129; Burke, *op. cit.*, p. 111.

52. Slawson, J., *op. cit.*, pp. 223 et seq.; Healy and Bronner, *op. cit.*, pp. 151–153; Burt, C., *op. cit.*, pp. 284 *et seq.*, 555; Cooley, *op. cit.*, p. 79; Glueck, B., "A Study of 608 Admissions to Sing Sing Prison", Mental Hygiene, Vol II (1918), pp. 86 *et seq.;* The Classification of the Prison Inmates of New York State, Commission to Investigate Prison Administration and Construction, New York, 1931, p. 7; Burke, *op. cit.*, pp. 26, 92–93.

53. Sutherland, *op. cit.*, p. 177; Cooley, *op. cit.*, p. 88; Report of the Crime Commission, 1928, *op. cit.*, From Truancy to Crime, p. 494 (separate pagination 58).

54. Report of the Crime Commission, 1928, *op. cit.*, A Study of Environmental Factors in Juvenile Delinquency, pp. 629 *et seq.* (separate pagination 53 *et seq.*).

55. Healy and Bronner, *op. cit.*, pp. 179, 181–182; Report of the Crime Commission, 1928, *op. cit.;* A Study of Environmental Factors in Juvenile Delinquency, pp. 585–586, 616 *et seq.*, 627 *et seq.* (separate pagination 9–10, 40 *et seq.*, 51 *et seq.*), and *id.*, Individual Studies of 145 Offenders, pp. 325–326 (separate pagination 17–18); Burke, *op. cit.*, p. 110.

56. Consult references mentioned in notes 51 and 52; Cooley, *op. cit.*, pp. 89–90; Bailey, *op. cit.*, p. 76; Burke, *op. cit.*, pp. 26, 97, 111.

57. The official figures of recidivism indicated in the reports are not complete, since they frequently do not include offenses committed outside the jurisdiction, or offenses for which persons might have been

arrested or convicted but for some reason or other were not. See Glueck, S. and E. T., "500", Chap. V; and Five Hundred Delinquent Women, New York, 1934, Appendix A. But making due allowance for these weaknesses in official figures, the picture presented is not one to flatter society about the effectiveness of its peno-correctional efforts. Thus, 59.8 per cent of offenders entering Massachusetts penal and reformatory establishments in 1927 were recidivists, 70.8 per cent of those entering Connecticut institutions in 1925–26 were repeaters. The Massachusetts offenders, 18,204 in number, had had a total of at least 59,104 prior commitments, or an average of 5.43 per capita. — Sutherland, *op. cit.*, p. 546.

58. Alexander, F., and Staub, H., The Criminal, the Judge, and the Public, New York, 1931, pp. 56 *et seq.*

CHAPTER VII

1. Llewellyn, K., Introduction to Hall, J., Theft, Law and Society, Boston, 1935, p. xxxiii.

2. Harvey, C. P., Solon or the Price of Justice, London, 1931, p. 8.

3. Kenny, C. S., Outlines of Criminal Law, Thirteenth Edition, Cambridge, Eng., 1933, p. 544.

4. "Learning and Science", in collected Legal Papers, by O. W. Holmes, edited by H. J. Laski, New York, 1920, p. 139.

5. *Id.*

6. Computed from data in letter of February 10, 1936, from Frederick A. Moran, Executive Director, Division of Parole, State of New York, to author.

7. Annual Report of the Commissioner of Correction for the Year ending November 30, 1934, The Commonwealth of Massachusetts, Public Document No. 115, pp. 196, 73, 177.

8. Federal Offenders 1933–34, U. S. Department of Justice, Bureau of Prisons, Washington, pp. 92–93.

9. Glueck, S. and E. T., 500 Criminal Careers, New York, 1930; and One Thousand Juvenile Delinquents, Cambridge, 1934.

10. The Mortality from External Causes, Monograph 3 in a Twenty-Year Mortality Review, Metropolitan Life Insurance Co., New York, 1935. It should be pointed out that this study, following the practice

in vital as opposed to criminal statistics, includes excusable and justifiable killing of a person by another, as well as felonious; it excludes accidental deaths involving criminal negligence, which are embraced in criminal statistics. — *Op. cit.*, p. 30.

11. Chicago Police Problems, by the Citizens' Police Committee, B. Smith, director of staff, Chicago, 1931, p. 3.

12. I have begun a research calculated to test roughly the deterrent effect of the threat of the existing system. Thus far, questionnaires applied to special classes under controlled conditions seem to indicate that so far as college students are concerned chief motives in socially acceptable behavior in addition to the threat of punishment are the fear of personal and family disgrace and, to a less extent, the influence of religious and ethical upbringing. This study will not be ready for publication for some time, as it calls for the testing of many and varied samples. The above conclusions should, therefore, be taken as highly tentative and subject to modification. See note 15.

13. Pound, R., Criminal Justice in America, New York, 1930, pp. 121–122.

14. A System of Penal Law, for the State of Louisiana, by Edward Livingston, Philadelphia, 1833, p. 7.

15. Professor von Hentig has keenly analyzed the psychologic misapprehensions behind an excessively deterrent aim of punishment: "Theoretically punishment must invariably be effective, always restraining man from a projected punishable action, for only thus can this artificially created danger exercise regularly its full deterrent effect. This effect depends upon the fulfilment of two conditions. First, the threatened damage must affect human instincts as a pain stimulus. Where, however, man's instincts of self-preservation are weakened, senile, or perverted, they will seek rather than avoid pain stimulus. Secondly, the artificial threat to existence inherent in the punishment must surpass any prospective gain, in the widest sense of the word, if it is to act as a deterrent. The legislator here proceeds from the concept of an average, which is not often to be found in real life. It is always possible that an expected gain will appear greater or more certain than the prospective punishment, especially since the danger threatened by a state power is no natural phenomenon with automatic incidence but one which can be affected only through a lengthy process of police and judicial investigation. The large number of attempted and successful suicides and a whole series of self-destructive

perversions of the instincts show that in modern civlization, perhaps contrary to the situation prevalent in primitive society, the instinct of self-preservation is not sufficiently stable and unchanging to make punishment a guaranteed part of the mechanism of social compulsion. Furthermore certain physiological conditions, such as puberty, and the desire for adventure characteristic of many chronically infantile natures can convert danger from a deterrent into an incitement. Finally, the polarity of a slight danger and great pain can have undesired effects. Even uncertainty of punishment connected with certainty of the desired gain or the remoteness in time of the punishment linked with the immediacy of the fruits of crime may sometimes introduce additional complications into the psychological problems involved in punishment." — von Hentig, H., "Punishment", in Encyclopædia of the Social Sciences, Vol. XII, p. 712. See also the writings of Freud, particularly Civilization and its Discontents, The International Psycho-Analytical Library, No. 17, translated by J. Riviere, London, 1930, and Alexander, F., and Staub, H., The Criminal, the Judge and the Public, translated by G. Zilboorg, New York, 1931.

16. The origins of punishment are many, and its motivation at any stage of civilization has not usually been single. "Specific forms of punishment have been extremely diverse. They exhibit a jumble of purposes: vengeance, deterrence, expiation and, finally, reformation." — von Hentig, *op. cit.*, p. 713.

17. Insanity and the Criminal Law, New York, 1923, pp. 13–14. See also Alexander and Staub, *op. cit.*

18. Bentham, J., Traités de Législation civile et pénale, edited by Ét. Dumont, Tome I, 1802, p. 101, translated and edited as The Theory of Legislation by C. K. Ogden, London, 1931, p. 62.

19. See Malan, G. H. T., "The Behavioristic Basis of the Science of Law", American Bar Association Journal, Vol. VIII (1922), pp. 737 *et seq.*, and Vol. IX (1923), pp. 43 *et seq.*; Lévitt, A., "Extent and Function of the Doctrine of Mens Rea", Illinois Law Review, Vol. XVII (1922–23), pp. 578 *et seq.*

20. It should be pointed out, however, that inconsistently enough a similar verdict is found in some jurisdictions even when a mentally ill defendant has been acquitted as not criminally responsible. In England in 1883, the Trial of Lunatics Act provided that upon an acquittal on the ground of insanity the jury should return the somewhat inconsistent verdict of "guilty, but insane", under which the defendant

could be legally controlled by the Home Secretary. By the Criminal Appeal Act of 1907 the Court of Criminal Appeal was empowered to quash the sentence of an appellant found guilty who was, however, in its opinion insane, and to order the appellant to be confined as a "lunatic", as if a special verdict had been found under the 1883 act. The defendant is not released until the Home Secretary so decides. In America the practice varies, but in Massachusetts, inconsistently with the verdict of *not* guilty by reason of insanity, the court must order the acquitted defendant in a murder or manslaughter case to be committed to a mental hospital "during his natural life", this amounting to a life sentence, usually in an institution that is to all intents and purposes a prison more than a hospital. — See Glueck, S., "Insanity — Criminal Law", Encyclopædia of the Social Sciences, Vol. VIII, pp. 64 *et seq.*

Under the system discussed in the text, the notion of guilt, which carries with it an ethico-theologic stigma, might be replaced by the determination of a treatment status, as in the case of juvenile offenders. The latter are declared, by the findings of the court, to be "juvenile delinquents"; the former might be found, upon trial, to be "adult offenders." Where it would be shown that the offense was attributable to genuine ignorance or mistake of fact, the result, as at present, would be the discharge of the defendant.

21. Such, for example, are the distinctions in varieties of arson found in the New York Penal Law (Secs. 221–223), dividing the crime into three degrees, dependent largely on the type of structure burned and whether the burning was by day or night; the familiar practice of breaking up burglary into degrees, depending upon whether or not the entry is accompanied by one or more of the common law requisites of burglary; the division of murder and manslaughter into degrees based on such mental and other accompaniments of the homicide as whether or not the act was done with "deliberately premeditated malice aforethought" (Mass. Gen. Laws, 1921, Chap. 265, Sec. 1), whether or not it was committed in the perpetration or attempted perpetration of specified other crimes, such as rape, arson, robbery or burglary, whether the means were poison (Pa. Act of April 22, 1794, Sec. 2), or interference with railroad tracks (N. Y. Penal Law, Sec. 1044), and like considerations.

22. It is desirable to retain the point of view of the trial judge because a good judge gets to be a shrewd judge of men and because the

magistrate, having heard the evidence, some of which would be repeated before the treatment tribunal, would be in a position to give valuable impressions regarding both the offense and the offender. This would mean that the nonlegal members of the treatment tribunal would sit in all cases to pass upon sentences, being joined in different cases by the particular judge who presided at the trial.

23. Where retained, "the jury would still pass upon the mental element of the crime — the *mens rea;* — but the work of scientific determination of the *peno-correctional consequence of conviction* . . . would be lodged in a skilled, administrative board specially qualified for such a task." Glueck, S., *op. cit.*, p. 486. So practical a statesman as ex-Governor Alfred Smith of New York urged the adoption of a treatment board device as a fundamental reform of existing practice. See New York Times, December 8, 1927 (address before the New York Crime Commission); *id.*, January 5, 1928 (Annual Message).

24. Livingston, in his System of Penal Law, *op. cit.*, pp. 9–10, provided that decisions, with reasons, should be recorded at least at the request of either party.

25. The Nicomachean Ethics, Book V, VIII, 1137 a.

26. General Laws of Massachusetts, Chap. 123, Sec. 113. This law is applicable at any time prior to the final disposal of a case in which the court might impose sentence to one of a series of peno-correctional institutions "for any offence not punishable by death or imprisonment for life", the person being committed on application of one of several enumerated public officials, including the district attorney or a probation or welfare official, and a hearing on the application.

27. The English Criminal Appeal Act (7 Edw. VII, 1907, Sec. 3 (c) and 4 (3)) provides: "A person convicted on indictment may appeal under this Act to the Court of Criminal Appeal . . . with leave of the Court of Criminal Appeal against the sentence passed on his conviction, unless the sentence is one fixed by law. . . . On appeal against sentence the Court of Criminal Appeal shall, if they think that a different sentence should have been passed, quash the sentence passed at the trial, and pass such other sentence warranted in law by the verdict (whether more or less severe) in substitution therefor as they think ought to have been passed, and in any other case shall dismiss the appeal." An important feature is that the court may of its own initiative hear fresh evidence. One of the effects claimed for the work of the court is that "its judgments . . . have tended to create a standard

throughout the country for the administration of criminal justice and to introduce some measure of uniformity in the character of sentences"; that is, it has permitted the retention of individualization of punishment while correcting "grossly disproportionate sentences due, in large part, to the varying standards which characterize particular courts."—Howard, P., Criminal Justice in England, New York, 1931, p. 284. See also Sixth Report of the Judicial Council, of New Jersey to the Governor, 1935, Appendix H.

I have recently analyzed a large sample of the decisions of this court, and find that while certain sentencing principles have been evolved for the guidance of trial courts, they are disappointing in not being sufficiently grounded in psychologic and sociologic considerations.

In the United States, an appeal from the sentence is generally not allowed. See, however, "Relief from Disproportionate Sentence Within Maximum Limits Prescribed by Criminal Statute", 42 Yale Law Journal (1933) p. 453. The American Law Institute's Code of Criminal Procedure (Sec. 427) provides that "an appeal may be taken by the defendant only from: (*a*) A final judgment of conviction, (*b*) a sentence, on the ground that it is illegal or excessive."

28. Even if concessions have to be made to public opinion in such matters as murder and rape (that is, even if, as to certain serious offenses, *minimum* limits of an indefinite sentence have to be retained), and even if concessions have to be made in regard to such crimes as larceny (that is, even if, as to certain less serious offenses, *maximum* limits of an indefinite sentence have to be retained), the proposed system ought to operate more satisfactorily than the existing one.

29. Glueck, S. and E. T., 500 Criminal Careers, New York, 1930; One Thousand Juvenile Delinquents, Survey of Crime and Criminal Justice in Boston Conducted by the Harvard Law School, Vol. I, Cambridge, Mass., 1934; Five Hundred Delinquent Women, New York, 1934. See also, Hart, H., "Predicting Parole Success", Journal of Criminal Law and Criminology, Vol. XIV, pp. 405 *et seq.;* Bruce, Harno, Burgess, and Landesco, "Workings of the Indeterminate-Sentence Law and the Parole System in Illinois, Chap. XXX; Glueck, S., and E. T., "Predictability in the Administration of Criminal Justice", Harvard Law Review, Vol. XLII, pp. 297 *et seq.;* Vold, G. B., Prediction Methods and Parole, Sociological Press, Hanover, N. H., 1931; Lanne, W. F., "Parole Prediction as Science", Journal of Criminal Law and Criminology, Vol. XXVI (1935), pp. 377 *et seq*. Most of

these studies pertain to prediction tables for use by parole boards, but as we have pointed out they are also feasible for judges in imposing sentence.

30. The coefficient expressing the relationship of the socio-psychiatric factors with outcomes after treatment ranged from .44 to .68; that expressing the relationship of the nature of the offense to outcome was but .11, and that expressing the relationship of its seriousness to subsequent criminal behavior was but .05. — Glueck, S. and E. T., "Predictability", etc., *op. cit.*, p. 327.

31. Crimes and Punishments.

32. "We know that the old analysis of act and intent can stand only as an artificial legal analysis and that the mental element in crime presents a series of difficult problems." — Pound, R., Criminal Justice in Cleveland, 1922, p. 586.

33. Glueck, S. and E. T., One Thousand Juvenile Delinquents, *op. cit.*,

34. See State of New York Law Revision Commission "Recommendations and Study made in relation to a Uniform Extradition Act", Legislative Document (1935), No. 60 (D); "Uniform Act to Secure the Attendance of Witnesses from Without the State in Criminal Cases", Drafted by the National Conference of Commissioners on Uniform State Laws, Chicago, 1931, and mimeographed materials on interstate cooperation in the field of law enforcement issued by the Interstate Crime Commission of New Jersey.

35. National Commission on Law Observance and Enforcement, Report on Lawlessness in Law Enforcement, Vol. IV, No. 11, pp. 5–6. Pound, R., "Legal Interrogation of Persons Accused or Suspected of Crime", Journal of Criminal Law and Criminology, Vol. XXIV (1934), pp. 1014, 1017.

36. There may be instances where, in the discretion of the prosecutor, either the preliminary hearing or the grand jury proceeding, is peculiarly suitable.

37. See Stephens, H. M., Administrative Tribunals and the Rules of Evidence — A Study in Jurisprudence and Administrative Law, Cambridge, 1933.

38. See Final Report of Samuel Seabury, Referee, in the Matter of the Investigation of the Magistrates' Courts in the First Judicial Department and the Magistrates thereof, and of Attorneys-at-Law Practicing in said Courts, New York, 1932, pp. 247, 248, 251, which illustrates

the ready opportunity for abuse of power that exists in adult courts where trial procedure is too informal. It is of course not a matter exclusively of procedure, but also, and perhaps most importantly, of personnel; but procedural safeguards are valuable curbs on arbitrariness or corruption.

39. Wigmore, J. H., A Treatise on the Anglo-American System of Evidence in Trials at Common Law, Second Edition, 1923, Vol. I, pp. 125–126.

40. "At present in some forty-two states the trial judge is prohibited by constitution, statute, or controlling decision from commenting upon the weight or credibility of the testimony. In some of them the judge must give to the jury only such instructions as are requested by counsel, and these before the arguments of counsel. In some he may review the evidence, but he must not indicate his opinion on it; and in none of them can he say a word as to the credibility of a particular witness. In some half dozen states the court has the privilege of comment, but many trial judges make little or no use of it. In the Federal Courts the privilege is unimpaired, but the great majority of Federal trial judges, following the state practice, do not avail themselves of it. The prevailing practice is unwise." — Morgan, E. M., and others, The Law of Evidence, New Haven, 1927, p. 9.

41. This is one place where, instead of departing from the historic past, a return to it seems indicated. "Trial by jury . . . is a trial by a jury of twelve men, in the presence and under the superintendence of a judge empowered to instruct them on the law and to advise them on the facts. . . ." — Capital Traction Co. v. Hof, 174 U. S. 1, 13 (1898). See also the authorities cited in Morgan, *op. cit.*, pp. 9–10, which establish the power to superintend the trial and comment on the weight and credibility of the evidence as running back to at least the third quarter of seventeenth century England, as described by Sir Matthew Hale.

42. "It is interesting to note that in England there is practically no expenditure of time in selecting a jury, and to ponder whether the privilege of comment, so vigorously used there, is not a contributing cause to this desirable end." — Morgan, *op. cit.*, p. 21.

43. *Id.*, pp. 20–21.

44. Morgan, *op. cit.*, pp. 16–17.

45. Revealing data on one branch of the problem of administration have recently been presented by N. F. Baker and E. H. De Long, in a

series of articles on the Prosecuting Attorney in the American scene. See Vols. XXV and XXVI of the Journal of Criminal Law and Criminology. J. J. Robinson has drafted a very suggestive "Manual of Legal Principles and Administrative Practice Governing Criminal Cases", Fourth Edition (mimeographed), Indiana University School of Law, 1928.

46. M. C. Goldman, who has been very active in the public defense movement, has recently urged the system of general public defense in an address at the Section of Criminal Law of the American Bar Association, July 15, 1935, "Should the Public Defender be Substituted for Defense Counsel in All Criminal Cases?"

The constitutional right of counsel is involved in the system discussed above. The Federal Constitution, Sixth Amendment, provides that "in all criminal prosecutions the accused shall enjoy the right to . . . have the assistance of counsel for his defence", and state constitutions have similar provisions. But it is questionable whether this right would be essentially abridged by compelling all defendants to choose counsel from a public panel. A wide choice would still be available. But assuming unconstitutionality, it may some day be found that the reform is so fundamental and might have such a tonic influence on the entire system of criminal justice that constitutional amendment would not be too high a price to pay for it.

47. There is, to be sure, some danger in such a system of a new form of log-rolling. Would not certain public defenders make deals with public prosecutors in the exchange of mutual favors? Here is a problem which, with many others of the system of justice requires control by some central supervisory agency, — a point discussed in the last chapter.

48. For interesting illustrations of the possibilities of this method in the fields of delinquency and criminality, see Aichhorn, A., Wayword Youth, New York, 1935, and Alexander, F. and Healy, W., The Roots of Crime, New York, 1935.

49. That the sense of honor can be appealed to in the case of the vast majority of prisoners has been shown by such forward-looking correctional administrators as T. M. Osborne and H. Gill. After the above was written, the press carried the announcement that some 500 convicts released on "Christmas paroles" from Alabama prisons voluntarily returned to the institutions, all but a very few having kept their "man-to-man agreement" with the Governor.

50. See the thoughtful and practical study by A. W. MacCormick, The Education of Adult Prisoners — A Survey and a Program — The National Society of Penal Information, New York, 1931.

51. Glueck, S. and E. T., One Thousand Juvenile Delinquents, *op. cit.*

52. See Aichhorn, *op. cit.*

CHAPTER VIII

1. There are a few exceptions to this general picture, notably in Rhode Island and in the federal Department of Justice.

2. See Pound, R., "Organization of Courts", Journal of American Judicature Society, Vol. XI, No. 3, October, 1927, pp. 69 *et seq.*

3. Roscoe Pound, in his numerous writings on this subject, has abundantly indicated the historic reasons for the existing practices, their advantages in the past, and their inadequacy in coping with modern crime.

4. This is not a new office on the Continent, and a number of English publicists long ago urged the adoption of some such instrumentality as an indispensable regulator in government. Early in the nineteenth century, Jeremy Bentham, in his treatise on a constitution for a republican form of government, though not developing all the implications of such an organ in the body politic, devoted considerable space to discussion of its importance and general functions. — Bentham, J., Works, Edinburgh, 1843, Vol. IX, pp. 597, *et seq.* It was again urged by Lord Chancellor Westbury in the middle of the nineteenth century. — Nash, T. A., The Life of Lord Chancellor Westbury, London, 1888, Vol. I, pp. 189–193. That learned lawyer and able administrator drew some odious comparisons between other disciplines and the law.

"Why is there not [he demanded] a body of men in this country whose duty it is to collect a body of judicial statistics, or, in more common phrase, make the necessary experiments to see how far the law is fitted to the exigencies of society, the necessities of the times, the growth of wealth, and the progress of mankind? There is not even a body of men concerned to mark whether the law is free from ambiguity or not; whether its administration is open to any objections; whether there be a defect either in the body or conception of the law, or in the machinery for carrying it into execution. The consequence is, that in the moral science of the law we never make an advance, because we never generalize, and have not persons who (as moral, political, or scientific men do in their peculiar line) interest and concern themselves in observing the effect of the law; whether the instrument we have destined for a certain duty is calculated to perform it well." — *Id.*, p. 191. The department of justice was to be "furnished with a sufficient staff to accomplish the three great objects in view — a general superintendence over the administration of justice in all its departments; the effective prosecution of amendments of the law; and the giving prompt and effectual assistance in conducting the business of current legislation." — *Id.*, p. 190.

A ministry of justice was also urged later by Lord Haldane's important Machinery of Government Committee. — Ministry of Reconstruction, Report of the Machinery of Government Committee, London, His Majesty's Stationery Office, 1918, reprinted 1925, pp. 63 *et seq.* Ten years ago, in a valuable volume, Professor Harold Laski urged as one important function of such a ministry the utilization "much more creatively than we now do" of "the knowledge and experience of the judiciary." — Grammar of Politics, New Haven, 1925, p. 581. In the United States, Dean Roscoe Pound and Mr. Justice Cardozo have for some time been urging the establishment of state ministries of justice. — Pound, R., "Juristic Problems of National Progress", American Journal of Sociology, May, 1917, pp. 721 *et seq.*, "Anachronisms in Law", *op. cit.*; "Law and Laws", The University of Missouri Bulletin, Vol. XXVIII, No. 47, December 1, 1917, pp. 25, 37. Cardozo, B. N., "A Ministry of Justice", Harvard Law Review, Vol. XXXV, pp. 113 *et seq.* See also my "The Ministry of Justice and the Problem of Crime", American Review, March–April, 1926, pp. 139 *et seq.*, in which I attempt to show the significance of such an agency in the field of criminal justice.

It was largely due to the vision, enthusiasm and leadership of Judge Cardozo that the nearest American approach to this much-needed reform was originally made. In 1923 Governor Alfred Smith of New York appointed a commission "to investigate defects in the law and its administration." That distinguished body unanimously adopted the report of Judge Cardozo's sub-committee, of which the chief recommendation was the establishment of a "permanent law revision commission", somewhat similar to a ministry of justice both in organization and in some of its functions. This recommendation was embodied in a bill which then came near to enactment.

It provided for a permanent state law revision commission, appointed for a five-year period, the five members required to be attorneys admitted to practice in the courts of New York, and at least two of them required, in addition, to be members of the law faculty of a university or law school within the state. In this manner it was hoped to bring to a focus of continuing activity on behalf of the public the practical judgment of lawyers, and the scholarship and research experience of professors of law. A major weakness of the proposal was that it did not provide for even a single member representing the "social science" group of disciplines.

The duties of this proposed law revision commission were to be as follows:

1. To examine the common law and statutes of the State and current judicial decisions for the purpose of discovering defects and anachronisms in the law and in its administration and recommending needed reforms.

2. To receive and consider proposed changes in the law recommended by the American Law Institute, the commissioners for the promotion of uniformity of legislation in the United States, any bar association or other learned bodies.

3. To receive and consider suggestions from judges, justices, public officials, lawyers and the public generally as to the defects and anachronisms in the law or in its administration;

4. To recommend, from time to time, such changes in the law as it deems necessary to modify or eliminate antiquated and inequitable rules of law and methods of administration, and to bring the law of this state, civil and criminal, into harmony with modern conditions;

5. To report its proceedings annually to the legislature. — See New York Law Journal, February 15, 1924, for a copy of this bill and for the Commission's report embracing the report of Judge Cardozo's sub-committee.

While a number of the functions of a ministry of justice as conceived by Bentham and Lord Westbury were provided for in the New York law, it still left untouched the basic problem of an effective integration of the processes of justice, particularly those dealing with crime.

See also The Report of the Commission on the Administration of

Justice in New York State, Legislative Document, 1934, No. 50, pp. 51–56, which strongly urges establishment of a "law revision commission" along the lines of Judge Cardozo's committee.

In 1934, New York finally established a Law Revision Commission, consisting of the chairmen of the senate and assembly judiciary committees *ex officio* and five members appointed by the governor, the chairman to be named by the governor from the appointed members. It was provided that four of the appointive members should be attorneys admitted to practice in the state, and at least two, members of law faculties. The duties listed in the statute are substantially in terms of the report of Judge Cardozo's committee report, except that in item No. 3 no reference is made to anachronisms in the *administration* of law. — Laws of New York, 157th Session, 1934, Chap. 597, Article 4–A, pp. 1289–90.

5. While the recently adopted amendment to the Constitution of California gives an opportunity for improvement of the processes of justice through centralized oversight, and is therefore a step in the right direction, its does not approach in comprehensiveness the authority of the Continental Ministry of Justice:

"Sec. 21 (to Article V). Subject to the powers and duties of the Governor vested in him by Article V of the Constitution, the Attorney General shall be the chief law officer of the State and it shall be his duty to see that the laws of the State of California are uniformly and adequately enforced in every county of the State. He shall have direct supervision over every district attorney and sheriff and over such other law enforcement officers as may be designated by law, in all matters pertaining to the duties of their respective offices, and may require any of said officers to make to him such written reports concerning the investigation, detection, prosecution and punishment of crime in their respective jurisdictions as to him may seem advisable. Whenever in the opinion of the Attorney General any law of the State is not being adequately enforced in any county, it shall be the duty of the Attorney General to prosecute any violations of law of which the superior court shall have jurisdiction, and in such cases he shall have all the powers of a district attorney. When required by the public interest, or directed by the Governor, he shall assist any district attorney in the discharge of his duties. In addition to appropriations made by law for the use of the Attorney General, the Governor and the Controller may in writing authorize the setting aside and the payment in accordance with law, from moneys in the State treasury not otherwise appropriated, of such sums as they consider proper for the necessary expenses of the Attorney General in performing the duties imposed by this paragraph.

"He shall also have such powers and perform such duties as are or may be prescribed by law and which are not inconsistent therewith. . . .

"All provisions of this section shall be self-executing, but legislation may be enacted to facilitate their operation."

According to R. W. Harris, Chief Deputy Attorney General of California, "insofar as the amendment purports to confer upon the Attorney General powers and duties in relation to the district attorney, the amendment does not in that respect substantially add to those powers and duties which were vested in the Attorney General prior to its adoption, such powers and duties being defined very broadly in sections 470 and 472, and other sections, of the Political Code. However all of the matters in the amendment relating to his powers with reference to the sheriff are new.

"While the amendment does not suggest with particularity in what manner he shall exercise such powers over the sheriff, measures have been introduced at the present session of the legislature conferring upon the Attorney General the power to appoint investigators, and to supersede the sheriff by one of the Attorney General's appointees in any criminal case under investigation, leaving the sheriff to the performance of his regular duties in other matters falling within his jurisdiction. Until such legislation is enacted and there has been some occasion to operate thereunder it would be difficult to say whether the system contemplated will be fruitful of beneficial results. It is hoped however that through some such system there will be more coordination in the accomplishment of beneficial results in the administration of the criminal laws of this state." — Letter to author, dated March 28, 1935, quoted by permission.

See, also, "How to Make Prosecuting Effectual", by H. Caldwell, Journal of the American Judicature Society, Vol. XVI (1932), pp. 73 *et seq.*; and Willoughby, W. F., Principles of Judicial Administration, The Brookings Institute, Washington, 1929, pp. 119–124. See also, De Long, E. H., "Powers and Duties of the State Attorney-General in Criminal Prosecution", Journal of Criminal Law and Criminology, Vol. XXV (1934), pp. 358, 380–381.

6. In most of these respects it roughly resembles the federal Department of Justice, but in as much as it is much smaller and the territory of Belgium is limited, it can give more intensive oversight.

7. The report of my Belgian investigation, entitled The Ministry of Justice, with Especial Reference to the Belgian System, is now in preparation. I am greatly indebted to the Harvard-Radcliffe Bureau of International Research for financial aid in connection with this study.

8. In all this, as Laski wisely cautions, care would have to be exercised in sketching the details of administration by the Department of Justice to prevent a confusion of powers between the executive and the judiciary. "Our effort must never involve such a connection between the judiciary and the executive as will break that independence in the former which lies at the root of civilized justice." — Grammar of Politics, *op. cit.*, p. 581. But while purely judicial functions would remain independent, the many administrative duties of the courts would be supervised in a businesslike fashion by the Department of Justice. So also, while a bureau in the Department might serve as an aid to the legislature in drafting legislation more in harmony with existing law, the proposed office would not be permitted to interfere with the exercise of legislative power.

9. Better Government Personnel, Report of the Commission of Inquiry on Public Service Personnel, New York, 1935, p. 3. See also, Wilmerding, L., Government by Merit, New York, 1935.

10. Better Government Personnel, *op. cit.*, p. 17.

11. Richardson, J. D., Messages and Papers of the Presidents, Vol. II, Washington, Government Printing Office, 1896, p. 449.

12. Frankfurter, F., The Public and Its Government, Yale Lectures on the Responsibilities of Citizenship, New Haven, 1930, p. 149.

13. Better Government Personnel, *op. cit.*, p. 17.

14. *Id.*, p. 18.

15. *Id.*

16. The Public and Its Government, *op. cit.*, pp. 157–158. See also the well-reasoned demurrer to Lord Hewart's familiar indictment of the "new despotism", by John Willis, The Parliamentary Powers of English Government Departments, Harvard Studies in Administrative Law, Vol. IV, Cambridge, 1933.

17. The Public and Its Government, *op. cit.*, p. 159.

18. Better Government Personnel, *op. cit.*, pp. 19–29.

19. *Id.*, p. 21.

20. *Id.*, p. 25.

21. Rogers, J. G., "The Dream of a New Legal Profession for America", American Bar Association Journal, Vol. XXI, No. 3 (March, 1935), p. 143.

22. Boyd, E., "Druggéd Individualism", The American Mercury, Vol. 33 (1934) pp. 308–309.

23. But see Perry, S. H., "Shall We Appoint Our Judges?" The Annals, Vol. CLXXXI, 1935, pp. 97 *et seq.*

24. Better Government Personnel, *op. cit.*, pp. 4, 30.

25. *Id.*, p. 13.

26. See Thomas, W. I., and Thomas, D. S., The Child in America, New York, 1928, p. 331. See also Myerson, A., Social Psychology, New York, 1934, p. 99.

27. Parmelee, M., Criminology, New York, 1918, p. 37.

28. The arguments in favor of sterilization and the progress of the movement in America are set forth in *Collected Papers on Eugenic Sterilization in California*, The Human Betterment Foundation, Pasadena, 1930. See, however, the judicial appraisal in J. H. Landman, Human Sterilization, the History of the Sexual Sterilization Movement, New York, 1932.

29. "We assume that the Legislature would not feel justified in compelling any persons to submit to sterilization, unless it could be shown beyond reasonable doubt that some at least of their offspring would either be mentally defective or would develop mental disorder. In the present state of knowledge no such proof can be produced. While the results of our enquiry and the other statistics we have collected may justify some prediction as to the average results in a large group of cases, it would be hazardous to attempt to forecast the genetic results of any particular union." — Report of the Departmental Committee on Sterilization Presented by the Minister of Health to Parliament by Command of His Majesty, December, 1933, London, His Majesty's Stationery Office, 1934, p. 37. This report is admirable for its objectivity and lucidity. See also the carefully reasoned Report of the American Neurological Association Committee for the Investigation of Sterilization, Abraham Myerson, Chairman, Boston, June 5, 1935.

30. See Glueck, S. and E. T., Five Hundred Delinquent Women, New York, 1934.

31. Lenroot, K. F., "Old and New Methods of Dealing with

Vagrants and Delinquents", Address before the Attorney General's Conference on Crime, Washington, December 13, 1934, p. 1 (mimeographed).

32. "Just as soon as public opinion can be made to realize that certain forms of vice represent not the human weaknesses of the participants but the commercial interest of the exploiter, vigorous and effective repressive action becomes possible." — Johnson, B., and Kinsie, P. M., "Prostitution in the United States, Journal of Social Hygiene, Vol. XIX (1933), p. 489, quoting Flexner.

33. Keynes, J. M., Laissez-Faire and Communism, 1926, pp. 134–135.

34. The Life and Letters of Lord Macaulay by his Nephew G. Otto Trevelyan . . . in two volumes . . . New York (popular edition, two volumes in one), 1877, Vol. 2, pp. 409–410, "Appendix. Lord Macaulay on American institutions", letter dated Holly Lodge, Kensington, London, May 3, 1857, writing apropos his opinion of Thomas Jefferson, to H. S. Randall, Esq., author of the "Life of Jefferson."

35. Graham, F. P., "Adjusting Democracy — Constitutionally and Otherwise", The American Scholar, Vol. 4 (1935) pp. 428, 430.

36. De Tocqueville, A., Democracy in America, translated from the French by Henry Reeve, Cambridge, 1862, Vol. II, p. 412. While this statement is in terms of the nineteenth century naive conception of free will, De Tocqueville may be said to have meant that a democratic people can consciously plan a good deal of its development.

37. Dewey, J., "A Critique of American Civilization", in Recent Gains in American Civilization, Edited by Kirby Page, New York, 1928, pp. 255 *et seq.*

38. See recent numbers of the American Bar Association Journal.

39. The work of Attorney General Homer S. Cummings and Governor Herbert H. Lehman, for example.

INDEX OF NAMES

TOPICAL INDEX